YOUR
SLEEPLESS
BABY | THE RESCUE
GUIDE

ROWENA BENNETT

To the countless babies and parents who struggle to get the sleep they so desperately need. This book is for you.

YOUR SLEEPLESS BABY | THE RESCUE GUIDE

ROWENA BENNETT

Registered nurse
Registered midwife
Registered mental health nurse
Certified child, adolescent and family health nurse
Graduate Diploma in Health Promotions
International Board Certified Lactation Consultant (IBCLC)

www.babycareadvice.com

ISBN 978-1505468090

Contents

Important Disclaimer

Your Sleepless Baby is designed to help parents and caregivers obtain general information about caring for, and promoting the health of babies and children. Information, opinions or judgments in this book are not intended as a substitute for medical advice. The content is provided for general use and may be unsuitable for people suffering from certain conditions, diagnosed or otherwise.

Accordingly, no person should rely on the contents of this publication without first obtaining appropriate medical advice. This publication is sold entirely on the terms and understanding that the author and/or consultants and/or editors are not responsible for the results of any actions taken on the basis of information in this publication, nor for an error in or omission from this publication, and further that the publisher is not engaged in rendering medical, paediatric, professional or other advice or services. The publisher and the author, consultants and editors expressly disclaim all liability and responsibility to any person, whether a purchaser or reader of this publication or not, in respect of anything and of the consequences of anything done or omitted to be done by any such person in reliance whether wholly or partially upon the whole or any part of the contents of this publication. Without limiting the generality of the above, no author, consultant or editor shall have any responsibility for any act or omission of any other author, consultant or editor.

About the author

Rowena Bennett is a child health nurse who specialises in helping parents resolve care problems of healthy babies. She is a registered nurse, midwife and mental health nurse, has been certified as a child, adolescent and family health nurse, is an International Board Certified Lactation Consultant (IBCLC) and has a graduate diploma in Health Promotions.

Married with three children and two grandchildren, Rowena, like countless parents, struggled with infant sleep problems with all three of her children. She attributes her resulting chronic sleep deprivation to developing postnatal depression after the births of her second and third child. Having experienced the strain that infant sleep problems can have on family life, and how it feels to suffer from chronic sleep deprivation and depression, Rowena wanted to help others facing similar dilemmas. Her journey eventually led to her becoming a child health nurse.

While working as a child health nurse at a residential parenting education centre in Queensland she learned about the causes and solutions to infant sleep problems and other baby-care problems that commonly trouble healthy babies, and cause a great deal of stress for their parents. At the centre she worked side-by-side with families for eight-hour periods over several days. This provided innumerable opportunities to observe babies, their sleeping patterns and behaviour, and how they responded to different settling strategies. It quickly became obvious that no single solution would work for every baby or every family.

In 2002 Rowena went into private practice as an online parenting consultant. At this time she developed what she calls a 'gentle settling plan'; a gradual way to improve infant sleeping habits *and* minimise any upset baby might experience. With more than 15 years of experience at the centre, nine of which included time in private practice, Rowena is able to help parents understand their baby's sleep, identify the cause of their baby's sleep problems and the steps they need to take to resolve the problem.

> **Child health** is a specialty area that provides parenting education to support parents to care for their *well* babies and children aged from birth to 18 years. Australia is one of only a handful of countries that trains nurses to facilitate well-baby health checks and provide parenting education. Child health is different to paediatrics, a specialty area focused on the care of *sick and disabled* babies and children from birth to 18 years.

Acknowledgements

I would like to express my appreciation to my good friend, Maureen O'Driscoll. Without your ongoing encouragement I doubt I would have started or completed this book.

I would like to thank my husband, Bruce, children, Hayden, Jessica and Caitlin, and grandchildren, Elijah and Willow for their patience and support. I apologise for my messy house, overgrown garden, not walking the dog, too many take-away meals and not spending enough time with you while writing this book. I promise to remedy this situation.

To my colleagues Marie-Ann Nelson, Kathy Hennessy, Regina McNevin, Hillary Warnett and the many other wonderful health professionals I have consulted while researching this book, I thank you for so generously sharing your wealth of knowledge and experience.

Last but not least, I extend my gratitude to Jessica Perini, my editor. Your passion for helping parents matched my own. You constantly challenged me to do better, and because of this I have managed to achieve more than I ever dreamed possible.

Rowena Bennett

Brisbane, 2012

Introduction

People who say they sleep like a baby usually don't have one.
– Leo J Burke

Sleep is something we tend to take for granted, that is, until we become parents. It's then elevated to something that is often foremost in our thoughts, sometimes it can feel like a permanent pre-occupation. But it needn't be; often we just need to follow some logical steps outlined below.

Decide if a problem exists

An infant sleep issue is only a problem if the wellbeing, health or happiness of any family member is compromised. If your baby is happy, healthy and thriving and you're happy with the current situation, there's no need to change a thing. However, if:

- your baby regularly suffers distress as a result of overtiredness
- you're feeling stressed or exhausted from supporting your baby's sleep
- you're not enjoying the time you spend with your baby because you're suffering from ongoing fatigue
- you're starting to have negative feelings about your baby, or thoughts of harming your baby
- you find you have no time, energy or patience for your other children
- your relationship with your spouse/partner is strained because of ongoing stress owing to chronic sleep deprivation
- you're feeling at your wits' end as a result of caring for a distressed or excessively demanding baby day after day

… then a problem exists. If you, your baby or other family members are suffering as a result of your baby's sleeping patterns or wakeful behaviour, then this book is for you.

Infant sleep problems

The six most common complaints parents voice about their baby's sleep are:

1. Difficulty getting baby to fall asleep.
2. Brief or non-existent day-time naps.
3. Frequent night-time awakenings requiring help to be soothed back to sleep.
4. Baby staying awake until very late.
5. Baby awakens extremely early in the morning, ready to start the day.
6. Baby remains awake for extended periods during the night.

Causes of infant sleep problems

Babies become sleepless or wakeful for multiple reasons. These fall into three broad categories:

- physical and medical
- developmental and
- behavioural.

Physical and medical

Physical and medical problems are the least likely reason for healthy, thriving babies to experience sleep disturbance. But the possibility of these problems needs to be assessed first. Medical reasons – such as chronic conditions, acute illnesses or digestive disorders – can cause infant sleep problems, but these are typically only temporary, until baby recovers or the condition is treated effectively.

A medical condition does not exclude a baby from experiencing behavioural or developmental sleep problems. So if medical treatment has failed to improve your baby's sleeping patterns and behaviour, consider the possibility of coinciding developmental and behavioural reasons.

Developmental

When someone says 'it's normal' after you describe your baby's sleeping patterns or behaviour, they're saying they're due to developmental reasons. Developmental reasons for a baby to become wakeful include separation anxiety and achieving new developmental milestones, such as rolling and standing. As your baby develops physically, emotionally and intellectually, and her awareness of her surroundings and ability to remember develops, this can cause changes to her sleeping patterns and behaviour.

Provided there's no behavioural reason for sleep disturbance (and there often is) wakefulness due to developmental reasons is usually only temporary. Your baby will outgrow it.

Behavioural

The most prevalent of all reasons for physically well babies to experience sleep problems is behavioural. By 'behavioural' I am not implying that baby is deliberately being difficult. 'Behavioural' means the baby's behaviour occurs in response to her parents' child-care practices, in particular, infant feeding and settling practices, or to what's happening in the immediate surroundings. The three most common reasons for babies to experience behavioural sleep problems include:

1. when baby's tiredness cues are overlooked or misinterpreted, she may become overtired. Once overtired, she can find it difficult to fall asleep.
2. when baby learns to rely on negative sleep associations. Sleep associations are the conditions baby learns to associate with sleeping. Negative associations are those that change after she has fallen asleep. During light sleep baby may notice the change and this can cause her to wake prematurely.
3. circadian rhythm problems. A baby's internal body clock can become destabilised by parents' child-care practices (in particular, feeding and settling practices). This can have a negative impact on a baby's sleeping and feeding.

Studies have suggested that behavioural sleep problems don't spontaneously resolve.[1] If left untreated sleep problems can persist, even into adulthood. It is estimated that between 15 and 27 per cent of school-aged children experience sleep problems.[2] Babies and children need their parents' support to resolve underlying issues causing behavioural sleep problems.

Why are behavioural sleep problems so prevalent? I believe it is because parents in general are not made aware of their role in supporting their babies to self-regulate their sleeping patterns.

Sleep self-regulation

A person is a person, no matter how small. – Dr Seuss

Self-regulation involves doing something for ourselves to restore homeostasis, an internal state of harmony within the body. In order to self-regulate our sleep we need to be able to take ourselves off to bed, fall asleep and remain asleep independent of others' help. The ability to self-regulate our sleep does not mean that we don't awaken during sleep. But it does mean we don't depend on someone else to help us return to sleep.

Normal, healthy babies are capable of self-regulating their sleeping patterns in accordance with their biological needs, but they're semi-dependent on support from parents and caregivers to achieve this. For one, they can't take themselves off to bed when tired. A baby is dependent on others to recognise when she's tired and to provide the conditions she needs in order to sleep. Failing to do so places her at increased risk of becoming overtired.

Babies don't need parents' help to fall asleep, but as parents and caregivers we can inadvertently teach them to depend on our help. If your baby learns to depend on your help to fall asleep this means she may also depend on your help to remain asleep. Repeatedly assisting your baby to fall asleep means you're accepting (knowingly or unknowingly) the responsibility to regulate her sleeping patterns. Her learned dependence on your support to fall asleep means your sleep is likely to be broken in order to help her to return to sleep, and this may place you at increased risk of sleep deprivation. It also means she's at risk of waking every time you remove your help. If after accidentally teaching your baby to depend on your help to sleep you find you're unable to provide the support she needs on a 24-hour basis, she will also be at risk of suffering from sleep deprivation.

More than lack of sleep

For many babies an infant sleep problem does not remain solely a sleep problem. Broken sleep and sleep deprivation can trigger a chain of events that can cause a great deal of stress for the baby and her parents. A sleep problem can cause infant feeding problems. Infant feeding problems can then be responsible for abdominal discomfort and gastrointestinal symptoms commonly displayed by newborn babies. These are often mistakenly attributed to medical conditions such as colic, reflux, milk allergy or intolerance. As a consequence the baby may be given medications she doesn't need; a breast-fed baby might be switched to formula; and a formula-fed baby may undergo multiple formula changes, until eventually one of these strategies masks the baby's gastrointestinal symptoms (but fails to resolve the underlying sleep problem).

As a child health nurse and early parenting educator, I meet hundreds of parents every year who are looking for a solution to their baby's sleep problem. The baby is miserable owing to lack of sleep, and the parents are stressed and sleep-deprived. They talk of the heartache of witnessing their baby's distress and feeling powerless to make a difference. They speak of the physical and emotional tolls this has taken on their lives, the lives of their partners, and their baby's siblings. They explain how their relationship with their partner has been strained, some to the point of breakdown. For some parents, chronic stress and sleep deprivation causes an anxiety disorder or depression. And some admit to having negative feelings towards their baby as a result of being forced to parent in a constant state of stress and sleep deprivation.

Caring for a normal, healthy baby doesn't need to be difficult or stressful. To avoid this heartache often all you need to do is:

- learn to be more accurate in interpreting baby's behavioural cues
- understand baby's sleep needs and
- support baby to self-regulate her sleeping patterns.

Please keep reading to find out how to do this.

What's in this book?

This book describes various infant sleep problems, what can cause these to occur, how you can recognise each one, and what steps to take to manage or resolve each problem. In this way, your ability to pinpoint the reason(s) for your baby's sleep troubles is increased. Developmental, behavioural, physical and medical reasons for infant sleep problems are explained so you can readily recognise each problem and find solutions.

The information is not slanted towards one particular style of parenting, for example, Attachment Parenting or an authoritarian style involving rigid feeding and sleeping schedules. Irrespective of whether you choose to share your bed with your baby or have your baby sleep alone, whether you prefer to follow your baby's lead or suspect your baby may benefit from your guidance, you will find the information helpful.

The case studies and emails that appear in this book are based on real stories, but the names have been changed. I have substituted names with the names of some of the many child health nurses and other professionals that I have had the pleasure to work alongside. The terms 'parent' and 'caregiver' are interchangeable. The pronouns 'he' and 'she' are alternated for each chapter.

What to keep in mind

You should keep in mind these two important things as you read this book:

- Babies can experience more than one problem at a time.
- There's usually more than one solution to any given problem.

By all means, skim through the pages first and read anything that sparks your interest. But then come back and thoughtfully read the entire book from cover to cover. Consider all potential reasons for your baby's sleep problem(s) and all possible solutions for resolving an individual problem before taking action.

The time you invest in understanding how, as a parent or caregiver, you influence your baby's sleep may not only prove beneficial in resolving your baby's problems, but may also prevent future sleep problems.

Physical and developmental reasons for sleep disturbance

Topics

Is baby hungry?
Is baby suffering pain?
Does baby have an illness or medical condition?
What are the non-medical reasons for discomfort?
Might developmental changes be causing baby's upset?
Could the problem be separation anxiety?
Do you have unrealistic expectations?

Hunger and pain are typically among the first things blamed when a baby displays wakeful or sleepless behaviour, because these are common reasons for adults to experience sleep disturbances. But these reasons are not the most likely cause of infant sleep problems. The most common reason for a well baby to experience broken sleep relates to the absence of his sleep associations. However, discomfort or pain due to illness, medical conditions and non-medical reasons can also cause sleepless or wakeful behaviour, as can developmental reasons, like a young baby's biological need to feed during the night, reaching new developmental milestones, or separation anxiety. All these things need to be assessed *before* assuming a behavioural problem is to blame.

Hunger

> My five-month-old baby boy wakes every one to two hours during the
> night wanting a breastfeed. I have tried feeding him more often during
> the day and I have started him on solids but it hasn't helped. How can
> I get him to go longer between feeds at night? – Zarina

Most babies under the age of six months require feeding during the night.
However, feeding every one to two hours is excessive. If a healthy, thriving
baby demands an excessive number of feeds during the day or night, or
continues to demand night-time feeds beyond the age of six months,
something besides hunger is likely the culprit.

Parents often ask how many times their baby should feed. This varies
depending on the baby's developmental stage and growth pattern. As a
general guide, a healthy baby will require fewer feeds as he matures.

Table 1.1 depicts the average number of feeds for healthy, thriving,
breast-fed and bottle-fed babies according to age, based on my experience.

Table 1.1:   Average breast- and bottle-feeds

Age	Average number of feeds in 24-hour period		Average number of feeds overnight		Period of decreased appetite during the night	
	Breast	Bottle	Breast	Bottle	Breast	Bottle
Up to 1 month	7–12	6–8	2–4	2–3	2–3.5	2.5–4
1–3 months	6–8	5–7	2–3	2	3–7 hours*	
3–6 months	5–7	5–6	1–3	1–2	5–8 hours*	
6–9 months	4–6	4–5	0–2	0–1	8–12 hours	
9–12 months	3–5	3–4	0–1	0	10–12 hours	

*The longer break between feeds at night usually occurs at one period only.
It's not the time between each night-time feed.

Of course, there are exceptions. Preterm babies, babies who are not gaining sufficient weight, babies who are sick or disabled, or those who have certain medical conditions that affect their growth may need to feed more often than average. Babies who struggle to gain sufficient weight may benefit from continued feeds overnight. However, in most instances, additional feedings during the day or night do little to increase a normal, healthy baby's overall milk intake. He may simply take less at each feed if he is offered feeds more often. And continuing night-time feeds beyond when a baby is developmentally mature enough to go through the night without feeding often decreases his appetite the following day.

Hunger is typically the first thing we suspect when a baby fusses or wants to suck, and when he wakes unexpectedly during the day or night. Indeed, hunger is a valid reason for such behaviour. But it's usually not the reason for a healthy, thriving baby's desire to repeatedly feed sooner than expected. So why would a healthy baby feed more often than he needs to? The following are the most common reasons:

- Babies under the age of five months often have a strong desire to suck: when they're tired, stressed, uncomfortable, bored, overstimulated, or simply because they love to suck. A baby's desire to suck for these reasons is often confused with hunger.

- Normal awakenings during the night are often mistakenly attributed to hunger; we assume baby has woken hungry without considering other potential reasons for him waking.

- If a baby learns to associate having his mother's breast or a bottle in his mouth with falling asleep, he's going to want it each time he needs to fall asleep and as a way to return to sleep when he wakes. This was the reason Zarina's baby wanted to breastfeed every one to two hours during the night. It's also the most common reason for a baby to demand night-feeds long after he's considered old enough to go through the night without feeding.

- Baby has developed a dysrhythmic day-night feeding pattern (one that is out of sync with a normal day-night pattern). As a result of feeding more often than he needs to during the night this decreases baby's appetite the next day. So the next day he eats very little, as a consequence he then wants to feed regularly during the night. This type of feeding pattern typically develops because of a feeding-sleep association, discussed above.

- Baby may have developed a grazing feeding pattern where, because he is offered frequent feeds, he only feeds a little at a time.

- A breast-fed baby experiencing problems owing to oversupply syndrome will want to feed more often than expected. Oversupply syndrome is a common breastfeeding problem that will discussed in greater detail further in this chapter.

These problems are not mutually exclusive: a baby may want to feed more often than expected for *one or more* reasons. Feeding more often than average will not cause your baby any harm, provided he can self-regulate his dietary intake to meet his growth and energy needs. However, offering feeds too often may cause problems for newborn babies who are vulnerable to overfeeding owing to the presence of their suck reflex. Once your baby's suck reflex has faded – around three to four months of age – he will be better able to self-regulate his dietary intake and the risk of overfeeding is reduced.

Growth spurts

Growth spurts are often blamed for a baby's increased wakefulness. A more fitting description of this phenomenon would be 'appetite spurts' because an appetite spurt clearly defines the underlying cause of baby's restless behaviour.

If your **breast-fed** baby is going through a growth/appetite spurt, then breastfeed more often. Your body will respond within a couple of days to his increased demands for milk. Fussiness or the appearance of insatiable hunger beyond three days is likely to be due to other reasons. A growth spurt need not cause a **bottle-fed** baby any fussiness, and it's seldom responsible for the appearance of insatiable hunger displayed by bottle-fed babies, as the situation is easily remedied simply by offering baby a little more milk at each feed.

What to do

The solution to these problems involves understanding your baby's nutritional needs, the reasons for his behaviour, and how your parenting practices, particularly the way you settle your baby to sleep, influence his feeding and sleeping patterns. All these will be covered in greater depth in this book.

Pain

Second to hunger, pain is the next most commonly suspected cause for a baby's unexplained crying or wakefulness and should be assessed as a potential cause. Many parents ask me, 'How can I tell if my baby is experiencing pain?' The checklist on the next page can help you assess whether your baby is in pain.

Diagram 1.1: Pain checklist

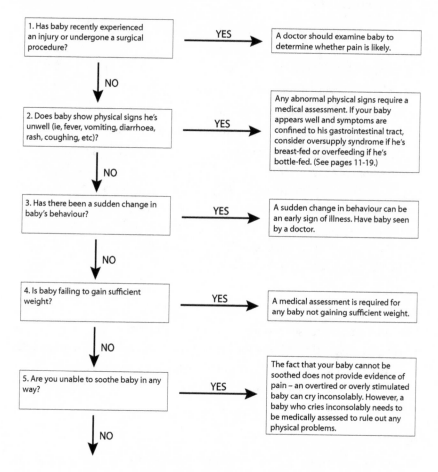

1. Has baby recently experienced an injury or undergone a surgical procedure? — YES → A doctor should examine baby to determine whether pain is likely.

NO ↓

2. Does baby show physical signs he's unwell (ie, fever, vomiting, diarrhoea, rash, coughing, etc)? — YES → Any abnormal physical signs require a medical assessment. If your baby appears well and symptoms are confined to his gastrointestinal tract, consider oversupply syndrome if he's breast-fed or overfeeding if he's bottle-fed. (See pages 11-19.)

NO ↓

3. Has there been a sudden change in baby's behaviour? — YES → A sudden change in behaviour can be an early sign of illness. Have baby seen by a doctor.

NO ↓

4. Is baby failing to gain sufficient weight? — YES → A medical assessment is required for any baby not gaining sufficient weight.

NO ↓

5. Are you unable to soothe baby in any way? — YES → The fact that your baby cannot be soothed does not provide evidence of pain – an overtired or overly stimulated baby can cry inconsolably. However, a baby who cries inconsolably needs to be medically assessed to rule out any physical problems.

NO ↓

If baby can be comforted in some way, such as being picked up, cuddled or fed, then he's probably not in pain. Comforting does little to offset true pain. If he quickly settles back to sleep, it's unlikely that pain was the reason for him awakening.

If baby calms quickly after being picked up, but soon starts to cry again even while being held in your arms, this may mean he wants or needs more than a cuddle. He may be hungry, still tired, overtired, overstimulated or bored.

If you suspect your baby is experiencing pain, have him examined by a medical doctor. Next, we will examine the most common medical reasons for babies to experience pain.

Illness and medical conditions

Unexplained infant crying and sleeping problems are among the most common reasons for parents to access health services,[3] especially when babies display gastrointestinal symptoms, such as vomiting, diarrhoea, abdominal cramps and bloating.[4]

Virtually any illness or medical condition that can cause a baby discomfort or pain can also cause broken sleep and irritability. If baby is currently suffering from an illness or an untreated medical condition, he's likely to be fussy or distressed at times, want to be held constantly, have difficulty sleeping during the day and wake more than usual during the night.

The types of illnesses and medical conditions your doctor will consider when examining your baby and taking a detailed history from you include:

- acute illnesses, eg, gastrointestinal, middle ear, urinary tract and respiratory infections
- dermatitis
- asthma
- airway obstructions, eg, inflamed tonsils and/or adenoids (any snoring requires a medical assessment)
- food allergy or intolerance
- acid reflux
- chronic illnesses
- neurological problems and
- recent surgical procedures, eg, circumcision.

These medical conditions generally only cause infant distress and sleep disturbance in the short term, until the illness passes or the condition is effectively treated or managed.

If you're wondering why teething hasn't been included in this list, surprisingly, scientific studies reveal that teething rarely disrupts the sleep of babies.[5] Infant irritability and wakefulness often attributed to teething is usually related to a behavioural sleep problem. I find parents who take steps to prevent or resolve behavioural sleep problems rarely complain about their babies being troubled by teething pain.

In 2000 a three-month study conducted at the Riverton Early Parenting Centre where I worked, revealed that 95 per cent of babies admitted to the centre during the study period had previously been diagnosed with between one and five medical conditions to explain their crying and wakeful behaviour. Less than five per cent of these babies actually had a medical condition.[6] Most babies responded favourably to behavioural techniques aimed at changing the baby's sleep associations and/or the timing of sleeps, indicating that medical conditions are infrequently the cause of a healthy baby's sleep problems.

What to do

If your baby displays any abnormal physical signs that might indicate an illness or a medical condition, such as fever, vomiting, diarrhoea, rash, coughing, poor appetite, irritability or lethargy, or if you're worried that a physical problem is disrupting your baby's sleep, have him examined by a medical doctor.

A point to consider if your baby has been diagnosed with a medical condition is that this does not preclude his simultaneously experiencing broken sleep due to behavioural or developmental reasons. So don't limit your search to medical solutions.

Non-medical reasons for discomfort and pain

Angus is six weeks old and breast-fed. He screams all day and barely sleeps. He even wakes up screaming. I can tell he's in pain. We've tried a number of different colic and reflux medications and I have eliminated all the likely suspects from my diet. My doctor suggested I try him on a hypoallergenic formula. I don't want to stop breastfeeding but don't know what else I can do. – Louise

When your precious baby is bawling his eyes out and has trouble falling asleep despite obvious signs of tiredness, or wakes still tired and immediately screams, pain could be a reason. However, the most common reasons for physically well babies to experience discomfort, pain and distress relate to non-medical problems. These include the following:

- becoming too hot or too cold
- wet clothing due to a wet nappy or bringing up milk
- a soiled nappy, which could scald a baby's bottom
- nappy rash and
- needing to burp.

Because these problems are easy to identify, they can be quickly remedied. Therefore they're not usually responsible for unexplained crying or ongoing sleep problems. The most frequent non-medical reasons for healthy, thriving babies to experience repeated discomfort and pain, or display distressed behaviour (easily mistaken as pain) are due to what I call the Big Os: overtiredness, overstimulation, oversupply syndrome and overfeeding.

Overtiredness

Sleep deprivation is the most common reason for unexplained crying, as well as fussy, demanding and distressed behaviour displayed by healthy babies and children. It is a major cause of stress for babies and children, as well as adults. Sleep-deprived babies cry, and cry often.

As a sleep-deprived parent, you know all too well that lack of sleep causes stress. What you might not be aware of is that crying is one way our body releases the tension we feel when stressed. Dr William H Frey, a biochemist and author of *Crying: The mystery of tears*, proposed that people feel better after crying. He claims humans benefit from shedding tears while crying because emotional tears contain higher than normal levels of certain hormones, which our bodies produce when we are stressed.[7] Crying helps us re-establish homeostasis – an internal state of harmony within the body – more quickly. As adults, we don't usually cry when we become sleep-deprived, but we can often feel like we're on the verge of tears. And it doesn't take much to tip us over the edge.

Screaming and frantic body movements displayed by sleep-deprived babies can be easily mistaken for pain. Chapter 2 describes the behaviour displayed by sleep-deprived babies, explains why babies become overtired, and why lack of sleep causes distress.

Overstimulation

Another common source of distress for babies is overstimulation. Overstimulation occurs when a baby's nervous system becomes overloaded by too much sensory stimulation. Baby becomes overwhelmed by too much happening to him or around him. Too much stimulation is stressful for a baby who is powerless to remove himself from the situation. Stress triggers the release of stress hormones, which activate a baby's fight or flight response. He then either withdraws by tuning out or falling asleep (if he can) or, alternatively, he screams and thrashes his body around.

When we're feeling dog-tired, we want peace and quiet. This is because we don't enjoy or handle sensory stimulation very well when we're feeling this way. Your baby is no different. If your baby is not getting enough sleep, he's going to be sensitive to any sort of sensory stimulation, like bright lights, loud or sudden noises, getting dressed or undressed, having a bath or massage, or being jiggled or patted. If he's is a newborn, he's even more vulnerable to overstimulation owing to immaturity of his nervous system. Overtired/overstimulated newborns can continue to cry, despite parents' best efforts to soothe them, for what can feel like or literally be hours on end.

Pain is typically suspected of being the cause of an overtired/overstimulated baby's inconsolably crying. **But baby is distressed rather than in pain.** Distress is more likely to occur in the evenings when a baby's sleep debt – which accumulates if he does not get enough sleep earlier in the day – is at a peak. Colic is frequently blamed for the evening screaming sessions displayed by overtired/overstimulated babies. Unfortunately, the situation can be made worse if the reason for baby's crying is mistaken as pain. Strategies to relieve a baby's perceived pain, such as warm baths, tummy massage, burping, etc, may further stimulate his already overloaded nervous system, prolonging his distress. Resolve the problem causing overtiredness and you can minimise the risk of your baby suffering distress as a result of overstimulation.

Oversupply syndrome

Oversupply syndrome (also called hyperlactation syndrome) is a poorly recognised breastfeeding problem outside of breastfeeding circles. It can occur where a breastfeeding mother with an overly abundant supply of breast milk and a forceful let-down reflex – which many breastfeeding mothers have in the early weeks – switches her baby from one breast to the other too soon.

The fat content of breast milk varies from feed to feed depending on how full the mother's breasts are. In general, the emptier a mother's breasts, the higher the fat content of her milk. An oversupply of breast milk means a mother's breasts produce large volumes of milk, more than her baby needs. In the case of oversupply, by switching sides too soon this limits the amount of high-fat hindmilk the baby is able to access. Instead, he receives large volumes of low-fat breast milk. Baby then needs to feed more frequently owing to the lower kilojoule/calorie content of low-fat milk.

A healthy newborn baby's immature digestive tract can digest enough lactose for healthy growth, but may not be able to digest all the lactose received from frequent large volume, low-fat feeds. Low-fat milk travels through baby's intestinal tract faster than milk with a higher fat content. The milk can be pushed through baby's small intestines so quickly that there is insufficient time for all the lactose to be digested. So baby develops gastrointestinal (GI) symptoms owing to lactose overload (not to be confused with lactose intolerance). The medical term for lactose overload is 'transient lactase deficiency'. It's not a medical condition, rather it relates to the mismatch between the baby's immature digestive system and the parent's infant feeding practices. Symptoms of lactose overload in a breast-fed baby include intestinal spasms, frequent watery, frothy or 'explosive' bowel motions, which may sometimes be green in colour. The baby may have an excoriated area around his anus because his stools become acidic owing to the fermentation of lactose in his large intestine. Blood or mucous can appear in a baby's stools if this problem is severe and prolonged. GI symptoms often vary in degree depending on the how much lactose is present in baby's intestinal tract at the time. Many, but not all, babies will regurgitate milk if their stomach becomes overly extended by large volume feeds. Despite these symptoms, the baby usually gains average or above average weight. Other symptoms include irritability and sleep disturbance due to abdominal discomfort. Baby wants to feed frequently in an attempt to soothe his aching belly. Many breastfeeding mothers with an oversupply of breast milk mistakenly interpret their baby's demands for frequent feeds as a sign of low milk supply. The problems related to oversupply syndrome don't end here.

Health professionals in general, including medical doctors who have not undergone specialised breastfeeding education, often fail to recognise this problem. As a consequence, the symptoms associated with oversupply syndrome are typically misdiagnosed as reflux, lactose intolerance or cow's milk protein allergy or intolerance. What distinguishes oversupply syndrome from these conditions is the fact that baby is gaining average or above average weight, something that does not occur when a baby has an untreated medical condition affecting his digestive tract.

Owing to misdiagnosis, countless breastfeeding mothers are mistakenly advised to eliminate certain foods from their diet, or give their babies medications or specialised infant formula. Unfortunately, any infant formula that is lactose-free or lactose-reduced (which includes anti-colic, anti-regurgitation (AR) and hyper-allergenic formulas) will reduce or relieve the GI symptoms associated with oversupply syndrome and this causes parents and health professionals to believe the misdiagnosis was correct. This is unfortunate because baby then misses out on the countless benefits that breastfeeding offers and the health professional who made the misdiagnosis may go on to recommend a similar course of action for other breast-fed babies troubled by oversupply syndrome.

A breastfeeding mother does not need to stop breastfeeding or restrict her diet to manage this problem. She simply needs to 'finish the first breast first' before switching her baby to the other side, thus enabling her baby to obtain more of the calorie-dense, high-fat hind milk which comes as her breast empties. Some mothers with an overabundance of breast milk need to 'block feed'. This means feeding baby consecutively from the same breast a number of times before the breast has emptied sufficiently. When the fat content of the milk is higher, baby does not need to consume as much milk, and thus the GI symptoms associated with lactose overload are reduced or alleviated. If you suspect your baby may be troubled by oversupply syndrome, see a qualified lactation consultant for individualised breastfeeding advice. Feeding management alone has been shown to cause a partial or complete resolution of GI symptoms in 79 per cent of babies with this problem.[8] But feeding management won't resolve distress due to overtiredness, which occurs as a result of a behavioural sleep problem.

Overfeeding

Another problem often overlooked is overfeeding, possibly due to the misperception that only fat babies are overfed babies. But a baby's size and shape is irrelevant. Tiny premature babies, lean babies and chubby babies can all overfeed. Overfeeding can be problematic for formula- and breast-fed babies who are given bottle feeds, irrespective of whether the bottle contains breast milk or infant formula.

Overfeeding is not just about weight. The symptoms associated with overfeeding occur due to overnutrition. Overnutrition means a healthy baby receives more nutrients (protein, fats and carbohydrates) than he needs for healthy growth. Overnutrition can cause a baby's immature digestive tract to be swamped with more nutrients – lactose in particular – than it is capable of digesting. Symptoms of overnutrition include frequent sloppy bowel motions for formula-fed babies, or watery explosive bowel motions if the baby receives mostly breast milk, intestinal spasms, excessive and often smelly intestinal gas, eight or more heavily wet nappies each day and irritability and sleeplessness owing to abdominal discomfort. Some babies may throw up small or large volumes of milk owing to hyperextension of their stomach, a common problem if baby feeds too quickly. An overfed baby will gain average to above average weight, however, weight gains won't necessarily appear excessive. The baby's homeostatic mechanisms – that correct or maintain the proper balance within the body – will attempt to compensate for overnutrition by regurgitating milk or pushing undigested nutrients through the intestinal tract.

The GI symptoms associated with overfeeding and overnutrition are often misdiagnosed as reflux, lactose intolerance and cow's milk protein allergy or intolerance. Lactose-free or lactose-reduced infant formula, 'anti-colic' and AR formulas, and hypoallergenic infant formulas can mask the intestinal symptoms associated with overfeeding, but fail to fully address the underlying reasons for it. And, so, the baby may continue to overfeed, regurgitate small or large amounts of milk, and continue to gain large amounts of weight. Fixing the symptoms is not the same as fixing the problem.

The problem of overfeeding is common in the newborn period owing to a number of factors. Hunger is typically the first thing suspected when a baby cries for unknown reasons, when a baby wakes prematurely from sleep, and whenever a baby wants to suck. Babies under the age of three months are especially vulnerable to overfeeding because of their suck reflex. A newborn's suck reflex can be automatically triggered by pressure on his tongue and palate by the teat of a feeding bottle, his mother's nipple, a pacifier, baby's fist or a parent's finger. If baby's suck reflex is triggered, he will suck because he can't not suck. Thus, a newborn baby has limited ability to control the flow of milk or stop when he has had enough, and, so, sucking is not proof of hunger.

Another common reason for overfeeding to occur is when a baby feeds too quickly. The ideal time for a newborn baby to complete a bottle feed is 20–40 minutes. The faster the feed, the greater the risk is that the baby will overfeed. Additionally, many societies mistakenly consider chubbiness in infancy to be an indication of good health. Yet, it's important to remember that we don't consider chubbiness at any other age to be a sign of good health.

The problem of overfeeding can be easily resolved by slowing down your bottle-fed baby's feeding, spacing feeds out to three- to four-hour intervals during the day, preventing baby from falling asleep while feeding, and satisfying baby's desire to suck using other means, for example, a pacifier or your finger. Feeding management strategies will usually resolve the GI symptoms associated with overfeeding, however, they won't necessarily improve a baby's contentment or sleeping patterns if his distress or broken sleep relates to a behavioural sleep problem.

How the Big Os connect

A newborn baby could experience one, two or three of the Big Os at the same time. Sleep deprivation alone is enough to cause a baby varying degrees of distress. Throw overstimulation, oversupply syndrome or overfeeding into the mix and this could take baby's distress to a whole new level.

More often than not, the initial reason for a well baby's wakefulness is due solely to a behavioural sleep problem. Wakefulness then creates a sleep debt that accumulates over the course of the day. Hunger is typically blamed for a baby's wakefulness, at least in the early stages. Parents then take steps to increase the amount of milk their baby receives, offering more frequent feeds, larger volumes, both breasts at each feed, or bottle feeds in addition to breastfeeds. This can cause a newborn baby to develop GI symptoms related to oversupply syndrome and/or overfeeding. The baby's intestinal tract becomes overloaded from receiving large volume, low-fat breastfeeds or consuming too much formula. The baby suffers abdominal discomfort or pain owing to intestinal spasms, and may throw up any milk his tiny, over-stretched stomach is incapable of holding. A vicious cycle develops. Abdominal discomfort prevents baby from falling asleep and increases his wakefulness and desire to suck as a way to soothe. This is mistakenly interpreted as hunger. Baby is offered another feed. This further overloads baby's already overloaded digestive tract, perpetuating his GI symptoms. And finally, lack of sleep and the strategies that parents use to attempt to relieve their baby's discomfort actually increase the risk of baby becoming overstimulated. The end result is you have one VERY distressed little baby on your hands.

When you consider this sequence of events, it's easy to see why a health professional might mistakenly diagnose a medical condition. But healthy growth distinguishes these problems from medical conditions, such as reflux, milk protein allergy or lactose intolerance. A medical condition affecting a baby's digestive tract will cause poor growth until such time as the condition is treated or managed effectively. But don't assume that poor growth provides proof of a medical condition. Eighty per cent of babies who experience poor growth have no underlying medical or physical cause.[9]

A misdiagnosis can – and often does – cause added problems for the baby. In some cases the recommended strategies to treat the diagnosed condition can contribute to baby's distress. For example, many parents are advised to hold babies allegedly suffering reflux upright for 30 minutes following feeds. But this can cause two major headaches for parents:

- their baby may become upset due to tiredness, boredom or overstimulation or
- their baby learns to fall asleep in this position and then finds it difficult to sleep any other way, and awakens when his parents try to put him down to sleep.

Medications can alter the natural chemistry and/or functioning of a baby's body causing additional problems further down the track. For example, antacids given to treat gastro-oesophageal reflux disease (GORD) in adults have been shown to block nutrient absorption, increase vulnerability to food allergies and gastrointestinal infections, and cause a problem called 'rebound acidity' where the stomach then produces excessive amounts of stomach acid. The question that has not yet been fully answered is: what long-term effect do antacids and acid-suppressing medications have on a baby's developing digestive system at a time when nutrients are needed to keep pace with rapid growth? Antacids and acid-suppressing medications may mask the symptoms of oversupply syndrome and overfeeding by slowing down the rate at which milk travels through a baby's intestinal tract – allowing more time for nutrients to be digested and absorbed – but they won't fix the cause.

Thomas's story below depicts an infant sleep problem that triggered a host of other problems.

Baby Thomas

From birth, Thomas would fall asleep while breastfeeding. For the first two weeks he would sleep well and have long naps. He was a very contented baby who demanded feeds around 2½–3½-hour intervals. His mother, Sue, thought she was lucky to have such a dream baby. However, when Thomas was around two weeks old his sleeping patterns changed; so too did his behaviour. He no longer took long naps; instead he would regularly wake, still tired, after a 20-minute nap. He was no longer a contented baby; rather he fussed and whined, wanted to be held continually and would cry if he was put down awake. By evening, he would cry regardless of whether held or not. Some evenings he would cry inconsolably for three hours or more before finally falling asleep.

Worried, Sue took him to a doctor who said, 'It's just colic,' and reassured her that Thomas would outgrow the problem by three months of age. Over the next few weeks, things progressively worsened. Thomas started to throw up increasingly larger amounts of milk up to two hours following feeds, yet gained 200–500 grams [7.05–17 oz] every week. His stools were frequent and watery, at times causing a bright red nappy rash. He was also very gassy, frequently expelling loud burps and farts. His fussiness now extended through the entire day. Even cuddling did little to comfort him. Sue commented that the only time he was not fussing or crying was when he was feeding or sleeping. Sue added that both she and her husband were thankful that Thomas slept well for the first part of the night. She could often hear him wake in the small hours of the morning, grunting, groaning and passing gas.

The stress of caring for a fussy baby all day long, day after day, was taking its toll. Sue was feeling at her wits' end caring for Thomas. She had the constant nagging thought that something more than colic was wrong with him. She took him back to the doctor, who diagnosed reflux and recommended an acid-suppressing medication. The doctor also suggested that Thomas be held upright for 15–30 minutes after all feeds. Things improved slightly, but not to the level that Sue had hoped. At the third visit, the doctor increased the medication dosage and recommended Sue avoid eating dairy, eggs, soy, nuts and wheat products, as he felt Thomas could be reacting to something that Sue was eating. This too proved to be a disappointment. At the fourth consultation, the doctor recommended that Sue stop breastfeeding and instead feed Thomas a hypoallergenic formula. Sue wanted to breastfeed Thomas and decided that because he was gaining weight well she would only take this step after she was confident that it was the only option left.

When Thomas was 10 weeks old, a friend of Sue's recommended she contact me. After asking about her infant feeding and settling practices, something her doctor did not do, what was troubling Thomas became clear. The distress he displayed, the large milk spills and gastrointestinal symptoms were two separate but related problems, namely overtiredness and oversupply syndrome, and not a result of colic, reflux or a reaction to the foods Sue was eating.

Thomas had lost the ability to self-regulate his sleeping patterns, learning instead to depend on Sue's help to fall and regulate his sleep. He also struggled to self-regulate his dietary intake because breastfeeding had become his way to fall asleep. This meant he wanted to feed not only when he was hungry, but also when he was tired. Sue had an overabundant supply of breast milk and a forceful let-down reflex. She was unknowingly making it difficult for Thomas to regulate his intake because she was switching sides too often. When he simply wanted to suckle to fall asleep, what he got was a large amount of milk flooding into his mouth.

In summary, Thomas was troubled by sleep deprivation due to his dependence on being breast-fed to sleep, which in turn caused feeding issues resulting in stomach pain. Sue needed to deal with both problems at the same time to succeed in relieving Thomas's discomfort. She followed my feeding recommendations to manage oversupply and encouraged Thomas to learn new sleep habits which enabled him to fall asleep independently and self-regulate his sleep patterns. Within a few days, he was a completely different baby, more relaxed when he fed and taking long naps during the day. He was bright, alert and contented when awake. He was a much happier little baby. With the permission of her doctor Sue ceased giving Thomas acid-suppressing medications and went on to successfully breastfeed him for over 12 months.

The risk of overstimulation and incidence of overfeeding and oversupply syndrome are reduced once a baby reaches three to four months of age. By then, increased nervous system development allows him to handle sensory stimulation better. The disappearance of a baby's suck reflex at that point increases his ability to control the flow of milk and self-regulate his dietary intake according to his needs, thus minimising the risk of overfeeding. Oversupply problems are usually resolved by three months of age, depending on how the mother manages the situation. In a small percentage of cases oversupply syndrome can take up to six months to resolve spontaneously if the problem has not been identified or effectively managed. This means, in most cases babies literally outgrow problems like overstimulation, overfeeding and oversupply syndrome by around three months of age. But you needn't wait for these problems to resolve spontaneously; they can be resolved or at least managed at any age.

You may find it difficult to resolve an infant sleep problem unless you also take effective steps to manage overfeeding or oversupply syndrome. Conversely, it may be difficult to effectively manage overfeeding, oversupply or overstimulation without resolving any behavioural sleep problem your baby might be experiencing. Babies don't outgrow a behavioural sleep problem. Your baby is powerless to change the situation without your guidance. How to resolve behavioural sleep problems is what this book is all about.

Developmental changes

> My baby has recently learned to roll. Now he keeps rolling onto his tummy in the night and then cries because he's stuck. No sooner do I turn him onto his back and he flips onto his tummy again. I had to resort to staying with him and patting him to sleep. Something I didn't need to do previously. – Mary

Mary recognised the reason why her baby had trouble falling back to sleep, but may not be aware of the developmental reasons why her baby may have started waking in the first place. Less obvious reasons for increased wakefulness relate to advancements in a baby's physical, intellectual and emotional development. As your baby develops this will affect the way he thinks, feels and reacts in different situations, including sleep time. The many developmental changes that can affect a baby's sleep patterns or behaviour include:

- **Intellectual growth spurts:** According to child development experts Hetty van de Rijt-Plooij and Frans Plooij, babies experience intellectual growth spurts roughly around the ages of five, eight, 12, 23, 34, 42 and 51 weeks, which are linked to changes in a baby's developing brain and nervous system.[10] These can be unsettling and may trigger increased wakefulness for a period of days or weeks.
- **Intellectual development:** Increased mental maturity makes a baby become increasingly more aware of his surroundings. His memory and ability to recognise consistencies and inconsistencies in the care he receives is enhanced. For example, while the loss of a pacifier during sleep might not bother a newborn baby, by the time he reaches four months of age, it could cause him to wake.
- **Developmental milestones:** New skill acquisitions – like rolling, sitting, standing, crawling or walking – are typically associated with increased wakefulness. Like Mary's baby, your baby might choose to practise his newfound skills during the night.

- **Increased ability to express emotions:** Increased physical, intellectual and emotional development around the age of three months means a baby is able to express a broader range of emotions through cries and behaviour. By three months of age, healthy babies can express both delight and anger.[11] The latter involves intense crying, easily mistaken as pain.
- **Changing emotional needs:** Day-time clinginess and night-time wakefulness can occur due to separation anxiety.

Your baby is continually developing, physically, intellectually and emotionally, and his emotions and reactions change accordingly. Settling methods that work well while he's a newborn may no longer be effective by the time he's six or 12 months old.

What to do

- The only way to determine whether the reason for sleep disturbances or changes in sleeping patterns is due to developmental reasons is to first rule out physical reasons, such as illness, medical conditions, or over- and underfeeding, and behavioural reasons, such as dependence on negative sleep associations or a circadian rhythm sleep problem.
- Be patient. If no physical or behavioural reasons exist, then the problem of wakefulness will usually resolve spontaneously in a matter of days or weeks.
- Provide opportunities for your baby to master new developmental skills, such as rolling and standing, during the day. Offer him lots of floor play opportunities so that he can stretch his muscles and practise new skills.
- Take care not to encourage your baby to learn to depend on negative sleep associations in your haste to encourage him to fall back to sleep, ie, anything that involves you helping him fall asleep, or sleep aids that can fall out, turn off or change after he has fallen asleep. This could lead to behavioural sleep problems which result in wakefulness that continues long after the original cause has disappeared. Mary started patting her baby to sleep,

unaware that, by doing so, she was teaching him to rely on patting to fall asleep. Once he did, which can happen in a matter of days, the problem worsened. He then started waking multiple times during the night. In a light sleep phase he could recognise he was no longer being patted.

Separation anxiety

Bryce (aged 4 months) wants to be carried all day and cries whenever I try to put him down for more than a few minutes. At night he won't let me put him back into his cot while he's awake. Is this separation anxiety? – Ruth

Even though Bryce cries whenever he's not in Ruth's arms, he's too young to experience true separation anxiety. Separation anxiety begins at about six months, peaks between nine and 18 months, and diminishes by about 2½ years of age.[12] The reason Bryce doesn't want to be put down during the day may be because he has learned to associate sleeping with being in close physical contact with Ruth or another warm body. Hence, during the day he cries if he's not being cuddled.

A baby will typically cry when experiencing separation anxiety, but don't assume that crying for attention during the night is due to separation anxiety. First consider how your baby behaves during the day. Is it consistent with separation anxiety? Behaviour that may indicate separation anxiety includes:

- crying when the main caregiver (usually the mother) is out of sight
- an unwillingness to be left alone even for a few moments
- clinginess, wanting to be held constantly in unfamiliar situations
- increased anxiety around strangers, as this usually develops around the same time as separation anxiety.

Many parents suspect separation anxiety when their baby begins to cry as soon as he is placed into his cot, or wakes and cries during the night until they return, and for day-time clinginess. While separation could be responsible, usually other reasons are involved, especially when such behaviour is extreme. For example, sleep-deprived babies often cling and cry every time they're put down. Babies who are dependent on others to satisfy their innate desire to suck will appear like they're suffering from separation more than babies who suck on their own fists or fingers. The most common reason for well babies to wake prematurely and cry until their parents return is because they have learned to rely on their parents' help to fall asleep, and thus require the same help to return to sleep. So your baby isn't necessarily experiencing anxiety over being separated from you. Rather he may be upset because you're not there to help him soothe or to fall asleep in the way he has learned to expect. In each of these scenarios and in the case of Connor below, the baby is crying to fulfil a want or need, not exhibiting separation anxiety.

Baby Connor

When Connor was 10 months old his mother, Kerry, returned to work full time, leaving him in the care of his father, Nick, who planned to work part- time from home. From the first day, Connor did not cope well with Kerry's absence. He barely slept and was miserable, fussing and whining. It took Nick's full attention to distract and console him. By the time Kerry returned home, Connor was distressed and so was Nick. Connor would fall asleep almost as soon as she started to breastfeed him. During the night he woke frequently to be breast-fed back to sleep, more than twice as often as before Kerry returned to work. Kerry was physically exhausted from working full time and being woken up to five times a night to breastfeed Connor. Nick was exhausted from trying to placate Connor most of the day, and was unable to do any of his own work. And Connor was miserable for most of the day.

Kerry believed Connor's distress was due to separation anxiety and asked if I could suggest some strategies to reduce his anxiety. But I suspected Connor's distress was the result of a breastfeeding-sleep association. Connor had learned to depend on suckling at this mother's breast as a way to fall asleep. Nick was not able to get him to sleep in the same way, so Connor would stay awake until he was too exhausted to remain awake any longer. He became increasingly more miserable as the day progressed owing to lack of sleep.

As long as Kerry continued breastfeeding him to sleep, reinforcing his dependence on breastfeeding as a sleep association, nothing would change. Kerry decided to breastfeed Connor when she could, and express milk for Nick to give to him, but she no longer allowed him to fall asleep while breastfeeding. Instead, Kerry and Nick encouraged Connor to fall asleep independently. In a matter of days, he settled to sleep with ease, napping between one and two hours, twice a day. Now that Connor was no longer burdened by sleep deprivation, he was once again a happy baby. Nick could work while Connor napped, and he was a joy for Nick to care for. He also began sleeping through the night for the first time since his birth. Kerry got to spend enjoyable evenings with him, as he was no longer distressed due to sleep deprivation. Connor had not been suffering from separation anxiety after all.

Babies and toddlers aren't the only ones to experience anxiety as a result of separation. Many parents, mothers in particular, can suffer anxiety when they're separated from their babies. If you're feeling anxious about being separated from your baby, you may project that and believe, rightly or wrongly, that your baby is experiencing the same anxiety.

What to do

It is unlikely that a baby wakes because of separation anxiety, but, after waking due to other reasons, he can express such anxiety. By ensuring your baby's sleep associations remain consistent throughout his entire sleep, you may minimise the risk of his waking prematurely. Like Kerry, you may discover that what you thought was separation anxiety was in fact something else entirely.

Unrealistic expectations

Unrealistic parental expectations could lead you to believe your baby has a sleeping problem when his sleeping patterns are – in fact – normal, and to be expected for his stage of development. I occasionally meet parents who have tried to encourage or force their baby to achieve something he's developmentally not capable of achieving. Examples include:

- withholding night-time feeds to encourage a baby to sleep through the night before he's mature enough to do so
- expecting a baby to sleep longer than he physically needs
- expecting a baby to sleep in multiple settings
- expecting a baby to comply with rigid feeding and sleeping schedules.

Baby Fergus

I received a telephone call from Robert, asking if I had any suggestions on how he could encourage his son, Fergus, aged 11 months, to sleep longer in the mornings. Fergus was waking consistently at around 5 am but Robert wanted him to sleep until about 8 am. I asked about Fergus's current sleeping patterns and behaviour. He had no trouble falling asleep. He napped twice a day. He settled to sleep at approximately 6 pm each night and would sleep soundly until close to 5 or 5.30 am. I suggested to Robert if he wanted Fergus to sleep later, he would need to gradually shift bedtime closer to 8.30 pm. Robert, however, wanted to keep Fergus's 6 pm bedtime. I explained that it would be unrealistic to expect Fergus to sleep for 14 hours overnight. Robert asked if cutting out one of Fergus's day-time naps would help. I advised him that at his age Fergus still needed two naps during the day and that eliminating one would not help him sleep longer during the night. Robert was not being unreasonable by investigating the possibilities. But it would have been unreasonable to attempt to force Fergus to sleep 14 hours overnight.

What to do

Before attempting to improve an infant sleep problem, make sure it's a genuine problem, and not a sleeping pattern consistent with your baby's stage of development. Also make sure you're not trying to get your baby to do something he's physically not capable of achieving. Check with your health professional if you're unsure.

Key points

- Medical conditions are not the only reason for babies to experience pain or discomfort. The Big Os are common reasons for healthy, thriving babies to experience abdominal discomfort or appear like they're suffering pain.

- Problems are not mutually exclusive. A baby may have a medical condition that is currently well managed and yet continue to display sleepless or wakeful behaviour due to a behavioural sleep problem or developmental reasons.

- Developmental reasons for sleep disturbance will normally resolve spontaneously, provided no underlying behavioural reasons are involved.

- Behavioural sleep problems can continue for months or years unless parents take effective steps to resolve the problem.

- Separation anxiety is often mistakenly blamed for wakefulness and crying when a baby has a behavioural sleep problem.

- The key is to explore all possibilities.

2

Overtiredness

Topics

Why babies become overtired

Signs that indicate babies are overtired

How lack of sleep affects babies' ability to sleep

Problems that can develop when babies are chronically overtired

My 8-week-old daughter, Georgia, cries constantly. I don't know what to do to comfort her. She hardly sleeps during the day, which I know is making things worse. She can be exhausted and crying her eyes out, but she can't seem to sleep. I am at a loss to figure out what's preventing her from sleeping, and so is my doctor. I have changed her formula four times and I have given her all sorts of medications (recommended by my doctor), but nothing has helped. Can you please help me? – Jess

Lack of sleep, without exception, is the most common cause of fussy or distressed behaviour displayed by healthy babies and children. More often than not, it's the stress associated with lack of sleep that makes it difficult for babies to fall asleep.

Unfortunately, getting enough sleep is not a simple process for babies or young children. I will explain why babies experience sleep problems that cause sleep deprivation in Chapters 3, 4 and 5, but, first, let's examine how sleep deprivation affects a baby's behaviour, as well as our own.

Why we need sleep

We know that we need sleep to feel energised, but sleep provides many more benefits besides restoring our bodies to a state of alertness. Sleep supports the optimal functioning of all our bodily processes. We need sleep to re-establish homeostasis, the state of harmony within our body. Lack of sleep is a source of stress to our body, affecting us physically and emotionally. Sleep is a basic human requirement that is as important to our physical wellbeing as nutrition.

How much sleep do babies need?

> Jenna is 3 months old. I am wondering if the reason she's so cranky is because she's not getting enough sleep. She gets around 11 hours a day. Is 11 hours enough at her age? – Gail

While there are average sleep times for babies, there's no required amount of sleep for a baby. Look for signs that your baby is well-rested. If your baby is healthy, thriving and generally content, then whatever amount of sleep she's getting is fine. If, on the other hand, your baby is irritable and not getting close to the average amount of sleep for her age (see Table 2.1 next page), then sleep deprivation may be a potential cause. Jenna is getting considerably less sleep than average for her age, plus she is cranky. So sleep deprivation is a potential reason for her crankiness. But it may not be the only reason.

Tips to help baby sleep

- Pillows are not recommended for children under 2 years of age. A pillow increases the risk of suffocation and SIDS.

- Exposure to daylight during the day can help a baby sleep better at night.

- The ideal temperature for sleep is between 18 to 22 degrees Celsius (or 65 to 70 degrees Fahrenheit).

The following table provides sleep averages for different ages. Use the figures as a rough guide only. Individual babies vary in the amount of sleep they need. Some sleep more and some less than average. Also day-to-day variations in the daily amount of sleep required are normal.

Table 2.1: Average hours sleep for age

Age	Average total sleep time (hours)	Average night sleep (hours)	Average day sleep (hours)
1 week	16½	8½	8
1 month	15½	8¾	6¾
3 months	15	10	5
6 months	14¼	11	3¼
9 months	14	11¼	2¾
12 months	13¾	11¾	2
18 months	13½	11¾	1¾
24 months	13	11¾	1¼

If you're not sure how much sleep your baby gets, keep a record for a day or two.

What happens when we don't get enough sleep?

What are the degrees of physical fatigue? When you're tired, you can easily fall asleep if given the opportunity. When you're exhausted, you can barely drag yourself around and have trouble keeping your eyes open. Overtiredness lies somewhere between tiredness and exhaustion. This diagram illustrates the progression.

Tiredness → Overtiredness → Exhaustion

Overtiredness means your body has gone beyond being ready to sleep. It involves a state of physical fatigue that disrupts homeostasis and activates your stress-response system. Stress hormones such as cortisol and adrenaline flood your bloodstream. These are often referred to as 'fight or flight' hormones because they increase your state of awareness, speed up your heart rate, raise your blood pressure and cause tension to build up in your muscles. Despite being physically fatigued, your mind is alert. You feel keyed up or agitated, ready to take flight or fight.

You become overtired when you're prevented from sleeping for some reason. You can feel so wrecked that you cannot wait to get into bed, but once your head hits the pillow your mind is racing. You toss and turn. You just can't seem to relax enough to switch off. You may even feel like crying.

Babies also find it difficult to switch off and go to sleep when overtired. But, unlike adults, who become lethargic when overtired, babies and young children become more active. It looks like baby is fighting going to sleep. But your baby wants to sleep, she needs to sleep, but her little body won't let her, because of the stress hormones circulating through her bloodstream.

Sleep debt

Sleep debt refers to lack of sleep. The larger the sleep debt, the more stress this places on your body. Sleep debt can be incurred in a single night or over many days. For example, if you miss out on two hours of sleep on Tuesday, you might cope okay on Wednesday. But if you also miss two hours of sleep on Wednesday, you will possibly struggle a little to get through Thursday. If the same thing happens on Thursday, then by Friday your ability to think and function effectively may be compromised. It gets harder and harder for you to cope because of the cumulative effect of an increasing sleep debt. Eventually, you need to repay the debt. So on Saturday, when your spouse/partner can care for your baby, you might get to catch up on at least some of the lost sleep, restoring your body's normal balance. Recovery from a cumulative sleep debt typically involves more deep sleep and not an hour-for-hour payback of lost sleep. If you fail to repay the debt and it continues, it will have a negative impact on the way you think and feel.

This principle also applies to babies. If, for example, a newborn baby misses an hour's sleep in the morning, it will probably make little difference to her behaviour. But if she misses another hour at her next nap, she might become unsettled and a little more demanding of your attention. If she misses more sleep at her afternoon nap she could have accumulated a sleep debt of several hours. By the evening she is going to be so strung out that it will take a mammoth effort to comfort her. A baby's cortisol level would normally drop in the evenings, enabling her to relax and fall asleep, but sleep deprivation causes a rise in cortisol, preventing her from relaxing.[13] What parents often refer to as the 'witching hours' between 6 pm and 11 pm is – in most cases – simply an accumulation of sleep debt built up over the course of the day or over a number of consecutive days.

What it feels like

When you're sleep-deprived, your symptoms might include:

- fatigue
- irritability
- tearfulness
- moodiness
- short-temperedness
- poor impulse control
- reduced alertness
- clumsiness – an increased risk of accidents due to slower reaction time
- disrupted sleep patterns
- difficulty in both falling and staying asleep
- loss of motivation
- poor concentration
- decreased ability to learn
- poor memory
- reduced efficiency at work
- difficulty making decisions
- decreased rational thought
- poor judgment
- numbness or functioning in a dream-like state
- chronic head or body aches
- weakness, nausea, dizziness or faintness
- over-eating or reduced appetite, and gastrointestinal symptoms.

Infant signs of sleep deprivation

A sleep-deprived baby:

- receives well below the average amount of sleep for her age (see Table 2.1 on page 29 for average sleep needs)
- appears to fight going to sleep
- is easily woken by even the slightest noise, eg, doors opening, talking
- sleeps very little during the day most days – day-time naps are typically very brief, eg, 20–30 minutes
- appears uncomfortable during feeds or periodically refuses to feed during the day, while feeding well during the night
- wakes excessively or sleeps unusually long periods during the night without waking for feeds
- is difficult to get to smile or engage in eye contact
- often has a worried expression
- is generally more content in the mornings than in the afternoons
- finds it increasingly more difficult to fall asleep as the day progresses
- cries often, ranging from whining to vigorous, inconsolable cries
- has a short attention span
- requires constant attention from you when she's awake
- wants to be held continuously, fusses in your arms, but cries whenever you put her down
- resists going into her pram, high chair, crib or car seat
- likes to be jiggled or rocked endlessly
- startles often
- experiences extreme separation anxiety
- displays frequent physical or crying outbursts
- has an insatiable appetite (these babies are often described as 'hungry babies')
- may feed briefly or fall asleep before the feed is completed.

Of course, all babies behave like this from time to time. It is the degree and frequency to which a baby displays these behaviours, plus the fact that she's getting much less than average sleep for her age, that points to sleep deprivation.

Exhaustion

But don't people fall asleep eventually? Yes, after a while our bodies restore the balance. Stress hormones return to normal levels. Breathing and heart rates slow, our minds become quieter, and our bodies relax.

After what could be hours of fussing or crying, your baby will eventually fall asleep, sooner if you're taking steps to help her relax, or longer if the steps you take further stimulate her. Once asleep, a physically exhausted baby may sleep for unusually long periods during the night, especially the first half. If her sleep debt is great you might not hear a peep out of her all night. She may not wake for night-time feeds that would normally be expected for her age.

If she gets enough sleep during the night to pay back her sleep debt, she will start the next day with a clean slate. But if she doesn't, then her sleep debt can be carried over to the next day, in which case, it might not take long before she reaches the point of overtiredness. Many fussy, distressed or demanding babies suffer from sleep deprivation on a daily basis, and encouraging their sleep can feel like a constant battle.

> **Sleep encourages sleep. Lack of sleep makes it difficult for us to sleep. Sleep is the only way to prevent overtiredness and exhaustion.**

Catch-up days

If your baby does not make up for a sleep debt during the night, she might occasionally have a 'catch-up day' instead. This is where a baby sleeps for unusually long periods during the day, after days of not getting enough sleep. She could sleep for three or four hours in one nap during the day or she might have a number of long naps. This is not something she decides to do; it just happens, to restore the balance. Once the sleep debt is repaid – which could take a day or two depending on how great her sleep debt had become – she will appear much happier because her body's natural balance has been restored. She feeds better, settles to sleep more quickly and is less tense and demanding of your attention. You tell others she is having a good day. She is, because she has caught up on missed sleep.

However, if the cause of her sleep deprivation remains unresolved, relief is usually only temporary.

Catch-up days are often a source of confusion. They provide stressed, sleep-deprived parents with much-needed relief. But they can also trick you into thinking that the situation is finally resolving itself or that whatever new strategy you might be trying, for instance a new settling method, dietary change or medication, is working. If it is just a catch-up day, then within a day or two you're likely to find your baby's behaviour relapses as her sleep debt builds once again. But don't despair. You will find the answers within these pages.

True or false?

1. Babies don't suffer from sleeping problems; only parents do.

FALSE: Babies suffer varying degrees of discomfort and distress due to insufficient sleep. Sleep deprivation can stress babies the same as adults. Some severely sleep-deprived babies suffer extreme distress on a daily basis. Chronically sleep-deprived babies face an increased risk of physical ailments because sleep deprivation can disrupt the normal balance and functioning of their body processes. See Table 2.2 on page 37 to discover what a sleep-deprived baby might miss out on.

2. Some babies don't need to sleep during the day.

FALSE: Some babies will sleep less than others, but all babies need to sleep during the day. Up until around three to five years of age, children generally require one or more day-time naps.

3. Some babies are naturally poor sleepers.

FALSE: Some babies do sleep better than others. This is not a natural occurrence, but rather due to circumstances. All healthy babies are capable of sleeping well. Often it is simply a case of changing your baby's sleep habits to promote better sleep. To achieve this, parents usually need to change their infant settling practices.

Problems linked to sleep deprivation

What came first, the chicken or the egg? Do physical issues cause infant sleep problems, or is it the other way around? We all know that physical problems can cause lack of sleep, but lack of sleep can cause physical problems. When we don't get the sleep our body needs to function at optimal capacity, we can suffer both mentally and physically.

More often than not, when physically well babies suffer sleep problems, sleep deprivation is the primary reason for their distress. But sleep deprivation can also be the underlying reason babies develop many problems, as listed in Diagram 2.1.

Diagram 2.1: Baby-care problems related to sleep deprivation

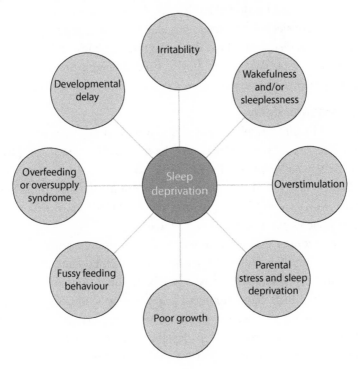

Chapter 1 discussed how a sleep problem could lead to overstimulation, oversupply syndrome and overfeeding. Other problems can also be linked to sleep deprivation.

Poor growth

Not all sleep-deprived babies overfeed. Some chronically sleep-deprived babies struggle to gain sufficient weight. A sleep-deprived baby can become too exhausted to feed effectively and therefore miss out on the nourishment she needs for healthy growth. Sleep-deprived babies often sleep for unusually long periods during the night, too exhausted to wake for night-time feeds.

Fussy feeding behaviour

When we are physically fatigued, it affects our coordination and we can become impatient and easily frustrated. Babies can have the same reaction when they're tired. While they may or may not experience poor growth, both breast-fed and bottle-fed babies can display fussy feeding behaviour owing to lack of sleep. Contrary to popular belief, arching the back during feeding is not evidence of reflux. Babies commonly back arch during times of frustration, especially when they're tired or being pressured to feed. Repeated pressure to feed can cause a behavioural feeding aversion.

Developmental delay

We have difficulty learning new skills and retaining new information when we're tired. And we may not have enough energy for physical activity when we're physically fatigued. So, it is possible that chronic sleep deprivation could delay a baby's development. This doesn't mean the baby won't catch up; simply that she might not learn new skills as quickly as she would if she was well rested.

At nine months of age Suzie was not even attempting to sit on her own. Suzie's mother, Hillary, described her as clingy, and claimed that Suzie would cry whenever she was not being held. By being constantly held, Suzie had little opportunity to practise new skills and develop the muscular strength she needed to sit without support. Suzie's clinginess was largely due to chronic sleep deprivation. Once her sleep problem was resolved, she happily played on the floor. Within a week she was sitting, unsupported.

Other problems

Much of what is known about the benefits of sleep comes from examining the impact of sleep deprivation on adults, as it would be unethical to deliberately deprive infants of sleep to study the effects. The following is only a small example of the benefits of sleep and what can happen when we don't get enough.

Table 2.2:   Sleep benefits

	Benefits of sleep	Problems linked to sleep deprivation
Nervous system	During sleep, blood flow to the brain increases, helping developing brains to grow.[14]	Adversely affected; increases depression and anxiety in both adults and children; increases ADHD in children; increases risk of marital conflicts for parents; lowers pain thresholds.
Endocrine system	Maintains correct hormone balance for proper organ and body system function.	Profound impact; predisposition to illness; linked to adult obesity and Type 2 diabetes.
Digestive system	Stabilises appetite and digestion via the nervous and endocrine systems.	Increased appetite; regurgitation (reflux) and impaired digestion linked or exacerbated.
Immune system	Sleep-wake cycles regulate the normal function of immune systems[15]	After several days, significant detrimental effects possible; weakens resistance to infectious illnesses and allergies.
Growth	Growth hormones are released during sleep.	Linked with excessive weight gain and poor growth; suppresses milk production in mothers.

	Benefits of sleep	Problems linked to sleep deprivation
Development	Vital. Well-rested babies are eager to engage with others, play and explore their environment.	Lack of energy and/ or motivation; increased frustration; less patience to face new challenges.
Memory and learning	REM sleep involves increased brain activity; facilitates learning and memory; increases attention span, memory, and processing and storing of new information.	Impairs attention span, memory, concentration and learning.
Mood and behaviour	Enhances overall quality of life; increases patience and tolerance.	Yields impatient, intolerant, short-tempered, accident-prone and impulsive behaviours. Sleep-deprived babies often whine, fuss, cry, cling; are demanding, irritable and intolerant of environmental stimulation.
Emotional development	Promotes feelings of physical and emotional wellbeing. When basic physical needs for sleep and nutrition are met, babies and parents are calmer, and smile and laugh more.	When physical needs (sleep) have not been met, emotional needs suffer; babies are difficult to soothe and parents struggle more to develop an emotional bond to a baby who is constantly whining, or crying.

As indicated, lack of sleep imposes significant stress on our bodies. We are unable to maintain homeostasis without adequate sleep. If someone tells you not to worry when your baby doesn't sleep, ignore them. Your baby needs sleep.

What can begin as sleep deprivation can lead to bigger and more complex problems for your baby. And a lot more stress for you.

Parental distress

Parental stress as a result of caring for a constantly crying baby or chronic sleep deprivation can be a problem for babies and children, because they're dependent on others for their care. Under the influence of fight or flight hormones, we have a natural tendency to act out aggressively or retreat. It is not surprising that babies and children are at increased risk of receiving unresponsive or hostile care when parents are stressed out or sleep-deprived. Sadly, this can happen.

Not all stressed parents provide unresponsive or hostile care, but it requires a far greater effort to provide responsive nurturing care for a baby when exhausted than when you're well rested. Even the most gentle, placid parents have limits when their bodies are under constant stress. It is important that your baby gets the sleep she needs to reduce her levels of distress. It's equally important that you, her parent or caregiver, receives sufficient sleep.

Key points

- Sleep is a basic physical need as important as nutrition to your baby's health.

- Once a baby has become overtired, it's hard for her to fall asleep.

- Lack of sleep is the most prevalent reason for distress in physically healthy babies.

- Chronic sleep deprivation can cause physical and other baby-care problems.

- To resolve other baby-care problems, you may need to first or simultaneously address the problem causing sleep deprivation.

- Your baby is powerless to change the situation. You're not.

3

Signs that baby is tired

Topics

What are signs of tiredness?
When to expect tired signs.
How to finetune your skills to pinpoint tiredness.

When I first trained as a child health nurse, I watched a video demonstrating how babies acted when they were tired. As I watched, it dawned on me that I had overlooked or misinterpreted all three of my babies' early signs of tiredness. By failing to notice, I had unknowingly made it harder for them to fall asleep.

I soon discovered that I was not the only parent or health professional to misread the signs of infant tiredness. Of all the parents I have worked with, few read all the cues indicating their baby's tiredness. Most parents were surprised when those cues were pointed out. Many expected heavy eyelids or yawning to be the first sign. Others thought that their baby would simply fall asleep when tired.

Signs of tiredness

Your baby can't tell you when he's ready to sleep, but he will display signs that indicate when he's fatigued. It's up to you to accurately identify these signs and respond appropriately by providing him with an opportunity to sleep.

Birth to three months

Young babies rarely display the typical signs of tiredness of children and adults. This is because their body movements are primarily controlled by reflexes; automatic, involuntary responses. Behaviour commonly displayed by babies younger than three months of age that indicate tiredness, and how they exacerbate, include:

- whining → crying → screaming
- glazed stare → looking away → turning head away (babies cannot turn their head away until about two months of age) → back arching (usually not until around three months of age)
- frowning → facial grimacing (a pained expression involving tightly shut eyes and an open mouth)
- tightly clenched fists
- pulling up knees
- waving arms and legs → jerking, quick arm and leg movements
- seeking comfort by sucking or feeding.

If your baby regularly falls asleep while breast- or bottle-feeding, he might appear as if he's hungry when he's actually tired. As discussed in Chapter 1, by repeatedly falling asleep while feeding he may have psychologically linked feeding with the act of falling asleep.

Babies over three months

By three months of age, many infant reflexes have faded and your baby has gained greater voluntary control over arm and leg movements. He no longer frantically flails his arms and legs when you lay him down. Behavioural cues that indicate tiredness are easier to recognise in this age group (compared to younger babies). These include:

- whining, crying, screaming
- loss of interest in toys or playing
- glazed stare
- sucking on fingers or hands
- pulling ears or hair
- rubbing nose or eyes
- yawning
- clinginess
- temper outbursts.

Yawning

Most babies don't yawn when they're tired. So if you're waiting to observe a yawn before settling baby to sleep, you could be leaving it too late.

Not all babies display the exact same signs or to the same intensity. A baby's temperament (inborn personality traits) will influence how he behaves in different circumstances. Some babies may only show subtle signs of tiredness, whereas others may appear to skip the subtle signs and bring out the big guns. But in reality most will display the early signs of tiredness. It's up to you to recognise when your baby is tired.

Look at the big picture

Alison misjudged her baby's tired signs as 'wind'. And as a result she could spend up to an hour trying to burp her baby, who became increasingly more upset. Tina confused her baby's desire to suck when tired with hunger, and mistakenly interpreted this to mean she was not producing enough breast milk. Angela mistook her baby's early signs for boredom. While burping a baby for an hour is excessive, wind, hunger and boredom can all be valid reasons for babies to display many of the same behavioural cues. So, how can you tell the difference? By gauging the context of the situation.

Behavioural states

The following behavioural states show the stages babies go through from sleep to wide awake and upset:

deep sleep → light sleep → drowsiness → quiet alertness → active alertness/
fussiness → crying

Identifying where your baby is on this continuum can help you determine the most appropriate course of action. Anticipate that he will progress to active alert state, a great time for play, following a quiet alert state. At some point in an active alert state he will start to show signs of fussiness. When he does, this means he wants or needs something. He might be tired and ready for sleep. But it could also indicate hunger, boredom, overstimulation or fright. Use the context of the situation to help you to decide on the most likely cause. Ask yourself the following questions:

- How long has it been since he last fed?
- Would it be reasonable to expect him to be hungry?
- How long has he been awake?
- Has he been sitting alone for too long?
- Could he be bored or overstimulated?

If you respond appropriately to your baby's behavioural cues when he first starts to fuss, you can avoid or minimise the next state, crying.

When to anticipate signs of tiredness

In addition to learning what behavioural cues to watch for, you may want to anticipate when your baby is likely to become tired. Below you'll find the average day-time periods spent awake before needing a nap. During the night you don't want to encourage any time awake, other than that required for feeding. Actively promoting such time, by way of bright lights, lots of talking or playful activities during the night, could come back to bite you if baby learns that night-time is party time with Mum or Dad.

Table 3.1:   Average time spent awake by age

Age	Estimated day-time awake (including feed)
2–6 weeks	1–1¼ hours
6 weeks–3 months	1–2 hours
3–6 months	1½–2½ hours
6–9 months	2–3 hours
9–12 months	3–4 hours

Consider the relevant timeframe, but watch for signs of tiredness before trying to get your baby off to sleep. If the timing is right and you notice signs that he's becoming unsettled, you should feel reasonably confident that tiredness is the reason.

The amount of time your baby can comfortably tolerate before needing sleep may vary. Generally, babies are awake for shorter periods in the morning versus afternoons or evenings. This may be the opposite of what you would expect after your baby has had a long night's sleep or a full day of activity. Day-to-day variations are also common, especially for babies younger than three months. If your baby has not been getting enough sleep, he'll probably be cranky, with very little time spent in a quiet alert state. A sleep-deprived baby might be ready to return to sleep much sooner than the suggested timeframe. Your baby will need to catch up on much-needed sleep before he will be able to enjoy his time awake. For these reasons, it's important not to become too fixated on timeframes; they're meant only as a guide.

How to hone in on infant signs of tiredness

It can be difficult to recognise the subtle signs of tiredness while a baby is being cuddled in your arms. When you anticipate your baby should begin to feel tired, slow things down. If he is a newborn, nestle him along your legs, facing you. If older, lay him on a play mat or blanket on the floor. Provide quiet activities: talk, read or sing to him, stroke, massage or calmly interact with him, versus more animated play. Once you notice him display any of the early signs of tiredness discussed here, it's time for sleep.

Key points

- Under the age of three months, babies' body movements are controlled primarily by reflex actions. This means they display similar behaviour for anything that troubles them.

- Babies seldom display the typical signs we associate with tiredness, for example, heavy eyelids and yawning.

- Many babies under the age of five months like to suck when tired.

- Infant signs of tiredness are commonly mistaken as hunger, boredom or pain.

- If early signs of tiredness are not recognised, your baby risks becoming distressed due to overtiredness.

4

Sleep basics

Topics

How babies sleep.
What happens during sleep.
What babies are aware of while sleeping.
Why babies wake during sleep.

It isn't hard to tell when your baby needs sleep. She wants you to hold her, to entertain her, to soothe her. She's tired, grumpy, demanding and impatient. She looks at you with startled, desperate eyes. You're on tenterhooks because you know any minute now she's going to burst into tears. You know it's not her fault; she wants to sleep. You try every trick in the book to help her. Eventually, after much effort on your part, you succeed. She's asleep. You breathe a sigh of relief. Finally. Now you have time to tend to your own needs. But, alas, no. She's awake again. She cries even before she opens her eyes. She's still tired, still cranky. You don't understand what keeps waking her. You ask family, friends and health professionals the same question: 'Why is she not able to stay asleep?'

The more you understand about how your baby sleeps, the clearer it will become how your actions (as a parent or caregiver) will influence her sleep.

Mechanics of sleep

The mechanics of sleep include the following:

- stages
- cycles and
- patterns.

Stages of sleep

> Why is it my baby can be asleep in my arms and the moment I put her down she's awake again? – Andrea

Sleep is a natural state of rest for the mind and body, in which consciousness is partially or completely lost. A baby's awareness of, and responsiveness to her sleeping environment differs depending on which stage of sleep she's in. Possibly, Andrea's baby awakens when put down because she's in a light sleep stage.

Sleep stages are dependent on brain development. Electrophysiological studies of newborn babies show they have two stages of sleep: REM (rapid eye movement) sleep, which is a light sleep stage, and deep sleep.[16] By around two months of age a sequence of five sleep stages, REM sleep and four non-REM sleep stages, can be identified. By observing your baby's behaviour, you may be able to tell what sleep stage she's in, helping you to make decisions about her care.

Stage 1: Non-REM sleep

Stage 1 non-REM sleep relates to wake-sleep transition – falling asleep. When your baby slips from drowsiness into a light sleep, she may have a dazed look; her eyes will roll back and her upper eyelids droop. She may suck, smile or grimace. Her eyes and mouth may close and then reopen. Her body may suddenly jerk in a normal 'sleep start', causing her to awaken.

As she drifts off to sleep, she's still semi-aware of what's happening within her immediate sleeping environment and can be easily woken. She can recognise any changes, such as if she's moved, loses her pacifier, or if you stop patting or rocking her. If she senses a change, her eyes might spring open or she might cry with eyes closed. This sleep stage lasts 30 seconds to about five minutes.

Stage 2: Non-REM sleep

Stage 2 non-REM is the initiation of true sleep. Your baby's heart rate slows and body temperature decreases. She may even need an extra layer of clothing or bedding when you put her down. Her breathing becomes more regular. She's less aware of her surroundings compared to stage 1, but she can still be woken and could startle or jump if you move her or make a sudden loud noise. Some babies will progress into the next stage, a deep non-REM sleep, quite quickly, while others can last in this second sleep stage for five to 20 minutes.

Stages 3 and 4: Non-REM sleep

There's only a discrete difference between stages 3 and 4 non-REM sleep. Your baby is deeply asleep in both. Her breathing is slow and regular, her muscles relaxed and her arms and legs limp. Her brain is less responsive to what's happening to, and around her. Sounds, movement, being touched and changes in temperature are unlikely to bother her now. It's very difficult to wake her and, if woken, she will be slow to react and easily fall back to sleep.

If Andrea was to wait and put her baby down while she's in a deep sleep she would likely stay asleep, at least for a little while, until she next enters a light sleep stage and is then able to recognise she has been put down.

Stage 5: REM sleep

REM is a light sleep stage when dreams occur. REM sleep in babies is often referred to as 'active sleep' because, unlike adults who remain motionless except for rapid eye movements during this sleep stage, babies move about. In addition to eye movement, your baby's heart rate and breathing speed up and become irregular, her face, hands or legs might twitch or jerk, and she might smile briefly or make fast sucking or swallowing motions. She can be easily woken from REM sleep.

At birth, babies spend about half their total sleep in REM, compared to adults who only spend 20 per cent.[17] By two weeks of age, your baby spends increasingly more time in deep sleep. By six months, deep sleep makes up about 70 per cent of your baby's sleep, and most of the remainder is REM sleep.[18] REM sleep emerges more regularly during a baby's sleep, resulting in shorter sleep cycles for babies compared to adults. Some researchers believe that the increased amount of REM sleep in young babies may be important to brain development.

Up until around three months of age, a baby will enter REM sleep first. For the rest of her life, she will maintain the normal cycle of four non-REM sleep stages first, with a period of REM sleep toward the end of the sleep cycle.

Sleep cycles

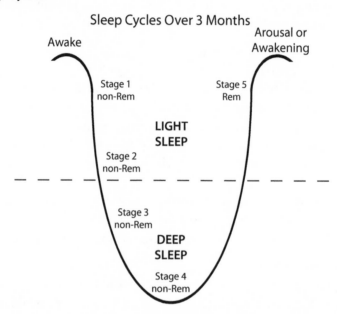

The five stages of sleep represent one sleep cycle. A single sleep cycle can take anywhere from 20 to 60 minutes depending on your baby's stage of development, how tired she is, and the time of day.

Day-time sleep

Sleep cycles during the day tend to be shorter than those in the early part of the night. The average length of time for one day-time sleep cycle is:

- 20–40 minutes for babies up to three months
- 30–60 minutes for ages three to 12 months and
- 60–90 minutes for over 12 months.

In general, the younger the child, the shorter the sleep cycle. A day-time nap can consist of one or more sleep cycles. In order to receive the necessary amount of sleep, babies usually require at least one or two of their day-time naps to consist of two or more sleep cycles linked together.

Night-time sleep

> Naeva usually sleeps at least five hours, sometimes as much as seven after she's finally settled for the night. But from around 2 am onward she keeps waking up every hour. Why is this? – Regina

What Regina describes is a fairly typical night-time sleeping pattern for a baby. From nine to 12 weeks of age, a baby spends the first half of the night mainly in deep sleep, the most energy-restorative sleep stage. More time in deep sleep results in longer sleep cycles. Longer sleep cycles mean fewer awakenings during the early part of the night.

During the final half of the night baby will spend more time in REM sleep, a light, active sleep stage, spending only short periods in deep sleep, so her overall sleep cycles will be shorter. Remember, your baby is more aware of her surroundings while in a light sleep stage, so she's more easily awakened during the early hours of the morning. This could explain why Naeva frequently awakens, beginning at 2 am.

Arousals and awakenings

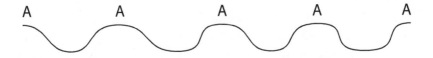

> Lucy keeps waking herself up. Sometimes she just stirs, moves around, grunts and moans and then goes back to sleep. But other times she wakes up crying and I can tell she's still tired. Should I leave her or get her up? – Michelle

What Michelle describes are arousals and awakenings between sleep cycles. Sleep cycles merge together into blocks of what appears to be uninterrupted sleep, however, they're actually separated by a partial arousal or a full awakening. It's possible for us all to wake before we have had enough sleep, babies included. Michelle should first give Lucy the opportunity to return to sleep if she wakes too soon.

Partial arousals

As adults, we regularly arouse between sleep cycles. We might change position during an arousal but, because we don't wake fully, we quickly progress into the next sleep cycle and continue snoozing. In the morning, we won't remember how many times this occurred.

Because babies have shorter sleep cycles, they arouse in their sleep more frequently than adults. You will recognise these arousals if you witness your baby moving about, perhaps opening her eyes, making sucking movements, and whimpering or crying briefly before returning to sleep seconds or minutes later. Newborns sometimes grunt, groan, even pass some flatus (gas) before dropping back to sleep during these arousals. It's especially obvious during the early hours of the morning.

When you observe baby making these movements, avoid the temptation to pick her up, thinking she's waking up. She might drop back into another sleep cycle. If you pick her up during an arousal you're likely to cause her to wake fully.

Full awakenings

We wake fully when we've had enough sleep. However, as you know, it's possible to wake fully before you have had enough sleep. If your baby has received sufficient sleep, upon waking she will be relaxed, waking gradually, opening her eyes and perhaps stretching. A young baby will remain quiet for only a brief period before starting to fuss or cry for attention. An older baby might quietly play before eventually crying for Mum or Dad. If your baby wakes still tired, she will cry almost immediately, perhaps even before her eyes are open.

The ability to wake during sleep is essential to our survival. For example, during sleep you could become hot or cold, or need to change your position, get a drink of water, or to go to the bathroom; all comfort remedies that require waking. But your comfort needs aren't all that your subconscious brain is monitoring during sleep, it's also scanning your safety needs. If, during an arousal, you sense a change in your immediate sleeping environment, for instance the light is now on, this can wake you fully. A change in your surroundings can indicate a potential threat, making it vital to your safety to wake fully to investigate. It might not turn out to be a genuine threat, but you won't know what, if any, actions you need to take until you awaken.

Your baby's subconscious brain monitors her comfort and safety needs, too. Comfort reasons include:

- hunger or thirst
- feeling hot or cold
- physical discomfort, ranging from a wet nappy to feeling pain.

As your baby cannot provide for her own comfort needs, she wakes and fusses or cries until you come to attend to her. You may think these are the most common reasons for babies to wake during their sleep. They aren't.

A physically well baby will wake repeatedly if she senses a change in the conditions she has learned to associate with sleeping. The change threatens her sense of security. So instead of smoothly moving from one sleep cycle to the next, she wakes fully and cries. As she matures she becomes increasingly more aware of any change that might occur. If you recognise this as the reason for her waking, you can re-establish the conditions she associates with sleeping.

How to support baby's sleep

Your baby partly depends on you or other caregivers to help her get the sleep she needs, when she needs it. Your child-care practices, in particular, your infant settling practices, affect her ability to do this. Table 4.1 describes ways you can support your baby to sleep and what might happen if she does not get the type of support she needs.

You wield considerable influence over your baby's sleeping patterns and behaviour. What your baby learns to associate with sleeping, combined with your ability to provide these as often as she needs, dictate whether she sleeps well or not. Being aware of these factors and encouraging good habits is key to your baby getting the sleep she needs.

Table 4.1:   What baby needs to sleep well

What baby needs	When baby doesn't get what she needs
Someone to recognise when she's tired and provide her with an opportunity to sleep.	If her signs of tiredness are overlooked or misinterpreted this increases the risk of overtiredness. Once stressed due to physical fatigue she will find it difficult to fall asleep.
A low-stimulating sleeping environment.	If the environment is too stimulating she may remain awake despite her readiness to sleep, thus increasing the risk that she becomes overtired.
Familiar sleep associations – the conditions she has learned to associate with sleeping.	Without her familiar sleep associations when she's ready to sleep, she may remain awake and risks becoming overtired.
She *may* need help to calm if she becomes upset while settling to sleep (this depends on her age, physical capabilities and self-soothing skills).	If you go beyond calming baby and actively assist her to fall asleep you will teach her to depend on your help to fall asleep. Expect that she will wake every time she notices the help you provide is missing.
She *does not* need help to fall asleep. She might *want* help to fall asleep because this is what she has learned to expect.	If you encourage her to rely on props or aids to sleep that either fall out, switch off or change after she has fallen asleep, she's likely to notice this during an arousal and wake prematurely.
Support to stabilise her biological/circadian 24-hour rhythm.	She may develop an abnormal day-night sleeping or feeding pattern, which can stress both baby and parent.

Key points

- Your baby is semi-aware of what's happening to her and around her while in a light sleep phase.

- It's normal for your baby to wake during sleep. Waking does not necessarily mean she's had enough sleep.

- During an arousal your baby's subconscious brain is checking on her comfort and security needs.

- If your baby notices a change in the conditions she has learned to associate with sleeping this will threaten her sense of security and cause her to wake prematurely.

5
Sleep associations

Elliot (aged 3 months) has trouble sleeping. He's not getting enough sleep and neither am I. Sometimes it can take me an hour to get him to sleep. No sooner do I get him down and he wakes himself up again. Most of the time he just wants his dummy and a pat to get back to sleep. If that doesn't work, I cuddle and rock him. He's not sick and doesn't appear to be teething so I can't figure out why he's having so much trouble staying asleep. Can you shed any light? – Jane

As parents and caregivers we exert a strong influence over our babies' sleep, more than you might think. Whether consciously or not, we teach our babies to associate certain conditions with sleeping. Promoting positive sleep associations minimises the chances your baby will wake too early, and reduces the risk of sleep deprivation for both him and you. If you unknowingly promote negative sleep associations, it might be a constant battle to keep him asleep. Elliot has learned to rely on negative sleep associations. That's why he keeps waking. Patting, rocking and cuddles are all, of course, nurturing things and essential to bonding, but Elliot has learned to depend on these to fall asleep. Elliot wakes every time his pacifier falls out, and as soon as he notices he is no longer being cuddled, rocked or patted.

Sleep associations have a profound effect on a baby's ability to fall and remain asleep. Understanding what sleep associations are, why we need them, and how they impact on us, can save you and your baby a lot of grief.

What are sleep associations?

Sleep associations are the conditions, activities and props that we psychologically associate with sleeping. We all have them. Some people like a firm bed and comfortable pillow. Some want to sleep on their side, others their back or stomach. Most prefer darkness and quiet. Each person relies on their own unique combination of sleep associations and may have trouble sleeping if these conditions are not present.

Babies, like adults, learn to depend on sleep associations to relax and go to sleep. Like you, your baby might have trouble falling asleep or staying asleep if one or more of his sleep associations are absent when he needs to sleep. Dominic (aged 6 weeks) likes to be rocked in his bassinette, positioned on his back, with a pacifier in his mouth, while his mother, Kate, makes and shoosh, shoosh sound. If one ingredient is missing, he will cry. Kate has learned what he likes and quickly figures out what's missing. But many parents are unaware of the impact that sleep associations have.

Your baby's sleep associations may include his sleeping environment, bedtime routines, your infant settling practices and any aids or props that you provide for him to support him to fall asleep. If you actively help him to fall asleep, then whatever you're doing leading up to your baby's sleep, and in particular at the moment he falls asleep, can and likely will become a sleep association. For example, if you rock him to sleep in his stroller, he learns to associate sleeping with being rocked in his stroller. If he's sucking on a pacifier as well, then he learns to associate sleep with sucking on a pacifier while being rocked in his stroller. If he always swaddled prior to being settled to sleep in his stroller then this is likely to be another sleep association.

How we learn sleep associations

From the day we are born to the day we die we constantly learn new things by association. Known as associative learning, we often don't even realise we're learning. Associative learning is making connections between things that happen.

For example, about 10 years ago I began turning on a fan when I went to bed. My children were teenagers, often up later than me, and I wanted to block out the household noise. I soon learned to associate the sound of a fan with sleeping. I still do. Now, it's harder for me to fall asleep without it. The hum makes me feel relaxed or drowsy, even when I'm not going to bed. Psychologists refer to this as a 'conditioned response'.

Associative learning is not limited to sleep associations. For instance, a red traffic light will immediately cause you to put your foot on the brake when driving without making a conscious decision to do so. Touch-typing is another example. Once you have learned to touch-type, you no longer need to look at the keys to know what to press.

How babies learn sleep associations

Among your baby's first learned associations are those related to sleeping and feeding, his primary activities. Through your actions, conscious or not, you encourage him to associate certain conditions, activities or props with sleeping. These become his sleep associations.

If your baby regularly falls asleep while being cuddled in your arms, he quickly learns to connect the two. In time, he will learn additional sleep associations or change them depending on his experiences and the care you provide. For example, as a newborn he'll probably be very happy to fall asleep while being cuddled in your arms as you sit. But, by the time he is three months old, he might prefer you to stand and rock or sway him while he's cuddled in your arms, if this is what you tend to do. He might learn to want a pacifier in his mouth as he's rocked in your arms. Whatever conditions, props or activities you provide for your baby at the time he falls asleep will be what he learns to associate with sleeping. He will then want these conditions, props or activities present each and every time he needs to sleep. Repetition creates habits.

You might think, 'Surely a newborn baby is too young to develop sleep associations.' In fact, newborn babies have an enormous capacity for learning, and they learn quickly! For example, when just days old, a baby can recognise his mother's smell, her voice, and even the difference between her and another woman's breast milk. He does this by means of associative learning. When you consider the reasons why we develop sleep associations, it's easy to understand why babies develop them at a very young age.

True or false?

It's possible to teach a baby to go to sleep in multiple different situations.

MAYBE: A baby could learn to depend on a number of varying sleep associations, but he will normally want them all to be present when he needs to sleep. It's usually not a matter of being able to switch back and forth between different methods. Attempting to settle a baby in different ways or in various places has a high risk of causing him to become overtired.

Why we develop sleep associations

We choose certain conditions for sleeping because these satisfy our or our baby's comfort needs. But the reason we psychologically associate certain conditions with sleeping is because the familiarity of our sleep associations provides us with a sense of security.

One of our most basic human needs is to feel safe. Your brain is constantly processing all sensory information – sights, sounds, smells, physical contact, tastes – on a subconscious level to confirm your safety, the exception being when you're in a deep sleep and are unaware of what's happening around you. When we're in unfamiliar situations or places, we are naturally alert even when we don't feel threatened; we have a heightened sense of awareness. In familiar situations or environments, ones in which we have already assessed as safe, we let our guards down and relax. We feel most relaxed when we're at home.

Familiar sleep associations act like a security blanket. We need them to allow us to relax enough to fall and remain asleep. During an arousal between sleep cycles, we can sense if our sleep associations are present or not. We will sleep in different places provided the conditions are similar to what we have learned to associate with sleeping, but we don't sleep as well as we do in our own bed in our own home.

Babies psychologically learn to associate certain conditions with sleeping for the same reason we do: the need to feel safe. But their need is even greater than our own, because they lack the experience to understand what is safe and what is not. It's the familiarity of sleep associations that provides your baby the sense of security to allow him to relax and fall asleep. Children thrive when life is familiar and predictable because it makes them feel safe.

How sleep associations affect baby's sleep

Most babies are good sleepers during the first few days or weeks after birth. A newborn baby will readily fall asleep in many situations and surroundings and will sleep for long stretches between feeds because he hasn't yet learned to associate any specific conditions with sleeping, other than the desire to feel contained, that familiarity of sleeping in the womb. Cuddling in your arms, swaddling, a baby rocker or swing, bassinette, baby hammock, baby car capsule – can make him feel contained and therefore secure. He will readily fall asleep in any of these places. He sleeps anywhere, any time he's tired. You could be lulled into a false sense of security believing you've been blessed with a good sleeper, without the need to foster good sleeping habits.

This changes, however, as your baby's awareness of his surroundings increases. Within days or weeks following birth, he begins to associate other conditions with sleeping. For example, he might regularly fall asleep while breastfeeding or while being rocked in a baby swing. If these situations are repeated often enough, he associates them with sleeping. In time he may learn even more sleep associations.

When baby learns to associate certain conditions with sleeping, his ability to sleep is no longer reliant solely on feeling contained. He now wants all of his sleep associations to be present when he's ready to fall asleep. By the time baby is two weeks of age or sooner, your good sleeper may become a poor sleeper, simply because of the type of conditions he has learned to associate with sleeping.

How to support baby to fall asleep

As an adult you can take yourself off to bed and set up your sleep associations the way you like them. Your baby cannot. He relies on you to recognise when he's tired and provide his sleep associations. Remember, by doing this you're letting him know it's safe to go to sleep.

When baby starts to display signs of tiredness, you have a small window of opportunity to provide his familiar sleep associations and encourage him to fall asleep with ease. This window opens when baby is physiologically ready for sleep; he won't sleep before he's ready. It closes when he becomes distressed, because he's overtired. The length of time this window remains open varies depending on age, time of day and whether your baby is getting enough sleep. It could be as little as 10 minutes for some or half an hour or longer for others. The key is to recognise early signs of tiredness.

If you accurately recognise your baby's tired signs and support him to fall asleep during this window of opportunity by reducing sensory stimulation and providing the conditions, props and activities he has learned to associate with sleeping, he will fall asleep with relative ease. However, if you overlook or misinterpret the behavioural cues that indicated tiredness, as many parents understandably do, or if you don't provide every one of his sleep associations in a timely manner, or if the environment is too stimulating, he might not fall asleep despite his readiness to sleep. (A stimulating environment might include any environment with bright lights, the sound of voices or loud or sudden noise.)

What does this mean in adult terms? Say, for example, you're usually ready for sleep at 10 pm. If you go to bed at this time and have all of your familiar sleep associations present – your favourite pillow or, like me, a whirring fan – you will likely fall asleep relatively quickly, provided you're not overtired or stressed. But if you're out dining with friends, even though you might feel tired at 10 pm, you don't allow yourself to fall asleep because the conditions aren't right for sleeping. This is the same for your baby. He needs to be tired and ready for sleep, but he also needs to have the right conditions to sleep, and this includes his sleep associations.

The longer your baby remains awake beyond the point where he's physiologically ready to sleep, the more tired he becomes. Once he's distressed and crying, it might be too late for a smooth transition into the land of nod. Once he reaches the point of overtiredness, even if you then provide his familiar sleep associations, he's going to find it difficult to fall asleep. It can appear like he's fighting sleep, because overtiredness triggers the release of stress hormones, which key him up. An overtired baby might need your help to calm and relax before he can fall asleep.

At some point, our need for sleep may become so great that it overrides our need for familiar sleep associations. Physical fatigue can accumulate to a point where we can no longer remain awake. So you fall asleep in places you would not normally sleep. You nod off watching the TV or a school play; you become dozy while catching the train from work; or have micro-sleeps while driving the car. Babies also reach a point where they will fall asleep without their familiar sleep associations, but not usually until their physical need for sleep becomes so great they can't stay awake a moment longer.

Tiredness	→	Overtiredness	→	Exhaustion
Baby requires familiar sleep associations to fall asleep.		Baby experiences difficulty falling asleep even with familiar sleep associations.		Baby's desperate need for sleep overrides his need for familiar sleep associations.

How to support baby to remain asleep

The conditions present when your baby falls asleep will have the greatest influence on his ability to remain asleep. Almost any sleep association can help your baby get to sleep, provided it is something he has learned to psychologically associate with sleeping.

Not all sleep associations are equal when it comes to supporting your baby to remain asleep long enough to get the amount of sleep he needs. Sleep associations that babies commonly learn to depend on fall into two categories, positive and negative. Table 5.1 shows how these two categories compare.

Table 5.1: Positive versus negative sleep associations

Positive sleep associations	Negative sleep associations
Present when the baby falls asleep and remain consistent throughout baby's entire sleep. These support smooth transition between sleep cycles.	Present when baby falls asleep but then alter in some way, disrupting the smooth transition between sleep cycles.
The presence of baby's sleep associations provide him with a sense of security.	The absence or change in baby's sleep associations may threaten his sense of security.
These support independent settling and sleeping. The consistent presence of positive sleep associations support baby to self-regulate his sleeping patterns.	**These encourage dependence on outside help to fall asleep.** Baby may wake every time he notices a change in his sleep associations, and cries to have these returned. Reliance on negative sleep associations may prevent baby from self-regulating his sleeping patterns. Reliance on negative sleep associations increases the risk of sleep deprivation for baby and his parents.

Sleeping through the night does not mean a baby does not wake. It means that, when he wakes, he can return to sleep independently, without waking others.

If you encourage your baby to learn positive sleep associations instead of negative ones, a poor sleeper can become a good one. On the other hand, a good sleeper can become a poor sleeper at any stage, if he subsequently learns to rely on a negative sleep association.

If you're having a hard time keeping your baby asleep, it's helpful to identify his sleep associations and know which category they fall into: negative or positive.

Positive sleep associations

Belinda prepares eight-month-old Noah for bed, dressing him in an infant sleeping bag. She dims the lights, draws the curtains and puts him into his cot while he's still awake. He snuggles his soft toy dinosaur, rolls onto his side and drifts off to sleep. Occasionally, he will fuss and Belinda returns. She pats him until he's quiet, reminds him it's sleep time and leaves while he's still awake. Belinda has consistently encouraged Noah to settle to sleep on his own since birth. The only change was to switch from swaddling to an infant sleeping bag when Noah was three months. She also gave him the soft toy to sleep with when he was six months old.

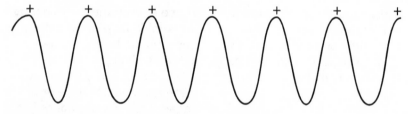

A positive sleep association is something that baby learns to associate with sleep when he first falls asleep and which is still there every time he enters into a light sleep stage and partial arousal. The presence of his sleep associations support him to smoothly transition from one sleep cycle to the next, minimising the risk of premature awakenings. Noah was settled in his cot in a quiet dark environment while sucking on his fingers, and later while cuddling his dinosaur. Other parents often comment to Belinda, 'You're lucky to have such a good sleeper,' but luck has nothing to do with it. Noah sleeps well because Belinda supports him to self-regulate his sleeping patterns by providing positive sleep associations.

Positive sleep associations include the following:

- a suitable and consistent sleeping environment
- baby's bed (cot, bassinette, cradle)
- swaddling

- infant sleeping bag
- thumb or finger sucking (when baby self-soothes by sucking his own hands)
- security objects
- safe sleep aids that remain consistent throughout baby's entire sleep.

Suitable and consistent sleeping environment

Baby's immediate surroundings will influence his ability to settle and stay asleep, as it does anyone's. If you want to support your baby to have longer or better quality sleep, you must provide him with a suitable, familiar and consistent sleeping environment.

A suitable sleeping environment is one in which your baby is safe and comfortable to sleep. Think about the type of environment in which you sleep. Most adults sleep best in a low-stimulation environment, one with reduced noise and lighting. External sensory cues, such as sights, sounds, odours and temperature, either annoy us when tired or stimulate brain activity that prevents us from falling asleep. Your baby, who is incapable of blocking out unwanted sensory stimulation as effectively as you are, also needs a low-stimulation environment.

Even in a generically ideal sleeping environment, we don't necessarily sleep well. It also needs to be familiar. The familiarity of our sleeping environment provides a sense of security. We tend to sleep best in our own beds in our own homes. Tents, hotel rooms, a bed at a friend's house, no matter how luxurious or comfortable, feel different, without the same sense of security as home.

Baby McKenzie

Three-month-old McKenzie was an unhappy baby. His mother, Brenda, worried that he had a problem with wind. McKenzie was not as good a sleeper as her older children, two and four years old now, had been when babies. When asked where he slept, Brenda responded, 'Wherever we are at the time: in his pram, baby car seat, back pack or on me.' He would only have one nap in his cot at home because they were out for most of every day. At night, he slept in a porta-cot in his parents' room. Brenda and her young family had an active family life. Brenda took McKenzie out with her older children to pre-school, play group, swimming lessons, shopping, and to visit Grandma. Brenda admitted she had been home a lot more when her other children were babies. No wonder they were better sleepers.

There was nothing physically wrong with McKenzie other than overtiredness. McKenzie was expected to sleep anywhere, simply not something he could do. Brenda had to make a very tough decision between curbing the family's activities temporarily or have a chronically cranky, overtired baby.

Your baby will sleep best in the place most familiar to him, the place where he regularly falls asleep. But a familiar sleeping environment is not necessarily a consistent one. Marcus, at 10 weeks, goes to sleep in Claire's arms. Familiar to him, he settles quickly. But, once asleep, Claire places him into his cot, changing his sleeping environment, and so he wakes. If in a light sleep, he wakes quickly; if in a deep sleep, he might not wake straight away, but he does when he next arouses between sleep cycles.

A consistent sleeping environment means baby wakes up where he fell asleep. The safest and most consistent place for a baby to sleep is in a bed designed for babies – a cot, cradle or bassinette. His immediate environment needs to be conducive to sleep. Consider what might make noise, cause movement or change lighting. Even subtle changes can be enough to disrupt a baby's slumber.

You can still go out. But, your baby's sleep may be delayed or cut short if it isn't a suitable, familiar and consistent sleeping environment. If he fails to catch up at his next nap, then he might be overtired by the evening.

Bed (bassinette, cradle or cot)

Babies who are put to bed tired – but before they've fallen asleep – are less likely to wake between sleep cycles and more likely to soothe themselves back to sleep when they wake, compared to babies who are put into their beds after they have fallen asleep elsewhere.[19] Putting your baby into bed when still awake and supporting him to fall asleep while he's there provides him with a consistent sleeping environment.

Imagine falling asleep in your bed and waking up to find yourself lying on the couch. You would be startled, even confused, perhaps. What if this happened repeatedly? You might even become apprehensive about going to sleep, unable to relax. Some babies will accept an inconsistent sleeping environment and still sleep well; others don't. Your baby will gain a greater sense of security if he gets to wake up in the same place as he falls asleep.

By allowing your baby to fall asleep while he's in his bed, he get to learn that his bed is a safe place to sleep. In time, he will learn to associate his bed with sleeping, the same way we do. Once he recognises that his bed means sleep time, he will long to go to bed when tired, like we do, and relax soon after being placed into it. It will take a many days of consistently falling asleep in his bed to learn to associate his bed with sleeping. He can only learn this if you give him the chance to learn.

This does not mean he can never sleep elsewhere, but try to provide a sleeping environment as similar to his bed as possible, such as another cot, portable cot, baby car capsule or his pram. If you're out shopping, for example, watch for signs of tiredness. Then, take him to a quiet environment, drop the back of his pram to make it as flat as possible, prepare him for sleep by swaddling if he's under three months of age, and reduce visual stimulation by placing a muslin wrap over the front of his pram. Avoid rocking him to sleep if possible, as this could become a negative sleep association if repeated. Rock to calm him, if necessary, but stop before he falls asleep. Once he's asleep, you can continue shopping.

Swaddling

Swaddling involves firmly, but not tightly, wrapping a baby in a swaddling wrap, cot sheet or lightweight blanket. Swaddling applies gentle pressure to baby's limbs, recreating the sense of containment and security he experienced in the womb.

Swaddling promotes more sustained sleep and reduces the frequency of awakenings for babies under the age of four months.[20] The feeling of containment soothes newborn babies. Also, newborns often startle as they drift off, and during arousals between sleep cycles.[21] Swaddling contains the involuntary limb movements associated with the startle reflex that can jerk baby awake. Ensure he remains firmly swaddled throughout his sleep. If it loosens, his environment has changed and he may wake. The trick is to learn how to swaddle him correctly. (See diagram facing page.)

The benefits of swaddling in relation to sleeping decline once your baby reaches three to four months of age. By then, your baby's startle reflex will have faded, and he will have greater control over his limb movements and be able to suck on his hands to self-soothe. If you notice your baby sucking on his hands, consider swaddling him with one arm out or cease swaddling altogether and dress him in an infant sleeping bag instead. Many parents mistake their baby's newfound ability to repeatedly suck on his fists at around three months of age as a sign of teething. It's got nothing to do with teething. Baby is self-soothing. A skill he lacked at an earlier age.

If your baby is more than eight weeks old and has not been swaddled for sleep before, it's not worthwhile if it upsets him. Try an infant sleeping bag instead.

How to swaddle a baby

- Lay the swaddling wrap, blanket or sheet squarely on a flat surface, such as a bed.

- Place your baby on his back centrally on the wrap with the upper edge of the wrap level with the back of his neck.

- Gently hold his left arm across his chest in a comfortable position with one hand. Pull the corner nearest to baby's left shoulder diagonally across his arm and body and tuck the edge under his back. Do the same for the right side.

- Fan out the bottom edge of the wrap slightly and pull it up towards your baby's chin, making sure his legs have room to stretch out.

- Tuck both corners under his back (one corner to the left the other to the right). Then tuck one end into the other, or pin or tape the end down, to prevent it from loosening.

There are many ways to swaddle a baby; this is only one. If you experience difficulties swaddling your baby, ask your doctor, community nurse or an experienced mother to show you how.

Using a wrap made from fabric that has a little give allows your baby to move a little without becoming unwrapped. Be sure to use a lightweight fabric, such as muslin, when it's hot.

Swaddling steps

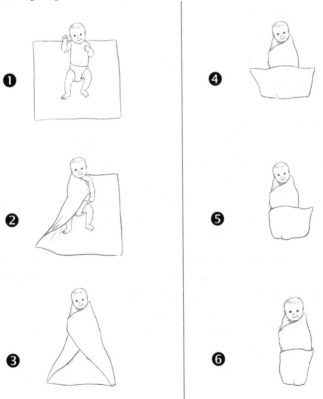

Infant sleeping bag

As your baby matures physically, he will naturally become more mobile. Once he begins to roll – generally around the age of four months – the risk of him rolling out from beneath his covers during sleep and waking feeling cold increases. An infant sleeping bag has sleeves or arm holes so that baby can freely move his arms, and are designed to provide warmth without other bedding.

Your baby can't escape from a sleeping bag, so, as always, you need to take care to prevent overheating. Some manufacturers provide a TOG (thermal overall grade) rating indicating how warm the bag will get, to help parents choose the right sleeping bag. The higher the TOG, the warmer the product. A TOG rating of:

- 0.5 is very light, for hot weather
- 1 is for lightweight summer sleeping bags
- 3 is for quilted or fleecy winter sleeping bags.

In addition, you must consider external factors when choosing a sleeping bag, such as the type of clothing worn, the room temperature, and your baby's state of health.

Thumb or finger sucking

Sucking is comforting for babies. It's the main way they soothe. Thumb or finger sucking enables a baby to self-soothe. It can also help him settle and resettle to sleep without help. A baby's ability to voluntarily control his arm movements and suck on a thumb or fingers when he chooses generally begins to develop around three months of age. But it takes practice before he will master the skills he needs to self-soothe.

Many parents prevent their baby from self-soothing by pulling his hand out of his mouth or by giving baby a pacifier, fearing future dental problems, but this is only an issue if a child continues once his permanent teeth start to emerge, usually after five years of age. Some parents think thumb sucking is unhygienic, but it's not if you keep your baby's hands clean. Keeping his nails short and smooth will also avoid scratches.

Security objects

Jean Piaget, a Swiss developmental psychologist, stated that, from around four months of age, babies become more aware of their environment, beyond their own bodies.[22] While three-month-old babies are more likely to suck on their thumbs and fingers to self-soothe, by six months they are more likely to use a soft external object to help them soothe.[23] The use of soft objects to aid soothing peaks some time after the first year of life.[24]

Psychologist, Dr Richard Passman has done extensive research into children's use of security objects and the effect these have on development. Through his research, Passman has found security objects offer positive benefits to babies and children. For example, they can reduce stress and thus crying, help them adapt to new situations and aid in their learning.[25] Babies who used soft objects had higher percentages of self-soothing compared to those who used other types of sleep aids or nothing.[26]

The American Academy of Pediatrics recommend parents give their child a security object at sleep time from four months of life.[27] SIDS and Kids Australia recommend that the safest practice is to have nothing in a child's bed before the age of two years. Given such differing opinions you must decide whether a security object will be safe and appropriate to use for your baby.

True or false?

Attachment to a security object threatens the emotional attachment baby has with parents.

FALSE: A security object will not impact on the special bond you have with your baby. His attachment stems from its familiarity. The smell and feel of his security object remind baby of the things he finds comforting: like cuddles in your arms. A security object helps baby to feel secure at times he is separated from you, like when he goes to bed, child care or is cared for by others. If it's not possible for you to be with your baby every minute of every day, would you not want him to have something that provides him a sense of security and comfort?

Positive sleep aids

Sleep aids can have a positive effect on a baby's sleep, provided they remain unchanged. An ideal sleep aid is something you can take with you if your baby is expected to sleep away from home.

Reproduced womb sounds, relaxation music and white noise, such as a low fan, air conditioner or low-volume radio, can help relax babies if they learn to associate these sounds with sleeping. Music and white noise can also buffer sudden or unwanted background noise, like household noise, early morning traffic, chirping birds or barking dogs. You can gradually reduce the volume over time so that your baby will learn to sleep without it.

> If your baby relies on even one negative sleep association, this can offset the benefits of positive sleeping associations.

Negative sleep associations

Heath, aged eight weeks, repeatedly wakes during his sleep. He naps only briefly during the day and is still tired when he wakes. At night, he wakes every two hours or so. His mother, Wendy, suspects a physical problem, but there's nothing wrong with Heath. His broken sleep is because he relies on a number of negative sleep associations. He's used to being cuddled in Wendy's arms and jiggled up and down. He also uses a pacifier. After he falls asleep, Wendy places him into his cot and, soon after, his pacifier falls out of his mouth.

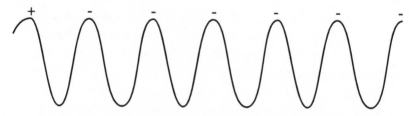

The absence of a baby's familiar sleep associations may cause him to wake fully and cry, to have these returned in order to fall back to sleep. By moving Heath after he has fallen asleep, Wendy unknowingly removes Heath's sleep associations. This would be like someone removing your pillow while you were in a deep sleep.

Negative sleep associations fall into several sub-groups:

- unsuitable or inconsistent sleeping environment
- parent-assisted settling methods
- negative sleep aids.

Unsuitable or inconsistent sleeping environment

It's a common misperception that babies will sleep whenever they're tired. Would you find it hard to sleep in a busy shopping centre, at a football match or a family BBQ? Probably. Your baby is no different. Of course, babies do sleep in these types of environments if they're exhausted. We, too, will sleep in unlikely places when our need for sleep becomes too great. Ever dozed off at an airport while waiting for a late-night flight? It isn't because the airport is particularly comfortable or relaxing; more likely you were so tired you could no longer remain awake. Most babies will sleep in unfamiliar places but won't settle or sleep as well as when they're in a familiar sleeping environment.

Changing your baby's sleep environment after he has fallen asleep will not provide the same sense of security as a stable sleeping environment. Sometimes this is unavoidable. Unavoidable or not if your baby misses out on sleep during the day, by evening he might become overtired and difficult to soothe.

Parent-assisted settling methods

Any activity that you do at the time your baby falls asleep could become a sleep association. For example:

- feeding, burping or cuddling
- carrying in a sling or a backpack-style infant carrier
- patting, stroking, or touching to let him know you're there
- rocking his bassinette, cot, baby hammock, pram or infant rocker
- lying next to him on the couch or bed
- driving
- pushing him in a pram during walks.

Whether deliberate or not, remember that all it takes is repetition for an association to be made. If you use one or more of these activities on occasion to encourage your baby to fall asleep, it won't necessarily become a sleep association. However, if your baby regularly falls asleep during one of these activities, he might learn to associate the activity with sleeping.

'But these methods work!' I hear you say. Yes they do. But, in the long run, they can deprive both your baby and you of sleep. The reason is learned dependence on others' help to fall asleep can prevent a baby from self-regulating his sleeping patterns. If your baby learns to rely on your help to fall asleep he may require the same help to *remain* asleep or *return* to sleep. He risks sleep deprivation if you can't provide this the entire time he needs to sleep on a 24-hour basis, you risk sleep deprivation if you do.

By helping your baby fall asleep you might minimise or avoid tears at the time he settles to sleep. However, if he's not getting enough sleep owing to his learned dependence on others' help to regulate his sleeping patterns, he's going to feel uncomfortable or miserable, and potentially cry even more at other times. If he becomes overtired he's probably going to cry even when you try to help him settle to sleep, so you might not avoid his crying after all.

True or false?

1. Babies need help to fall asleep.

FALSE: Babies are capable of falling asleep without outside help from birth. They settle to sleep without help while in the womb. The patterns of care parents provide unknowingly encourage babies to associate sleep with certain activities that require their participation. Babies then want help because that's what they have learned to expect. This is not the same as needing help to fall asleep.

2. Babies will eventually learn to sleep without help.

TRUE: Most children do learn to sleep independently, eventually. If they're not encouraged by parents to do this as infants, then the average age for this to happen is three to four years. Some children still want their parents' help to settle to sleep in the evening and during the night at seven years and older. Between 15 and 27 per cent of school children experience sleep problems.[28] Sleeping habits are learned. Parents can encourage and support healthy sleep habits during infancy and prevent years of stress for their child and themselves.

Negative sleep aids

Once your baby is dependent on your help to fall and remain asleep, you may become exhausted and try encouraging him to rely on some type of sleep aid instead. A sleep aid is any prop or device that soothes baby in your absence. Sleep aids include:

- pacifiers (dummies)
- mechanical infant swings
- music, CD lullabies or radio
- white noise, eg, fans, vacuum cleaners or hair dryers
- wind-up mobiles
- baby hammock
- devices that rock or vibrate a baby's cot, cradle or bassinette.

Once your baby has learned to depend on a particular sleep aid to go to sleep, the sleep aid must remain present; changes can disrupt his sleep. If the aid doesn't remain present and unchanged throughout your baby's entire sleep then it likely falls into the negative sleep association category. If the aid isn't portable, your baby may find it difficult to sleep elsewhere. Choose sleep aids with that in mind.

Pacifiers

Pacifiers are the most widely promoted of all sleep aids. Many parents will provide a pacifier during the early weeks of life, when baby can't quite get his little fist to his mouth to satisfy his sucking needs. Consequently, baby may learn to rely on a pacifier to fall asleep. Pacifiers do have disadvantages, including:

- **Delayed settling time (wake-sleep transition):** If baby has learned to associate sucking on a pacifier with falling asleep, as he starts to drift into stage 1 sleep, he will naturally stop sucking. Ironically, this pause creates a change in his sleep associations which could cause him to wake. He could repeat this numerous times before falling asleep. If it keeps falling out of his mouth while he's trying to settle to sleep, it's going to delay sleep's onset, especially if he has to cry to have it returned.

- **Wakefulness:** When baby drops into deep sleep, his body, including his jaw, relaxes, and his pacifier will fall out. Almost two-thirds of babies lose their pacifiers within 30 minutes of falling asleep.[29] Again, the change in his sleep associations, the absence of his pacifier, can wake him before he's had enough sleep. During the night most babies will generally return to sleep quickly once their pacifier has been returned. However, during the day, pacifiers can cause naps to last for only one sleep cycle. During day-time naps, once baby has woken and cried for his pacifier to be returned, he might be too upset or alert to return to sleep even if he's still tired. A brief nap can be enough to take the edge off his tiredness and prevent him from going back to sleep, but might not refresh him. He'll soon be fussing and need sleep again.

- **Infant sleep deprivation:** If your baby does not get sufficient sleep during the day, his sleep debt will accumulate. This causes unsettledness in the late afternoon or early evening.

- **Parental sleep deprivation:** The parents of babies who rely on pacifiers as a sleep association may suffer if they're woken multiple times during the night, often out of a deep sleep, to get up, find and return their baby's pacifier.

- **Inhibition of self-soothing skills:** When a baby uses a pacifier to satisfy his sucking needs, he has little incentive to learn to self-soothe by sucking on his fingers.

- **Breastfeeding problems:** Pacifier use is linked with problems establishing breastfeeding.[30] Pacifiers are also connected to an early cessation of breastfeeding.[31]

- **Oral thrush:** The use of unsterilised pacifiers is associated with increased risk of oral thrush.[32]

- **Ear infections:** Sucking on a pacifier while lying down is linked to an increased risk of middle ear infections in babies over six months.[33]

- **Speech delay:** The overuse of a pacifier has been associated with delayed speech.[34] It's difficult for baby to practise making sounds with a pacifier in his mouth.

- **Dental problems:** Prolonged pacifier use can cause crooked teeth.[35]

Pacifiers are not wholly negative. Babies who use pacifiers appear to have a reduced risk for Sudden Infant Death Syndrome (SIDS), possibly because babies who use pacifiers are lighter sleepers.[36]

Not all babies experience the disadvantages of pacifier use. Some sleep well, whether they have a pacifier in their mouth or not. Charlie and Nelson, however, didn't. Maria didn't suspect Charlie's pacifier was responsible for his 20-minute catnaps during the day because he would sleep for long periods during the night after it had fallen out. The reason Charlie slept so soundly at night was because he was not getting enough sleep during the day owing to his pacifier falling out and disrupting his naps. By night-time, he was simply too exhausted to fuss over his missing pacifier.

Nelson's mother didn't suspect his pacifier dependence to be the cause of his wakefulness during the night because Nelson had used a pacifier since birth, and, during the early months, he had slept well. But when he reached four months, he became excessively wakeful during the night. By that age, babies go through an intellectual growth spurt where their awareness of their surroundings expands.[37] What had not been a problem in the past now had become one, due to Nelson's increased awareness of his surroundings and his improved memory.

True or false?

1. Removing your baby's pacifier after he has fallen asleep will stop him from waking during his sleep.

FALSE: If your baby's sleep is disturbed because his pacifier is missing, it will make no difference whether it falls out or you remove it, it's still missing either way.

2. Placing one or more pacifiers in the cot within easy reach or attaching a pacifier to baby's clothing will allow him to find his pacifier.

TRUE: Between the ages of 12 and 18 months, many children start looking for their pacifiers when they awaken during their sleep, but to do so, they must be fully awake. Once your child wakes, chances are that he's not going to complete his nap during the day, therefore, he may miss out on sleep. At night he might cry to be reassured by Mum or Dad's presence.

Well-meaning health professionals and parenting educators routinely advise parents to settle their colicky or reflux babies by using one or more parent-assisted settling methods, or by providing a pacifier. However, by encouraging a baby to rely on negative sleep associations, this can contribute to, or be solely responsible for the baby's distress. Learned dependence on even one negative sleep association can increase the risk of sleep deprivation. The distress displayed by sleep-deprived babies is often mistakenly attributed to colic, reflux and other physical problems. You won't know to what degree negative sleep associations may impact your baby's sleep, and thus contribute to his unsettled behaviour, until he learns to sleep without them. You might discover that your colicky or reflux baby has suddenly been 'cured'.

Identify baby's sleep associations

Observe how your baby regularly falls asleep, noting each sleep association. Divide these into positive, parent-assisted and sleep aids, and note them in the appropriate tables below. Also, include any that you feel might be appropriate for his stage of development that you're not currently providing.

Table 5.2:   Positive sleep cues or associations

E.g., baby's bed, swaddling, infant sleeping bag, thumb/finger sucking, security blanket or toy.

Table 5.3:   Parent-assisted settling methods

E.g., feeding to sleep, falling asleep in your arms, sling, backpack, carrier, being patted, stroked, held, rocked, while in a moving car, or pram. (See page 73 for a full list.)

For the table below, remember that a sleep aid must remain consistent throughout baby's sleep in order to be classified as a positive sleep association. Note whether the sleep aid is positive or negative.

Table 5.4: Sleep aids

E.g., pacifier, swing, music, white noise, mobile and anything in the sleep environment that provides light, movement or noise when falling asleep. (See page 75 for a full list.)

Deciding on a course of action

There are no right or wrong infant settling practices. It's a matter of finding what works best for your baby and your family. If your baby is happy, healthy and thriving and you're satisfied with the way he sleeps, then you don't need to make any changes, regardless of what others might say. However, if things are not so rosy in your household – either baby is not getting the sleep he needs or you're not getting enough sleep owing to his sleep habits – then you must decide what to do.

Diagram 5.4: How to decide

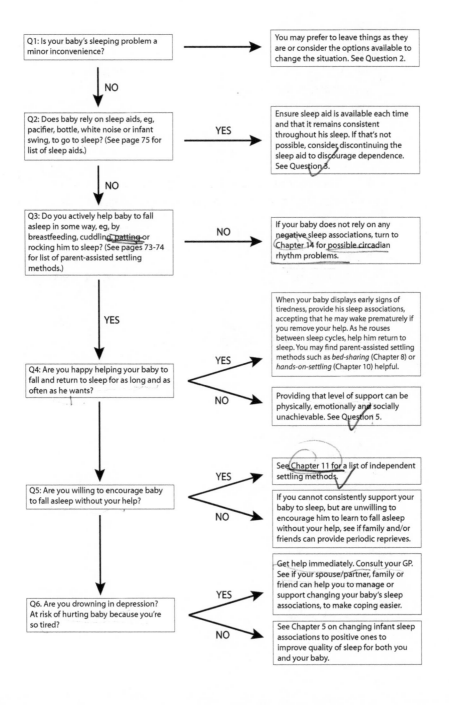

Key points

- A baby can learn sleep associations within a few days of birth. We teach them to rely on such associations by the infant settling practices we employ.

- Learned dependence on negative sleep associations is the most common reason of all for healthy thriving babies and children to experience broken sleep.

- Not all babies experience sleep disturbances when reliant on parent-assisted sleep associations or negative sleep aids.

- A baby will change sleep associations depending on the type of care provided by parents and caregivers.

- A baby requires guidance and support to change his sleep associations.

- If you feel depressed or have thoughts of harming your baby seek professional help as soon as possible.

6

Sleep training

Topics

What is sleep training?
What does it involve?
How does it work?
What age can sleep training begin?
The great debate: what supporters and critics say about
     sleep training.
Top five concerns about sleep training. Are these valid?

I was seated next to John on the plane and we got talking. He asked what I do. After telling him, he asked 'What do you think of sleep training?' Before I had a chance to respond, he continued, 'I think it's cruel. People have a baby and then stick it into a cot at the other end of the house so they can't hear it crying.'

'Do you have children?'

'Yes, one. He slept in bed with us every night until he was seven.'

'Seven months?'

'No, seven years.' He chuckled. 'Some nights I had to sleep in the spare bed, but we did what we needed to do. Children are meant to sleep with their parents. It helps them feel secure.'

John certainly had strong opinions about what parents should do based on his personal beliefs. I sometimes find I must challenge parents' preconceived beliefs about what sleep training is and what it involves. John was not experiencing a baby sleep crisis, however, so I changed the topic and enjoyed the flight.

The mere mention of the words 'sleep training' can send some people into a state of fury. They claim that it's inhumane, that it psychologically traumatises babies, breaks their trust, and trains them not to cry. If these things are true, why is sleep training promoted by so many health professionals knowledgeable in child development? And why do countless parents swear sleep training improves their baby's contentment, and quality of life for the entire family? Who's right?

For many years I was a firm believer that sleep training was ill-advised. My own babies were breast-fed or cuddled to sleep as newborns and, later, rocked or patted until they fell asleep. I didn't realise that I could teach them to fall asleep on their own without leaving them to cry it out. Leaving my babies to cry alone until they became so exhausted they fell asleep was not something I was prepared to do. Consequently, my children learned to depend on help to fall asleep. One or more would wake during the night and cry until my husband or I came to help them go back to sleep.

It took nine years from the birth of my first child until the youngest slept through the night. For nine years I parented, worked and survived in a chronically sleep-deprived state. I have no doubt that was a major contributor to the episodes of postnatal depression I suffered during that time. The depression and constant physical fatigue strained our family to the point where my marriage teetered on the edge of collapse.

Only when I became a child health nurse did my opinion about sleep training change. I got to witness first-hand the many benefits sleep training provided for babies and their families. I discovered that my previous concerns regarding sleep training were based on misconceptions.

What is sleep training?

Whether you realise it or not, you teach, in other words *train*, your baby how to sleep from the moment of her birth. Most babies learn to associate particular conditions, activities or props with sleeping within weeks or even days following birth. You probably already know your baby's preferred way of falling asleep: with a pacifier, bottle or breast in her mouth, in her cot or your arms, when patted or rocked to sleep or perhaps when driven around in the car.

Few parents think about how their actions influence their baby's sleep habits. Hence most babies are accidentally trained to associate certain conditions with sleeping. These could be positive or negative sleep associations depending on the actions of parents or caregivers when baby falls asleep.

> **Positive and negative sleep associations: what's the difference?**
>
> If something helps your baby go to sleep and is still present as she arouses between sleep cycles, it's a positive association. If it's gone when she rouses between sleep cycles, it's a negative association.

Babies who learn to rely on negative sleep associations are more vulnerable to sleep problems, including broken sleeping patterns and difficulty settling to sleep.

Your baby's sleep associations are learned. They can be altered by changing the way you settle her to sleep. It only takes consistent repetition for new associations to be learned. 'Sleep training' is a phrase coined by American paediatrician, Dr Marc Weissbluth, to suggest that parents can assist their child to learn the habits of how to sleep.[38] The difference between accidental training and sleep training boils down to awareness. Most parents only consider sleep training after they have discovered their accidental training has led to sleep problems.

Sleep training is designed to resolve a baby's sleep problems by discouraging reliance on negative sleep associations. If the baby's sleep problems relate to some other cause, such as a physical problem or timing of feeding and sleeping patterns, sleep training may not help.

How sleep training works

The most effective sleep training strategies involve the use of 'extinction', a behaviour modification technique. Extinction works on the principle that if a particular behaviour is no longer reinforced, it will fade and eventually disappear. So, when your baby depends on a negative sleep association, for example being cuddled to sleep, and you stop cuddling her until she falls asleep, her dependence on falling asleep this way fades and disappears.

Extinction is *not* something new. Parents have forever used it instinctively to modify children's behaviour. Renowned psychologist, BF Skinner, simply gave it a name. Extinction can be used in a number of ways to change a baby's previously learned sleep associations, including:

- **Unmodified extinction:** consistently withholding negative sleep associations and leaving baby to cry it out.
- **Modified extinction:** consistently withholding negative sleep associations, but consoling or reassuring baby from time to time if upset.
- **Gradual extinction:** withholding negative sleep associations sometimes, but providing them at others. For example, no longer helping your baby to fall asleep at night, but doing so during the day (or vice versa).

Gradual extinction usually takes longer and has a higher failure rate because the baby is provided with negative sleep associations intermittently.

What does sleep training involve?

Sleep training involves:

- changing infant settling practices
- a learning phase and
- maintenance to reinforce your baby's new sleeping habits.

Changing infant settling practices

Your baby is powerless to change her sleep associations without your guidance and support. Remember, your actions encouraged her to develop certain sleep associations, positive or negative, in the first place. As long as you continue to settle her to sleep in the same way, she will not learn new sleep associations, and any associated sleep problem will probably continue. Only by changing your infant settling practices will your baby get the chance to learn new sleep associations.

In the previous chapter, you identified your baby's sleep associations. Think carefully about which ones you want to target for extinction and which ones you want to encourage.

The keys to extinction are consistency, patience and perseverance. Sleep habits are not learned in a day; neither are they forgotten in a day.

Learning phase

Learning new sleep associations takes time. The learning phase can vary from a few days to weeks or even months. How long it takes depends on the type of settling method you choose and how consistent you are.

During the learning phase, consistency is the key to success. Inconsistency understandably breeds confusion. Without consistency, there's no way to be sure a baby's sleep habits will change.

Whether infant or adult, the time it takes to change our sleep associations is about the same. So, waiting until your baby is older won't make it any easier.

During the learning phase, expect resistance.

Protest crying

Your baby has *no* desire to change familiar sleeping habits to something that will initially feel strange to her. So she will understandably resist your attempts to change her sleep associations. During the learning phase, expect a 'post extinction response burst' (PERB): that is, escalating crying, otherwise known as protest crying. Protest crying will stop as soon as you enter the room, or when you pick your baby up, or if you restore her familiar sleep associations. In other words, she stops when she gets what she wants or believes she's going to get what she wants. (She will also cry if she's hungry so be sure to rule that out first.)

At what point your baby stops crying depends on her ability to link series of events. An older baby might stop crying as you enter the room, or as soon as you pick her up, but start again once she figures out you're not going to give her what she wants. A young baby might keep crying until you restore her familiar sleep associations or soothe her in a different way. Initially she will continue to protest until she gets too tired to protest any longer.

The reason she protests is because the conditions, activities or props that she has learned to associate with sleeping are no longer there to help her feel secure. Understandably, the change will cause her to initially feel confused, frustrated, angry or upset. From your baby's perspective, things are not right and she will let you know this. This does not mean you should not continue. Her state of confusion and upset will decline as new sleep associations are learned. Protest crying is usually temporary. Provided you're consistent and persistent in encouraging her to fall asleep in the new way, any protest crying will lessen as the learning phase progresses, and may even drop well below the amount of crying your baby was doing before you began sleep training, especially if she was previously sleep deprived.

Can crying be avoided?

No one enjoys hearing their baby cry! We would all like a quick and effective settling method that will fix baby's sleep problem without tears. Whether this is realistic or not depends on many factors, such as:

- the settling approach you choose
- the sleep association you want to discourage
- the presence of other sleep associations
- your baby's age
- your baby's temperament and
- whether your baby is already distressed due to sleep deprivation.

As a general rule, the quicker you want to resolve the problem, the more significant and abrupt the changes will be and the more likely your baby will cry in protest. But if you can take things slowly and make a number of small changes over a longer period, this may lessen her protest crying to minor fussing. However, whether your baby cries or not does not depend solely on your choice of settling method, but also on the one or more sleep associations you want to discourage. If, for example, your baby has learned to depend on feeding or sucking on a pacifier as a way to fall asleep this will be very difficult to change without protest crying. Once you no longer allow her to fall asleep while feeding or with a pacifier, there will be little to stop her from crying. If you persist, she may learn to self-soothe by sucking on her thumb or fingers if over three months old, or learn to fall asleep without sucking. Some – but not all – babies catch on very quickly.

The more significant or numerous the changes to your settling practice, the more likely your baby will protest. If you remove several negative sleep associations at once, she will probably cry. If you remove one at a time you may limit crying or fussing, but accept that it will take longer to resolve her sleep problem. If your baby is supported by positive sleep associations, like falling asleep in her bed, swaddling, an infant sleeping bag, finger sucking or a security blanket or toy, that she has already learned to associate with sleeping, these may help her settle with minimal fussing or crying when you withhold a negative sleep association. However, if she hasn't yet learned to associate these things with sleeping, they will require a learning phase.

The older your baby is, the greater an overall awareness she has. As she matures, she will recognise even small changes in your settling practices. This is why many parents find their baby's sleep deteriorates around the age of four months. In general, newborns (birth to three months) can be soothed in a different way without returning to the problematic sleep association. But from four months onwards a baby knows exactly what she wants, which is to have her familiar sleep associations returned, and she's probably not going to be calmed by something else.

How intensely your baby reacts during the learning phase also depends on her temperament. Babies with easy temperaments adapt more quickly to change. If you've got a baby with a spirited temperament, she'll have a lower frustration tolerance, won't as readily accept change, and will be inclined to protest vigorously at even the most minor changes. But even a spirited baby will eventually come around if you persist.

Irrespective of these considerations, if your baby is already fussing due to physical fatigue or is feeling distressed from overtiredness, you probably can't resolve her sleeping problem without her crying. Even if you manage to avoid her crying as she settles to sleep, her fussiness or distress will continue at other times until she gets the sleep she needs.

Maintenance

A habit must be reinforced or it will cease to be a habit. Think about the effort required to get fit. You need to exercise to get fit, but you also need to exercise to remain fit. This is the same for your baby's sleep habits. You need to consistently encourage your baby to fall asleep in the way that reinforces her new habits. Maintaining your baby's new sleep habits will not be as challenging for either of you as it was during the learning phase.

What to expect during maintenance

Even after the learning phase has passed, you may find your baby continues to cry when you put her to bed. Some babies and children are so inquisitive and active that they don't seem to recognise when they're tired. They can be irritable and clumsy due to physical fatigue and yet still protest when they're put to bed. Crying is usually only brief once the learning phase has passed, except when they have become distressed due to overtiredness. The key to avoiding overtiredness is to recognise your baby's early signs of tiredness and provide an opportunity for her to sleep.

When sleep habits might slip

At certain times, children's sleep habits notoriously regress, including:

- illness
- when achieving a new developmental milestone, eg, rolling, sitting or standing
- moving house
- overnight visitors
- holidays away from home
- starting at day-care or with a new sitter
- the birth of a sibling.

These are times when settling practices are likely to change. If you promote negative sleep associations you could expect your baby's sleep patterns and behaviour to regress.

If you find baby's sleeping patterns and behaviour deteriorating, make sure another caregiver isn't settling your baby using negative sleep associations like cuddling, rocking, etc.

There will be times, such as illness, when your baby may need extra comforting to fall asleep. Be aware that if this is repeated often enough it will encourage her to learn new sleep associations, ones that depend on your help. If this happens, expect increased wakefulness as a result. The pattern of broken sleep may continue long after your baby has recovered from the illness. This does not mean you should not comfort a sick child.

Babies and children need additional comforting when sick. It just means you need to anticipate that a behavioural sleep problem might develop and need to be remedied afterwards. If you want to promote healthy sleeping habits once your baby is well again, you'll need to start sleep training from scratch. It is important to wait until your baby is physically well, however; please don't do sleep training when your child is ill.

Although it's not technically any easier the second time around, and neither is the learning phase any quicker, parents usually find it easier, because they have been through the process before and know what to expect. But, even though your baby has been through it before, she's not going to be any happier about it or find it easier the second time around.

If you're wondering whether sleep training is really necessary, given that the learning phase can be stressful for baby and parents, it comes down to how much stress your baby's sleeping problem is causing your baby, you and other family members. Only you can decide if it's worth it or not. Sleep training is not your only option. See diagram 5.4 on page 81 for options.

At what age can sleep training begin?

Sleep training can be undertaken at any age. Cry-it-out and controlled crying are not recommended for babies under six months, other methods can be used for younger babies. A number of methods can be used successfully for babies of all ages, including newborns (see Chapter 7).

Bear in mind that most babies under the age of six months require night-time feeding, so sleep training should not be used to stop night-time feeds. However, if your baby appears to feed excessively during the night, there may be steps you can take (see pages 252-259).

The great debate

I am a health professional who works with mothers and babies. I strive to provide reliable information to parents so I read a lot. For every book that I've read that endorses sleep training there's another that claims it psychologically traumatises babies. Both sides make good points and sound very convincing. But two opposing views can't both be right. Are you able to shed any light? – Lisa

As health professionals we have a duty to families to provide evidence-based information rather than opinions based on personal parenting beliefs or someone else's. This can be a difficult task when we're exposed to conflicting information. With most parenting issues, there's some agreement on what provides the best care, but not when it comes to the topic of sleep training.

What supporters say

Around 60 per cent of parenting books support the use of sleep training.[39] For example:

- Dr Marc Weissbluth is the Professor of Pediatrics at Northwestern University in Chicago, USA, and author of several books that deal with sleep disorders in young children. In his book, *Healthy Sleep Habits, Happy Child*, Weissbluth promotes a cry-it-out settling method for babies over the age of four months. He states: 'Often I will refer to ignoring all crying or extinction [cry-it-out] as the preferred solution to help your child sleep better because I think this works best for the 20 per cent of babies who have extreme fussiness/colic; after four months of age'.[40] However, he does recommend that parents consider trying other options that involve less crying first.

- Dr Richard Ferber is an American paediatrician and the director of the Center for Pediatric Sleep Disorders at the Children's Hospital in Boston, USA, and author of *Solve Your Child's Sleep Problems* as well as many academic papers on children's sleep disorders. He is best known for his infant settling method called 'controlled crying', a modified form of extinction that involves scheduled times to check and reassure the child. Ferber states: 'Treatment of improper sleep associations is fairly simple and the change will be quite rapid. A young baby's sleep will show marked improvement usually in a few days, but at least within a week or two.'[41]

- Dr Jodi A Mindell is the Professor of Psychology at Saint Joseph's University, associate director of the Sleep Disorders Center at The Children's Hospital of Philadelphia, USA, and author of the parenting book *Sleeping Through the Night* and numerous other publications on children's sleep disorders. Mindell recommends the use of gradual extinction to resolve infant and child sleep problems related to negative sleep associations. She encourages parents to teach children to first learn to fall asleep independently when put to bed in the evening, but to help them return to sleep in their usual way during night-time awakenings.[42] This is based on the theory that once the child learns to settle to sleep without parents' help in the evenings she will eventually learn to return to sleep independently following night-time awakenings.

- Dr Harriet Hiscock is paediatrician, Senior Research Fellow at the Centre for Community Child Health, Royal Children's Hospital, Melbourne, Australia, and author of numerous academic papers on infant crying and sleep problems, prevention of early childhood behavioural problems, and postnatal depression. Hiscock promotes the use of controlled crying for babies over the age of six months to resolve infant sleeping problems and reduce the incidence, severity and longevity of maternal postnatal depression.[43]

These sleep disorder specialists all recommend the use of extinction, modified extinction or gradual extinction. A large number of studies show these methods to be effective.[44]

Again, cry-it-out and controlled crying are not generally recommended for babies under the age of six months.

What critics say

One-third of all infant sleep books oppose using any settling methods that involve ignoring a child's crying, even for brief periods.[45] Concern relates to the potential emotional and psychological effects of temporarily withholding your response to infant crying during sleep-time. Most opponents of sleep training advocate a quick response to the baby's or child's distress to soothe the child. They typically promote parent-assisted settling practices, such as bed-sharing, feeding your baby to sleep and cuddling or rocking your baby to drowsiness or sleep. (As negative sleep associations, such settling practices are often the reason why babies nap very briefly and awaken frequently during the night.) The following is only a tiny sample of what critics have to say about sleep training.

- Dr Margot Sunderland, director of education at the Centre for Child Mental Health in London, opposes sleep training methods that involve 'prolonged crying'. However, she does not define what constitutes prolonged crying. In her book, *The Science of Parenting*, Sunderland comments: 'A baby who is trained out of his instinct to cry on being separated from a parent should never be mistaken for being in a state of calm. His stress levels have gone up, not down ... Infants who are trained not to cry can often be seen staring into space with a fixed stare. Allan Schore, a neuropsychoanalyst, calls it "the back spot in going-on-being" or "conservation-withdrawal".'[46]

- Dr William Sears, American paediatrician and author of *Nighttime Parenting* claims, 'a restrained response to crying undermines the infant's trust'.[47] In *The Fussy Baby Book*, Sears states: 'Babies who are "trained" not to express their needs may appear to be docile, compliant, or "good" babies. Yet these babies could be depressed babies who are shutting down the expression of their needs.'[48]

- Robin Grille, psychologist and author of *Parenting for a Peaceful World* states: 'When controlled crying "succeeds" in teaching a baby to fall asleep alone, it is due to a process that neuro-biologist Bruce Perry calls the "defeat response".'[49]

- In their book *Helping Your Baby to Sleep*, psychologist Beth Macgregor and social scientist Anni Gethin state: 'In neurological terms sleep training forces an extended mis-attunement, or attachment rupture, within a baby ... If this is done repeatedly it will have a negative effect on the child.' They also claim: 'The essential ingredient of sleep training is the withholding of parental love and comfort.'[50]

- Pinky McKay, mother of five and author of *100 Ways to Calm the Crying*, states: 'There is emerging evidence that distress at being left to cry (abandonment) changes the physiology of the brain and may predispose children to stress disorders such as panic, anxiety and depression in later life.'[51]

These authors, most of whom are trained health professionals, make some very serious claims regarding the consequences of sleep training. But are these claims founded on evidence or opinion? Let's take a closer look.

Top five concerns

The top five concerns are:

- psychological harm
- brain damage
- teaches baby not to cry
- breaks baby's trust
- insecure emotional attachment.

Most claims stem from studies on the psychological (brain development) and neurobiological (brain chemistry) effects of negligent and abusive care-giving on children. Some writers even go so far as to compare the effects of sleep training to the trauma that devastated the lives of children in infamous Romanian orphanages during Nicolae Ceauşescu's dictatorship.

Romanian orphanages

During President Nicolae Ceauşescu's rule (1965–89), contraception and abortion for women under the age of 40 were banned. Ceauşescu wanted to increase the country's population by 50 per cent within a single generation. The general population was poor, and families were unable to provide for multiple children. Tens of thousands of children (most of whom were not orphans) where abandoned to state orphanages for which the country became notorious. The plight of these children did not come to light until Western journalists were permitted access in 1990. The world then got to see images of babies lying three or four to a bed, given no attention by the few staff on duty. Children were malnourished, some tied to their beds. They had been severely neglected, and physically and sexual abused. Many children had impaired brain development, and psychological and emotional problems. The children were so poorly treated that some orphanage mortality rates reached over 50 per cent in a single year.[52]

No-one disputes the physical and psychological effects on defenceless children maltreated at the hands of their alleged caregivers. But claims that sleep training results in similar harm to those children in the case study above are unsubstantiated. Let's examine these top five concerns more closely.

1. Does sleep training cause psychological harm?

In 2003, the Australian Association for Infant Mental Health (AAIMH) published a position paper expressing concerns that 'controlled crying is not consistent with infant need for optimal emotional or psychological health and may have unintended negative consequences'. Since that time, the two page AAIMH position paper has been viewed by some as evidence that controlled crying and, by association, other settling methods that involve delayed response to crying, psychologically traumatises infants. However, the paper does not provide evidence to support claims of psychological harm; it merely raises concerns.

A number of other studies have demonstrated that behavioural interventions, such as controlled crying, don't cause any discernable signs of psychological harm.[53] In fact, these studies identified positive effects of sleep training related to alleviating the stress of both baby and parents associated infant sleep problems. Perhaps the most compelling evidence that sleep training does not cause psychological harm comes from a six-year study completed by the Murdoch Children's Research Institute, Melbourne, Australia, in 2009. Dr Anna Price and associates assessed the health and emotional wellbeing, behaviour and child-parent relationships of 225 six-year-old children who had received controlled crying behavioural modification as babies. The study concluded that techniques such as controlled crying, don't lead to emotional or behavioural problems later in life. Price added that, 'without intervention, sleep problems are also more likely to persist into childhood, potentially leading to behavioural and cognitive problems including aggression, anxiety and attention and learning difficulties'. Price states 'health professionals can feel comfortable offering these interventions [instruction on how to use controlled crying] to families presenting with infant sleep problems. Parents can also feel reassured they will not harm their babies by using sleep interventions.'[54]

For more than 15 years I worked as a child health nurse at a residential parenting education centre where 20 new families were admitted each week for a period of four to five days and nights to resolve baby-care problems. Working with parents, I closely observed the behaviour of hundreds of babies as they progressed through the learning phase of sleep training. I did not witness any behaviour that would indicate a baby or a child was psychologically or emotionally traumatised as a result of settling methods that involved some crying.

When babies were admitted to the centre with their parents, their behaviour was typically clingy, whiny, fussy, irritable and demanding, most often because they were chronically sleep-deprived. Once these babies learned to fall asleep without their parents' help they got more sleep and were no longer burdened by constant fatigue. These same babies and children then played more readily, smiled and laughed more often than they had done before sleep training; not the behaviour of psychologically traumatised babies and children.

2. Can stress associated with sleep training cause brain damage?

Critics of sleep training will sometimes refer to studies by Allan Schore, Bruce Perry and others, which indicate that prolonged exposure to high levels of cortisol and other stress hormones can permanently impair the developing brain's processing of stressful stimulation. Dr Allan Schore is a leading authority in the area of psycho-neurobiology. In 'The effects of early relational trauma on right brain development, affect regulation, and infant mental health', Schore describes the effects of maltreatment on early brain development 'associated with abuse and neglect'.[55] Dr Bruce Perry, a clinician and researcher in children's mental health and the neurosciences, and an internationally-recognised authority on children in crisis, states 'physical or sexual abuse, living in the fallout zone of domestic or community violence, surviving a serious car accident, all have an impact on the child's development'.[56] Neither Schore nor Perry mention sleep training. It's a big leap to compare the experience of abuse and neglect with that of sleep training. The only logical explanation as to why critics of sleep training repeatedly cite information gained from studies on the effects of abusive and negligent care is that they hold the personal opinion that sleep training is a form of abuse or neglect.

Change is stressful. Changing sleep habits is not an easy task. None of us like change, even when we know it's good for us. Your baby cannot understand that changing her sleep associations will improve her quality of sleep and ultimately benefit her. She will get upset when you change your settling practices to modify her sleep associations. Your baby's stress levels will rise because she is tired and upset by the changes. A short-term rise in cortisol has not been shown to be harmful.[57]

If short-term stress resulted in brain damage, every time a toddler or child became upset because they were denied something, they would incur further brain damage. Chronic stress is harmful, but short-term stress has not been shown to be.

Parents do sleep training to alleviate the long-term stress that an infant sleep problem causes their baby, themselves and other family members. Parents must gauge what's less stressful in their particular situation, changing settling practices to resolve a sleep problem and risk increased stress during the brief learning phase, or continuing the settling practices that perpetuate their baby's sleep problem, and any stress this might incur and hope this somehow spontaneously resolves down the road.

Being a parent is not easy. Sometimes we need to make difficult decisions for the sake of our children. They're not always going to like the choices we make on their behalf. If your baby needed medications or surgery to fix a physical problem would you refuse to allow this because it would upset her? Of course not. You know the benefits of treatment will outweigh any short-term stress she will endure. If your baby experiences chronic stress or other problems related to insufficient sleep, she will be more than compensated for any short-term stress, which can occur while learning new sleep associations, by the benefits of improved sleep.

3. Does sleep training teach babies not to cry?
Many people believe sleep training teaches babies not to cry, citing what Schore calls 'conservation-withdrawal' and what Perry refers to as 'defeat response' to back up such claims. Schore and Perry, however, refer to neglected and abused children who learn not to cry when their cries

perpetually go unanswered. To claim that sleep training elicits this type of response shows a lack of understanding of the sleep training process.

It's not the baby's crying that is targeted for extinction during sleep training; it's the baby's learned dependence on negative sleep associations, which include cuddling, rocking, patting, feeding or reliance on pacifiers, their sole purpose being to facilitate sleep. Your baby is likely to cry in protest during the learning phase of sleep training, but, once that phase has passed and the new way of settling to sleep has become familiar, her protest crying will decline. Once your baby relearns how to self-settle, and go from a quiet state to falling asleep without your help, this means she no longer cries for your help to fall asleep, she doesn't need to. She does, however, still depend on you to recognise her signs of tiredness and provide her with positive sleep associations to support her to sleep independently.

Additionally, after your baby relearns how to fall asleep independent of outside help, she can move between sleep cycles on her own. The risk of her waking prematurely due to the absence of negative sleep associations is markedly reduced. If her sleep is no longer being broken, she suffers less from sleep deprivation, and, thus, her total crying time over the course of the day has lessened. If your baby also learns to self-soothe, say, by sucking on her hands and fingers or clutching her cuddly toy, crying when settling to sleep will be minimal or a non-event, unless she's overtired.

I say 'relearn' to self-settle, because, when a baby is first born, she can fall asleep without others' help, provided she feels securely contained, as if in the womb. She loses this ability when we teach her to rely on help to fall asleep. Babies would not need sleep training if we did not first accidentally train them to rely on negative sleep associations.

4. Does sleep training break a child's trust?
If only caring for a baby was as simple as giving her what she wants, then everyone would be happy. A baby learns to trust her parents when her needs are met in a compassionate and consistent manner. If she is tired and crying, it's because she needs to go to sleep. She wants her familiar sleep associations to ease her into sleep because this is what she has been taught to expect. Settling a baby to sleep in the way she has already learned to associate with sleeping will be the quickest way to get her to sleep. But

helping her fall asleep may not be the most effective way to get her to stay asleep long enough to provide for her sleep needs. The ability to fall asleep independently enables a baby to self-regulate her sleeping patterns, and is the most effective way to ensure she gets enough sleep. You needn't ignore your baby's cries to achieve this.

Imagine you're a small baby. You're tired and so you cry. Mum picks you up and cuddles you. You're feeling warm and safe in her arms. The sound of her voice and the gentle swaying as she rocks you lulls you to sleep. Once you're asleep, she places you in your cot. You sleep for a short while before beginning to rouse between sleep cycles. You need more sleep, but something's not right. Your eyes spring open. What's going on here? Where's my mum? You start to cry. Most times Mum comes to you quickly, but sometimes you're crying for what can feel like a long time before she comes. When she returns, she lovingly picks you up and kisses you. If she recognises you're still tired, she cuddles you back to sleep. If she doesn't, she gets you up. You haven't had enough sleep so you're soon fussing with tiredness again. She has taught you to depend on her help to fall asleep, but, when you need her help to move smoothly from one sleep cycle to the next, she's not there. What if this help is not always available when you need it? Do you think you will learn to trust that your needs will be met?

Now imagine yourself as a baby, tired and crying. Mum picks you up and cuddles you. You feel warm and safe in her arms as she rocks you. The sound of her voice relaxes you. You have learned what this means: it's time for sleep. Mum rocks you for a few minutes, and then places you into your cot. You would much rather be in her arms so you give a little cry. She strokes your head and whispers, 'It's time for sleep.' Her touch and the sound of her voice reassure you. You lie quietly for a few minutes. It's been an exciting day and you don't yet fall asleep. You start to cry. Your mum waits for a few minutes to give you a chance to calm on your own. You clutch your favourite cuddly toy, suck on your fingers and close your eyes. If you cannot calm yourself, Mum returns, reassures you once again, and leaves before you're asleep. You're tired and comfy so you drop off to sleep on your own. Because you know how to fall asleep without your mum's help, you can also move from one sleep cycle to the next on your own. When you've had enough sleep, you wake up feeling refreshed. You look around. Nothing's changed. You fell asleep in your cot alone and you're still in your cot. You've had enough sleep and you're ready to get up, so you cry for Mum to come and get you. She comes and lovingly picks you up and kisses you. Do you think that because your mum doesn't cuddle you until you fall asleep that you cannot trust her? Or, because she deliberately delayed her response to provide you with an opportunity to self-soothe?

Which settling approach is more likely to gain a baby's trust? The method that helps baby fall asleep and then removes this help after baby has fallen asleep and therefore is not aware, or the method that lets baby know from the start 'I am here, I will help you to soothe if you're not able to achieve this for yourself, but I will allow you to fall asleep on your own'?

5. Can sleep training cause an insecure attachment?
Attachment theory holds that secure attachments – the bond between baby and parent – and the attuned infant-caregiver interactions that produce them, are crucial to healthy psychological development.[58] Attachment theory is the joint work of British psychiatrist, John Bowlby and Canadian developmental psychologist, Mary Ainsworth.[59] John Bowlby's early work focused on the effects of prolonged infant-mother separation, such as that experienced by hospitalised and institutionalised children during the late 1940s, back when parents were not allowed to stay with their children in hospital. Bowlby concluded that prolonged periods of separation from the mother can be detrimental to the formation of a secure emotional attachment. Ainsworth's work related to the interactions between mother and baby. She studied maternal sensitivity to infant signals and its role in infant-mother attachment. Ainsworth claimed an insecure emotional attachment may develop when the child's needs are frequently unmet and the child comes to believe that communication of needs has no influence on the caregiver.

Critics of sleep training claim it involves prolonged periods of separation and that ignoring the child's cries, even for short periods of time, may result in an insecure emotional attachment. But is this the case?

Parents choose to do sleep training because a problem already exists. Their baby might be distressed and overtired, and parents and other family members may suffer from lack of sleep owing to baby's wakefulness. Sleep training aims to resolve such problems. It doesn't involve prolonged periods of separation or neglect. It involves parents withholding negative sleep associations responsible for their baby's pattern of broken sleep, and providing opportunities for their baby to learn new, positive, self-regulating sleep associations. The baby receives love, affection and attention at other times to reinforce emotional attachment, possibly more than before, once her parents are no longer burdened by chronic sleep deprivation.

Infant-parent attachment forms throughout your child's early years based on the countless interactions you have with her every day. It's not solely dependent on how you settle her to sleep. Well-rested babies and parents are in a better position to form a close loving bond compared to when they're chronically stressed and exhausted.

Dr Karyn G France, a clinical psychologist and senior lecturer at the University of Canterbury in New Zealand, compared the behaviour characteristics and security scores of 35 babies aged between six and 24 months treated with extinction for sleep disturbance, and concluded that there was no evidence of any detrimental effects on the treated infants and that, in fact, their 'security, emotionality/tension, and likeability scores improved'. Swedish paediatrician, Berndt Eckerberg examined the relationship before and after sleep training and concluded, 'According to parental ratings, family wellbeing and negative day-time behaviour also improved.'[60] Following the results of a Murdoch Children's Institute study on controlled crying methods, paediatrician and researcher, Dr Harriet Hiscock and associates stated 'The sleep intervention in infancy resulted in sustained positive effects on maternal depression symptoms and found no evidence of longer-term adverse effect on either mothers' parenting practices or children's mental health'.[61]

A recent study by the Flinders University, South Australia, found controlled crying did not increase stress levels of babies or lead to attachment disorders. The study found decreased levels of stress hormone cortisol in the saliva of babies that were subject to controlled crying. In the interview quoted in www.news.com.au, one of the lead reseachers, Dr Michael Gradisar from the Child and Adolescent Sleep Clinic, School of Psychology, at Flinders said that it seemed controlled crying 'helped to resolve their sleep issues'. He added that it was possible that with increased sleep mothers are also less stressed, resulting in better mother and child interactions.

It has been my observation that babies and parents are happier once the baby's sleep problem is resolved as a result of sleep training. Babies are generally more content. The total crying time after sleep training compared to before, when the baby was sleep-deprived, is significantly reduced, and many parents say they feel more confident and attuned to their baby's needs and behavioural cues. Some claim they finally enjoy caring for their baby, often for the first time since their baby's birth.

The Circle of Security, a program that helps parents build a healthy emotional attachment with their child, claims that healthy attachment is achieved by filling the child's 'emotional cup' each day. You fill your baby's emotional cup with all the wonderful loving interactions you have with her. If her emotional cup is kept topped up, it won't be depleted by short-term stressful events, such as during the learning phase of sleep training. And it is a lot easier to fill your baby's emotional cup with loving interactions once you and she are no longer sleep-deprived.

True or false?

1. Young babies are not capable of self-settling.

FALSE: Babies are born able to self-settle from a quiet, wakeful state to asleep without help, but not all babies can regain a calm state by self-soothing once they start crying. It's possible to encourage a baby to self-settle and yet assist her to soothe as often as required. You simply need to withdraw your help once she's calm, but before she's asleep.

2. Babies who are left to cry alone experience feelings of abandonment.

MAYBE: Once a baby has developed a strong emotional attachment to their main caregiver, typically after the age of seven months, she will then experience some degree of anxiety when separated. Bowlby's hypothesis is that the anxiety the child feels relates to fear of abandonment. Bear in mind that Bowlby was commissioned to study the effects of institutionalised children in orphanages and hospitalised children at a time when parents were discouraged from visiting based on claims this would upset the child. Short periods of solitude during sleep training in the familiarity of their own bed are not the same as extended periods of separation while suffering illness or injury in a foreign place surrounded by strangers. While babies can suffer separation anxiety, in most instances, it's not separation from parents that troubles the baby as much as separation from *parent-assisted sleep associations*, which the baby has learned to rely on to fall asleep. If you're concerned your baby might suffer from separation anxiety, you can effectively sleep train while remaining present in the room.

3. Sleep training aims to prevent baby from feeding at night.
FALSE: Sleep training does not mean night-time feeds are withheld. Your baby should be fed as often as she needs. The difference is that sleep training means baby is no longer fed to help her fall asleep. Feeding a baby to sleep, a negative sleep association, can result in your baby wanting to feed excessively day and night simply to achieve more sleep.

4. Sleep training goes against a mother's natural instincts.
TRUE: Humans are biologically programmed to respond to a baby's cries. The sound of a baby's crying triggers the release of stress hormones in all humans within earshot, but more so in the mother or caregiver, prompting us to respond and soothe the baby. If you have inadvertently trained your baby to need your help to fall asleep, she will cry if you withhold your help, and you will feel compelled to soothe her by providing that help. Acting on your instincts may help you to limit her immediate distress, but it may also prevent you from resolving an infant sleep problem that is causing you both long-term distress through sleep deprivation.

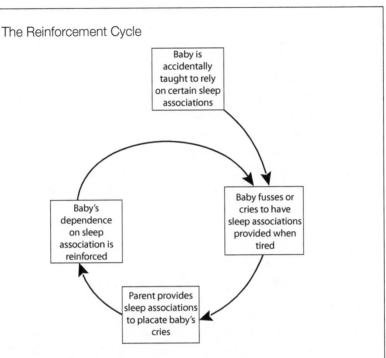

The Reinforcement Cycle

Baby is accidentally taught to rely on certain sleep associations

Baby fusses or cries to have sleep associations provided when tired

Parent provides sleep associations to placate baby's cries

Baby's dependence on sleep association is reinforced

5. Parents who do sleep training are selfish.

FALSE: People who have never experienced the seemingly endless stress associated with chronic sleep deprivation can understandably fail to appreciate just how debilitating it can be. Infant sleep problems are not only the most common reason for infant distress; they impact negatively on maternal health and wellbeing, as well as that of other family members. Parents who act to resolve a problem that is distressing their baby or family are not selfish.

6. Sleep training is cruel.

FALSE: Babies suffer varying degrees of distress caused by chronic sleep deprivation (see Chapter 2). Sleep training can be stressful in the short term for all involved, but when done properly, is not cruel. Failing to address the underlying cause of a baby's sleep deprivation is cruel (and potentially harmful if Mum or the baby's main caregiver is also perpetually physically exhausted).

Unfortunately, those who don't support sleep training often misrepresent information obtained from studies on abusive and negligent and parenting (or care) as evidence that sleep training is harmful. It is important to remember that there is no documented evidence (that I have found during extensive literature reviews) that behavioural interventions, such as controlled crying or other sleep training techniques, are physically or psychologically harmful. If there was such evidence, critics of sleep training would most definitely make it known.

Not every parent who attempts sleep training succeeds, however. (See Chapter 12 as to why some claim sleep training doesn't work.)

Key points

- Sleep training is effective when used correctly and appropriately.

- Sleep training is most effective when a baby is supported to fall asleep independent of others' help and without unreliable sleep aids.

- Extinction (cry-it-out) and modified extinction (controlled crying and responsive settling) are the most effective sleep training methods when used consistently. Gradual extinction (which involves withholding negative sleep associations intermittently) takes longer and has a higher failure rate.

- Studies that refer to psychological damage and attachment disorders are linked to negligent and abusive parenting, not sleep training.

Seven ways to change baby's sleep associations

Many people like to share their opinion on how parents should or should not settle their babies to sleep. One of the most hotly debated topics in parenting chat rooms, websites, parenting books and magazines is the best way to get babies to sleep. The truth is that there is no single way to effectively settle every baby to sleep. Your personality, parenting beliefs, physical and emotional health, responsibilities and commitments, family composition, lifestyle, home environment, baby's temperament, and most importantly whether you or your baby is sleep-deprived, all play a role in your choice of infant settling methods.

This chapter identifies seven settling methods to help parents manage or resolve an infant sleep problem stemming from a baby's learned dependence on negative sleep associations. Each method is explored in greater detail in ensuing chapters. Comparing methods may help you choose a settling method that best suits your baby and your family circumstances.

Settling options

> I have read a number of books on babies' sleep, and talked to my doctor, child health nurse and other mums. Everyone tells me to do something different. I feel so confused. I don't know what to do anymore. Can you tell me what's the best way to get my baby to sleep? – Philomena

Every parent and health professional may have a preferred way to settle a baby to sleep. People tend to naturally recommend the method they used with their baby or the method that fits with their personal parenting beliefs. You could read or be told about many different infant settling methods. This can be confusing. However, it becomes less confusing once the settling methods are grouped according to the goal achieved, how quickly the goal can be attained, and the recommended age. The following flow chart depicts how the different settling methods are grouped.

Diagram 7.1:   What do you want to achieve?

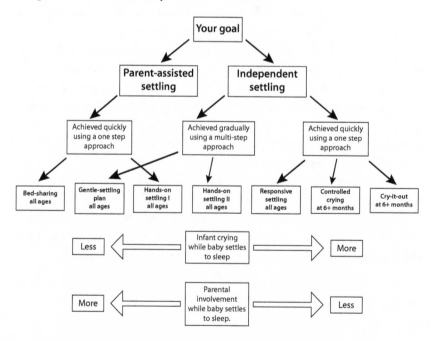

To pinpoint the settling method best suited to your baby and family, you need to:

- decide on your goal
- choose a one or multi-step approach
- select a settling method within that approach.

Your goal

If you're clear about what you want to achieve, you will more readily identify infant settling methods that match your goal. Therefore, the first thing you need to decide is whether you want parent-assisted versus independent settling: whether you're happy to help your baby to fall asleep, and also help him return to sleep if he wakes too soon, or if you want your baby to learn to fall asleep without your help, thus enabling him to move between sleep cycles independent of your help.

Your goal

↙   ↘

Parent-assisted settling   **Independent settling**

Knowing the potential advantages and disadvantages of parent-assisted and independent settling may help you decide if you can fulfil the responsibilities attached to parent-assisted settling methods, or alternatively, support baby to settle to sleep on his own.

Parent-assisted settling

Parent-assisted settling methods include any that involve actively helping a baby to fall asleep. This includes things like feeding, cuddling, rocking or patting baby at the time he falls sleep. (See page 73 for more examples.) Parent-assisted settling methods encourage baby to associate sleeping with the help that you or other caregivers provide.

The main advantage of parent-assisted settling methods is that they're often an effective way to get baby to fall asleep with minimal fussing or crying, which is why parents so frequently fall into this pattern. A major disadvantage is that your baby's risk of waking increases whenever you withdraw your help, which is what normally happens. **By withdrawing your help, you will be removing your baby's sleep associations.** During light sleep and arousals between sleep cycles, he may become aware of his immediate surroundings, including the presence or absence of his sleep associations. If he notices that his sleep associations are missing he will wake fully and cry until you to come and soothe him back to sleep.

By assisting your baby to fall asleep, you become responsible for regulating his sleeping patterns. Your baby will now depend on your help to fall asleep, and require that same help to remain asleep or return if he wakes too soon. Just how burdensome this responsibility will be for you depends largely on your baby's temperament. Some babies who receive help falling asleep sleep just fine and wake well rested. Others are sensitive to change, and will notice their sleep associations missing, unless they're too physically exhausted to wake, they rouse too early from their naps and wake excessively during the night.

Once you understand your responsibilities in regulating your baby's sleeping patterns using parent-assisted settling methods, you may find you can increase the amount of sleep your baby gets. So, if you enjoy helping your baby fall asleep and can readily commit to doing so every time, then you might like to consider trying a parent-assisted settling method like bed-sharing or hands-on settling I.

Bed-sharing

Bed-sharing, sometimes referred to as co-sleeping, is when your baby sleeps with you in your bed. Bed-sharing will not necessarily resolve a negative sleep association-based infant sleep problem. Some parents find bed-sharing to be convenient and enjoyable for their family, while others don't.

If your baby is wakeful during the night because he has learned to associate sleeping with close physical contact, for example, by being cuddled or breast-fed to sleep, then bed-sharing may be a way you can maintain his sleep associations throughout the night. One potential disadvantage to bed-sharing is that your baby might not sleep if you're unable to maintain physical contact with him the entire time he needs to sleep, both day and night.

Chapter 8 explains in greater detail what bed-sharing entails, the effect it can have on a baby's and parent's night-time sleep, and what impact bed-sharing at night could have on baby's day-time sleep behaviour. If you enjoy bed-sharing, you may learn new strategies to smooth over infant sleep problems. Alternatively, it may help confirm if bed-sharing is not a practical sleeping arrangement for your family.

Hands-on settling I

Hands-on settling I is actively assisting your baby to fall asleep while he's in his cot, cradle or bassinette, by patting, rocking or stroking him. The main advantage of this settling method is that, by falling asleep in his bed, your baby's sleeping environment remains consistent during his entire sleep. This can be enough to improve the quality of sleep for some babies, particularly newborns. Even if hands-on settling does not completely resolve your baby's sleep issues, learning to fall asleep in his bed is a huge step towards settling to sleep independently, something that can resolve excessive wakefulness for most well babies.

A disadvantage of hands-on settling is there may be some tears involved during the learning phase if your baby is not already familiar with falling asleep in his bed. If he currently favours sleeping elsewhere, like your arms, an infant rocker or swing, it will likely take him several days to become accustomed to falling asleep in his bed. See Chapter 10 to find out more about hands-on settling.

Independent settling

If you simply want to get your baby to sleep, you might choose a parent-assisted settling method, but if you want your baby to sleep better, then encourage independent settling. The most effective way to resolve an infant sleep problem based on negative sleep associations is employing a settling method that encourages baby to fall asleep without them. That is because settling methods that promote independent settling enable your baby to self-regulate his sleeping patterns, which improves both the quality and quantity of sleep. In general, babies who self-regulate their sleeping patterns suffer less from sleep deprivation compared to those who depend on others to help them to fall and remain asleep.

Even a newborn can self-regulate his sleeping patterns in line with his stage of development, but he needs support to achieve this. Revisit Table 4.1 on page 54 for what type of support your baby needs from you and other caregivers to get the sleep he needs.

Recognising and accurately interpreting your baby's early signs of tiredness and then providing him with an opportunity to sleep are key elements to supporting his sleep. But equally important is where your baby settles to sleep and the way he falls asleep. Three key elements are involved in supporting a baby to self-regulate his sleeping patterns. A number of my clients refer to these as Rowena's Golden Rules.

Rowena's Golden Rules

1. Provide baby with a suitable and consistent sleeping environment.

2. Withhold any unreliable props or sleep aids at sleep time.

3. Promote independent settling.

By placing your baby into his bed to fall asleep every time, you provide him with a suitable and consistent sleeping environment. The risk of waking too soon due to a change in his surroundings, or as a result of environmental noise, bright lights or visual stimulation is reduced. To gain the full benefits of a consistent sleeping environment, your baby needs to fall asleep while he's in his bed.

By no longer providing unreliable props or aids as your baby falls asleep, he learns to sleep without them. This may take a few days, and you must be consistent and persistent, but once he learns to fall asleep without unreliable props or aids, then his sleep will no longer be disrupted when they fall out or switch off.

By withholding your help at the moment your baby falls asleep, he re-learns how to fall asleep without your help. Then he will be less inclined to wake fully during arousals that occur between sleep cycles, a time when he is likely to realise that his parent-assisted sleep associations are missing. When he does wake, he will also be better able to settle back to sleep without your help.

Providing baby with positive sleep associations, ones that remain consistent throughout his entire sleep, like swaddling, using an infant sleeping bag or security object, depending on what's appropriate for your baby's stage of development, ideally support him to settle to sleep and move between sleep cycles independent of your help, once he learns to associate them with sleeping.

By achieving the three Golden Rules and promoting positive sleep associations, you support your baby to self-regulate his sleeping patterns. He will still wake to have his physical needs provided for, but the risk of waking prematurely is reduced, which means he will be get more of the sleep his little body needs.

If you decide to support your baby to self-regulate his sleeping patterns by promoting independent settling, then you must decide which approach you will employ.

Approach: one step or multi-step?

Every parent with an infant sleep problem wants to find a solution in the quickest possible time – yesterday is good! – *and* avoid upsetting their baby. Some settling methods will resolve your baby's sleep problem quickly, and others may minimise baby's tears. But there are no quick solutions without some tears.

To resolve a baby's negative sleep association-based sleep problem involves all caregivers changing their infant settling practices to achieve the three Golden Rules. Babies and children don't like change, however, so, if you change your settling methods, you must anticipate some resistance on your baby's part, until the new way of falling asleep becomes familiar.

This is where 'approach' comes in. You have a choice:

- **Resolve the problem quickly** by making all necessary changes at one time. This is likely to result in some short-term periods of intense crying during the learning phase.
- **Minimise your baby's upset** by making a series of smaller changes over a few days, weeks or months. This will take much longer

but if minimising your baby's upset is more important to you, and you can manage the risk of your baby's and your own sleep deprivation, this will be potentially less upsetting to your baby.

The various independent settling methods can be separated into two groups, the one step and the multi-step approaches.

Independent settling

↙   ↘

One step approach   **Multi-step approach**

To compare the one step and multi-step approaches, consider what happens when pulling off a child's Band-Aid. Some parents do this swiftly. There may be tears, but it's over quickly. Other parents prefer to do it slowly to lessen their child's tears, but this takes time. Similarly, a settling method that uses a one step approach can improve the quality and quantity of a baby's sleep within a matter of days, but is rarely achieved without some crying. It may be possible to change your baby's sleep associations and still minimise his tears, but, like slowly peeling off a Band-Aid, it's not completely painless and takes more time.

Each approach has its advantages and disadvantages. How these stack up depends on your circumstances.

One step approach

A one step approach is quicker, but you've got to achieve all three Golden Rules at the one time. This means you're no longer reinforcing your baby's dependence on negative sleep associations. Improvements can usually be seen three to five days, if you're consistent. One step settling methods include:

- responsive settling
- controlled crying
- cry-it-out.

When used correctly, these three settling methods are all effective. Again, the downside to making significant changes is that most babies will get very upset during the learning phase. The main difference between these three methods is when you're encouraged to soothe your upset baby.

Responsive settling

When using responsive settling, you go to your baby as often as you feel is necessary to check, console or reassure him, but, first, you give him an opportunity to self-soothe by resisting the urge to swoop in and rescue him at the first cry. You listen, interpret his cries, and determine if he needs your help to soothe him or a little more time to work things out on his own.

Responsive settling aims to encourage a baby to self-settle, to transition from a quiet state to asleep unaided. A very young baby is not expected to self-soothe, but he is given opportunities to learn and master the self-soothing skills that will eventually enable him to achieve this.

Because baby is not forced to self-soothe, this makes responsive settling suitable for babies of all ages. Because a baby's sleep problem can usually be resolved quickly, and parents get to soothe their baby whenever they feel is necessary, most parents choose this method. See pages 69 & 74–96 for more details.

Controlled crying

Controlled crying (also known as controlled comforting or Ferberizing) was made popular by Dr Richard Ferber, an American paediatrician and Director of the Center for Pediatric Sleep Disorders at Children's Hospital in Boston. It's a settling method that encourages you to check, console or reassure baby at pre-determined timed intervals; for example, after five minutes. Variations of this method involve gradually extending the time between visits.

This method is often a good option for anxious parents who have a tendency to rush in and sweep their baby up into their arms the moment he looks even remotely upset. Using controlled crying may be viewed as forcing a baby to self-soothe and, therefore, this **method is not recommended for babies under the age of six months.** (Such young babies generally have limited ability to self-soothe compared to older babies.) For more on controlled crying and variations in timed response intervals, see page 69.

Cry-it-out

Cry-it-out, as the name suggests, involves leaving a baby to cry without responding until he eventually falls asleep. Responding is done only if baby has physical comfort and safety needs that require attention.

Cry-it-out is an effective way to resolve an infant sleep problem related to negative sleep associations because there's little room for error. However, it can be stressful for babies and their parents during the learning phase. Because this method will force a baby to self-soothe, it is **not recommended for babies under the age of six months**. See page 71 for more details.

All the one step settling methods involve periods of intense crying on the baby's part during the learning phase of sleep training and, therefore, are not methods that every parent will find acceptable. Most parents prefer to avoid or at least minimise their baby's crying if possible. You can lessen any upset your baby experiences by using a multi-step approach instead.

Multi-step approach

You may be able to avoid tears by making a series of small changes over time using a multi-step approach. This aims to achieve all three Golden Rules, but does so one at a time rather than all at once. Two types of multi-step methods are my gentle settling plan and hands-on settling II.

Gentle settling plan

A gentle settling plan aims to encourage your baby to slowly and gently transition from sleeping in your arms, for example, to falling asleep in his bed, initially with your help and then without. You can use only some of the steps if you're happy just to get your baby willingly settling to sleep in his bed with your help. Or you might prefer to have him fall asleep in his bed on his own. It's up to you.

The main goal is to reduce any upset baby may experience while changing his sleep habits. How much crying you can avoid depends on whether your baby is already distressed by sleep deprivation. The disadvantage of using a multi-step approach like this one is that it takes much longer to resolve a baby's sleep problem. The time it takes to get your baby to independently settle can range from weeks to months, depending on how quickly you're able to support and encourage him to progress through all the steps.

This method is best suited for non-sleep-deprived babies, and parents who are not in a hurry to resolve their baby's sleep issues. See Chapter 9 for more on gentle settling.

Hands-on settling II

Hands-on settling II uses a three-step approach, with each step achieving a different objective. For example:

- **Step 1:** Provide baby with a consistent sleeping environment by settling him to sleep while he's in his bed.
- **Step 2:** Discourage baby's dependence on unreliable props or aids, like a pacifier.
- **Step 3:** Encourage baby to settle to sleep independently.

Hands-on settling II achieves the three Golden Rules one at a time, enabling baby to self-regulate his sleeping patterns. The advantage of using a multi-step approach like hands-on settling II is that, by making one change at time, this process may be more acceptable to baby and thus less upsetting than a one step approach. The disadvantage is that it takes longer to resolve your baby's sleep problem than a one step approach. Hands-on settling II can take from nine days to weeks or longer, depending on how quickly you achieve each step.

This, like my gentle settling method, is best suited for non-sleep-deprived babies and parents who are not in a hurry to resolve their baby's sleep issues. See Chapter 10 for more on hands-on settling II.

Your choice

Unfortunately, you can't waive a magic wand to resolve an infant sleep problem based on negative sleep associations. Sleep habits are learned. A baby can only learn new sleep habits with guidance from parents and caregivers. To guide your baby you must change your infant settling practices.

Only you can decide which method may suit your circumstances. Alternatively, you can continue doing what you're doing, the quickest way to get your baby to go to sleep in the short term with minimal upset, but it won't necessarily resolve your baby's sleep problems.

> **If you always do what you have always done, you will always get what you have always got.**

Keys to success

- **Consistency**: This is imperative to succeed. Inconsistency will send your baby mixed messages, which may impede his learning. Doing different things at different times may confuse and frustrate him. Following the same steps each time your baby settles to sleep, during the day, evening and night, is key to your success.
- **Persistence**: It takes time for a baby to learn new sleep habits and associations. Each settling method has a learning phase. Persistence on your part is necessary during this sometimes difficult phase.
- **Patience**: Your baby has no desire to change his sleep associations, and therefore will not be a willing participant. During the learning phase of sleep training *it may take him longer to fall asleep and in some cases baby might become more wakeful.* This is only temporary until the new, positive sleep associations become familiar. Throughout, you must remain calm and patiently continue to guide him, despite his protests.

Sleep safety recommendations

No sleeping arrangement is 100 per cent safe for a child. Whatever sleeping arrangement you choose, you should follow the relevant sleep safety recommendations to make his sleep environment as safe as possible.

- Make sure the cot or bed is positioned away from power points, heaters, electrical appliances, lights and windows.
- Keep it away from curtain cords or other cords or ropes in which baby could become entangled.
- Make sure nothing on the wall above the cot or bed can fall on your baby.

- Use a firm, well-fitted mattress, with no gaps between the mattress and the frame of the cot, or between the mattress and bedrails or wall.
- Avoid using soft bedding such as quilts, sheepskins, pillows or fluffy bed clothing.
- If baby is under 12 months, place him on his back to sleep. But expect that he might not stay there once he's learned to roll.
- Don't cover baby's head with hats, hoods or rugs when sleeping.
- Avoid overheating the room.
- If you swaddle baby, use only a light wrap to avoid overheating. Add additional blankets if necessary.
- Don't dress baby in clothing that contains an attached hood, long drawstrings, ribbons or cords when sleeping. Remove any bib. Ribbons used to attach baby's pacifier should be no longer than six inches.

If you choose to bed-share with your baby, you will find additional infant sleep safety recommendations on pages 143–144.

Diagram 7.2:   SIDS safe sleeping

Key points

- No one settling method is better than another or will suit all families. A settling method that is acceptable and achievable to one parent may be something another parent finds unachievable or unacceptable.

- You may need to choose between resolving your baby's sleep problem quickly and minimising crying during the learning phase. It's up to you.

- Don't feel pressured into a settling method you're not comfortable with. And don't feel guilty about choosing a settling method that others disagree with.

Bed-sharing

While attending a breastfeeding conference, a speaker broached the topic of infant sleep. As I expected, she endorsed bed-sharing as way to promote breastfeeding and better sleep for babies and parents. She cited other benefits, such as the ease of night-time breastfeeding and closer parent-child relationships. She claimed that bed-sharing is the 'natural' way to provide for children's sleep needs. She painted a rosy picture and made bed-sharing sound like an ideal sleeping arrangement for all families. As a lactation consultant, I had read and heard such claims many times before, and, as a child health nurse I have come into contact with thousands of families struggling under the strain of an infant sleep problem. As a result, I realise that bed-sharing is not the ideal solution to night-time parenting responsibilities that some profess it to be. While bed-sharing has advantages, it also has disadvantages. Much depends on your family's individual circumstances, so the choice is entirely up to you.

Definitions

- **Bed-sharing**, sometimes referred to as the 'family bed', is having your child in bed with you, sharing the same surface, during sleep.

- **Room-sharing** involves having your child sleeping in the same room as you, but on a different surface.

- **Co-sleeping** is often used to collectively describe bed-sharing and room-sharing. The term 'co-sleeping' can cause confusion because the benefits associated with room-sharing are often mistakenly attributed to bed-sharing and vice versa.

What bed-sharing involves

Many people are surprised to learn that bed-sharing is a form of sleep training. A baby learns to depend on parent-assisted sleep associations, in particular those involving physical contact with a parent, such as cuddles, breastfeeding, being patted or simply having a parent's hand reassuringly touching her in some way as she falls asleep. Whatever the conditions your baby learns to associate with sleeping will become her preferred way of sleeping during the day and at night.

Some parents plan to bed-share with their baby because of personal or cultural beliefs. Others are reactive bed-sharers who bring their baby into their bed as a response to a sleep problem that disrupts their and their baby's sleep. Willingly choosing to share your bed with your baby doesn't mean that bed-sharing will be a problem-free experience. Bed-sharing can enhance the sleep of some babies and parents, but can cause sleep deprivation for others.

Sleep problems related to bed-sharing

Think about bed-sharing in terms of sharing the same bed with or without physical contact with someone else. Some adults like to sleep while they're in contact with their partners. Others, though sharing the same bed, prefer to have their own space while sleeping. Bed-sharing with your baby can involve physical contact, or not. Your baby could be snuggled up next to your body or she might be within arm's reach but not actually touching you as she falls asleep.

It's not the act of sharing the same bed that causes sleep problems for babies and parents. It's that the baby learns to associate sleeping with being in bodily contact with others. Adults who regularly sleep while in physical contact with their partner will often complain that they sleep poorly whenever their partner is absent. This can be the same for babies. Babies complain by fussing or crying. If your baby learns to rely on physical contact with another person as a way to fall asleep, she could experience difficulty falling or remaining asleep when she's not in contact with someone.

The risk of sleep disruption for your baby occurs whenever physical contact is broken. If you separate from her after she has fallen asleep, for example, by placing her into her cot, by leaving her sleeping on the bed, or by simply rolling over, this may involve removing one or more of her sleep associations; even if she's the one who rolls over. Older babies and young children move about a lot in their sleep so contact is easily broken. Baby might not sense the loss of contact while she's in a deep sleep phase, but there's a good chance that she'll notice during the natural arousals that occur between sleep cycles.

Parents who bed-share with their baby often experience sleep disruptions as a result of their baby repeatedly waking them during the night to re-establish physical contact. Admittedly, it's easy to draw your baby close and restore contact while bed-sharing. So, although she may wake frequently, she can usually be quickly soothed back, often before she wakes fully. Parents may also be woken abruptly by a kick in the stomach or smack across the face from a child's movements during sleep. Some parents are not fazed by frequent disruptions to their sleep. Once they have restored contact, restoring their baby's sleep associations, they may drop back off to sleep so quickly that, by the morning, they can't remember how many times they were woken. But other parents find repeatedly being woken by their baby's movements or fussing to be soothed back to sleep burdensome. Not all parents return to sleep quickly after being woken. Some parents who bed-share claim they wake tired in the mornings as a result of repeatedly having to restore physical contact with their baby, and they remember exactly how many times they were woken, sometimes as many as 12 or more times a night.

The problems that can occur when a baby associates sleeping with being in contact with a parent are not restricted to overnight. Parents who bed-share often find it frustrating that their baby refuses to fall asleep in her cot during the day, or have a decent nap after she's been placed into her cot asleep. Babies sleep best when they're consistently comforted by the conditions they associate with sleeping. A baby won't understand why she's settled to sleep one way at night but not the same way during the day. But some will tolerate inconsistencies better than others depending on their temperament.

From a baby's perspective, learning to rely on physical contact with another person to sleep can have even greater consequences during the day than at night. The presence of baby's familiar sleep associations enables her to relax and fall asleep with ease. Without them, she may remain awake despite her readiness for sleep until she becomes so tired she can't remain awake a moment longer. So, if you don't help your baby to fall asleep during the day in the same or similar way as at night, she's at risk of becoming overtired. An overtired baby will become fussy or distressed and find it difficult to fall asleep even when her sleep associations are finally provided.

A newborn baby who bed-shares with parents at night might be content to be held or carried in a sling while sleeping during the day. But an older baby, who is generally more aware of her surroundings compared to a newborn, often associates specific conditions with sleeping, and might not be content to be held or carried when tired. She will want to lie next to you on the bed like she does at night, so you may need to change the way you settle baby to sleep during the day, as she gets older. From about four months of age, babies learn the difference between being cuddled by Mum versus by Dad, and most demonstrate a preference for whomever is the most familiar person, usually Mum. Dad might then find it more challenging to help his baby fall asleep and be forced to return the responsibility of settling baby to sleep to Mum.

Providing a baby's learned sleep associations is the quickest way for her to fall asleep. But it won't necessarily ensure she remains asleep for as long as she needs. She'll expect to find these associations still there as she arouses between sleep cycles. If physical contact is not maintained throughout, she's at increased risk of waking prematurely. If you place her into her cot after she has fallen asleep, or if you get up, leaving her sleeping on the bed, she may not sleep for as long as if you maintained contact.

Bed-sharing only at night does not provide the level of consistency that some babies require, and may be why babies who bed-share with parents only at night often appear to be poor sleepers during the day. But the baby isn't a poor sleeper; all healthy babies will sleep well if provided their sleep associations. Poor sleep occurs when a baby is not provided with the sleep associations she's been taught to rely on, in the way that supports her sleep. So, if you're not able or willing to provide the same level of physical contact during your baby's day-time naps as at night, she may become fussy or distressed because she's overtired.

Baby Alexis

Alexis's mother, Gabrielle, had shared her bed with her since birth and planned to continue to do so once she returned to work. Meanwhile, 10-month-old Alexis would be cared for at a local childcare centre. However, the childcare workers found it difficult to get Alexis to sleep during the day. Gabrielle suspected separation anxiety, but it was not; it was because Gabrielle breast-fed her to sleep at night, something she could no longer provide when she worked, and obviously something the childcare workers could not provide. Bed-sharing had worked for Alexis and Gabrielle previously, but the change meant it no longer worked for Alexis.

The way you settle your baby to sleep at night can become the way she wants to sleep during the day. But the opposite can also be the case. Parents who regularly help their babies to fall asleep during the day, intentionally or not, by providing close physical contact – breastfeeding or cuddling baby to sleep in their arms or on their shoulder while being burped, while in a sling, or by holding upright after feeds – may find their baby awakens whenever contact is broken. As a result of this during the day, many babies become wakeful during the night, when parental support is absent. After being woken repeatedly to help their baby fall back to sleep, many parents resort to bed-sharing, even though it may not be their choice to do so.

Baby Elsa

Amanda wanted help to resolve a problem she was experiencing with her daughter, Elsa. Elsa would only fall asleep while lying on Amanda's chest. She would wake as soon as Amanda tried to move her. During the day, Amanda sat in a recliner and cuddled Elsa until she woke. At night, Amanda resorted to sleeping in a semi-upright position in her bed, supported by pillows, unable to move for fear of waking Elsa who was sleeping on her. Elsa got plenty of sleep, but Amanda didn't. She was severely sleep-deprived and had recently been diagnosed with postnatal depression.

Some parents bring their baby into their bed and find their baby won't sleep. Liz commented, 'I got so desperate to get Abbey (nine months) to go back to sleep that I ended up taking her into bed with us. She thought it was big game and rolled about having a great time, but didn't go to sleep.' There are various reasons why, the most likely being that lying next to a parent on the parent's bed does not provide the conditions that baby has already learned to associate with sleeping. Perhaps baby has become distressed from overtiredness. Or she has developed a circadian rhythm sleep problem (see Chapter 14) and is simply not tired at that time, even though her parents were, as was the case for Abbey.

How to resolve sleep problems while bed-sharing

It's not all doom and gloom. In many cases, infant sleep problems can be resolved while continuing to bed-share by using one of the following strategies:

- Enhance your ability to identify baby's early signs of tiredness (see Chapter 3).
- Provide your baby's sleep associations once tired signs are recognised. This might include breastfeeding, cuddling baby,

carrying her in a sling while she sleeps, or lying next to her on the bed.

- If you plan to remove yourself after she has fallen asleep, wait between 5–20 minutes after she first falls asleep for her to reach a deep sleep stage. At that point, she will be motionless, her limbs limp and her breathing deep and regular.
- Expect her to wake prematurely if you don't maintain physical contact. If she wakes still tired, it may be necessary for you to help her to return to sleep in the same way. But once a baby has woken from a nap it can be difficult to get her to go back to sleep, even if she's still tired. If your baby wakes still tired and won't go back to sleep she may need another nap sooner than she would otherwise.
- If your baby often becomes irritable due to lack of sleep, she might require physical contact throughout her entire nap to ensure she remains asleep long enough to get the amount of sleep she needs. Babies require a lot of sleep, so this would be a huge commitment on your part, especially if you can't change position.

It can be extremely time consuming for parents to provide the level of support that a baby requires during the day when bed-sharing at night, and depends heavily on your baby's temperament, your own health, other responsibilities in addition to caring for her, and your individual family circumstances. Many parents can and do enjoy dedicating their time to their baby and find it relaxing to cuddle their sleeping baby; others understandably find it impossible to maintain such a high level of support over the long term.

If you enjoy bed-sharing with baby at night but find you're unable to support her sleep during the day or if you're becoming sleep-deprived as a result of her frequent awakenings, you might reduce the number of awakenings by taking the following steps:

- Stop breastfeeding your baby to the point where she falls sleep. This will discourage a feeding-sleep association. She will still awaken from genuine hunger, but it can reduce the number of times she wakes you to breastfeed just to sleep.
- If she continues to be wakeful after learning to fall asleep without breast contact, try teaching her to fall asleep without any physical

contact. You can take both steps at the same time if you choose to do so.

This does not mean you need to separate yourself from your baby. She can sleep within arm's reach by using a co-sleeper, a small soft-sided bed suitable for newborns that is placed in an adult bed, or sidecar cot, a three-sided cot for larger babies that firmly attaches to the side of your bed. You can also place a regular cot next to your bed or in the same room.

You must expect your baby to protest if you try to change her sleep associations by changing your settling practices, but this is usually temporary. If you're consistent and persistent, she will learn the new sleep associations that enable her and you to get more sleep. Note that if you replace physical contact with any other parent-assisted settling practices, such as patting, rocking, stroking, or shooshing her to sleep, she'll learn to associate these with sleeping and likely continue to wake just as often and cry for you to help her return to sleep. The best sleepers are babies who self-regulate their sleeping patterns by settling to sleep independently. By learning to self-settle, your baby's sleep will no longer be disrupted by loss of contact with you during sleep. (See Chapter 7 for ways to promote independent settling.)

Deciding if bed-sharing is for you

> We co-slept with our older son until he was about 3½ years old. We loved having him in our bed. He now happily sleeps on a mattress on our bedroom floor. We're co-sleeping with our 9-month-old daughter, which we have done since her birth. We have no plans to do anything different with her. I breastfeed her to sleep for naps and at night. It is the easiest, most natural thing to do. She wakes up every two hours to breastfeed through the night. I just plug her in and we both drift back to sleep. We both sleep better in the same bed. I can't imagine putting her into a cot to sleep. I think I'd be so paranoid that if she was in a separate room I wouldn't get any sleep.
> – Shannon

Shannon obviously enjoys bed-sharing and considers it the best way to provide for her children's and her own sleep needs. Like Shannon, you might find bed-sharing to be the best option for you and your children. However, not every parent feels this way. Rebecca found bed-sharing to be problematic.

> My daughter is now 7 months old. Since she was born she has just about always breast-fed to sleep. She is a horrible sleeper and

napper. If she doesn't have my nipple in her mouth she doesn't want to sleep. I have to lie down and breastfeed her to get her to have a nap. Whenever it slips out she wakes up and freaks out. So at night I am constantly being woken up to reattach her. I'm going insane. I can't take it anymore. My back aches from lying in the one position all night. I am completely and utterly exhausted. I feel like I am going to collapse or get sick or something. I don't know what to do. I am worried this will never end. – Rebecca

Rebecca liked the idea of bed-sharing but found it did not meet her expectations. She had thought she would only need to help her baby to fall asleep and all would be fine. She did not realise that, because her baby had learned to rely on physical contact with her to fall asleep, the responsibility of supporting her sleep would span 24 hours a day. Rebecca ultimately resolved her dilemma by teaching her baby to fall asleep independent of her help. She pushed her baby's cot next to her bed so that she could attend to her quickly during the night if necessary, but it seldom was. Within a week, to her relief, her baby started sleeping through the night.

As with many parents in western societies, Rebecca had read about the positive aspects of bed-sharing, but was unprepared for the possible negative consequences associated with it.

The bed-sharing controversy

Just as sleep training rouses debate between critics and supporters, so too does bed-sharing.

Dr James McKenna PhD, Professor of Anthropology at Notre Dame University and the director of the Mother-Baby Behavioural Sleep Lab, is a leading figure in the pro-bed-sharing debate. McKenna is also the author of *Sleeping with Your Baby: A parent's guide to cosleeping*, as well as many related academic papers. Other supporters of bed-sharing include American paediatrician and Attachment Parenting guru, Dr William Sears, and breastfeeding associations such as La Leche League International and the Australian Breastfeeding Association. Proponents claim that bed-sharing:

- is a natural sleeping arrangement
- promotes better sleep for babies and parents

- helps establish and maintain breastfeeding
- enhances a baby's emotional development and promotes a secure attachment with parents
- reduces the risk of Sudden Infant Death Syndrome (SIDS).

In the early part of this chapter I explained how bed-sharing can be responsible for sleep deprivation rather than better sleep for many babies and their parents. Might there be another side to these other declared benefits of bed-sharing?

Historical and cultural perspectives

Dr McKenna claims that, from an anthropological perspective, co-sleeping – which he defines as having baby sleep within arm's length – is a natural way for families to sleep. He points out that throughout human evolution babies have fallen asleep while being breast-fed, they fell asleep while they were held or carried during the day, and they sleep lying next to their mothers at night.[62] In most cultures worldwide today, co-sleeping is considered to be a normal and expected sleeping arrangement, with the notable exception of western culture; us. Many parents in western societies place their babies in cots to sleep, either in the parents' bedroom or in a separate room. McKenna claims that parents from cultures where bed-sharing is the norm don't usually complain about infant sleeping problems, unlike parents living in western societies. Co-sleeping is often promoted to western families as a more natural sleeping arrangement and a solution to infant sleep problems.

From a survival perspective, it is essential for a baby to remain close to someone who can protect her and provide for her needs. As parent or caregiver, that's your responsibility. But just how close do you physically need to be? Is it necessary to have baby share your bed? Is it alright if she sleeps on a different surface but within easy reach? What if she sleeps in a cot in the same room as you? Can she sleep in a cot in a separate room, provided you can hear her if she cries?

Our environment dictates an acceptable proximity that needs to be maintained to provide protection and respond to baby's needs. The observation that the majority of parents today, as in the past, share their bed with their children may have more to do with necessity than choice.

According to UNICEF, one billion children, half the world's population of children, currently live in poverty.[63] Imagine caring for baby while living in a hut or shanty. It may not be safe to put a baby down or leave her alone for any length of time. There could be rats, snakes, spiders, or other insects or animals able to gain access to your home and your baby. She has no means to defend herself. For her safety it would be essential that you remain very close to her at all times, including at night. How different is this to your home? It's likely that your baby can be safely left alone while you're in the next room, without the threat of attack. But you must be near to provide for her needs. The structure and security of your home enables you to decide the distance you need to maintain in order to protect your baby and respond to her needs. Affluence affords you freedom of choice; poverty inhibits choice. This does not imply that it's better for a baby to sleep alone, it simply explains why our ancestors co-slept with their children, and why it's considered the norm in most other cultures today.

In 1975, after spending two and a half years living deep in the South American jungle in a village belonging to the Yequana tribe of Venezuela, Jean Liedloff, an American author, wrote a book about her experiences entitled *The Continuum Concept*. In this she described the contentment of the village babies. She attributed this to what she called the 'In-Arms Phase', which consists of the baby being in physical contact with either an adult or older child 24 hours a day, beginning at birth and ending when the baby starts to crawl, generally around the age of nine months. The parenting strategies described by Liedloff have become the foundation for many Attachment Parenting books, all of which promote breastfeeding on demand, bed-sharing and carrying baby in a sling during the day. Unfortunately, many western parents find that these don't promote the level of infant contentment described by Liedloff. What's more, some mothers suffer from physical exhaustion when they attempt to maintain physical contact with their baby 24 hours a day. Why? Because you cannot pick and choose elements from one culture and insert them into another and expect identical results. Often overlooked is the major advantage, among the countless disadvantages, that parents in many other cultures have, which we typically don't: the ready availability of hands-on support from extended family members living within the same household or in close proximity. Babies raised in a village are often carried while sleeping during the day. While they are rarely put down, they are at times hung up, suspended to the rafters or a tree branch in a sling. They sleep next to others at night, but it's not always the mother who provides for her children's cares 24 hours a day. Grandmothers, aunts, siblings and neighbours share the responsibility for childcare. Breastfeeding women will at times feed other babies if the mother is unavailable. Village babies, who learn to rely on physical contact to sleep, remain asleep because contact is seldom broken. Therefore, these babies don't experience distress associated with overtiredness. And village mothers who share child care responsibilities with others are less likely to suffer sleep deprivation. Hence, these parents are unlikely to complain about infant sleep problems.

'In-Arms Phase' involves 24-hour holding. Once a baby learns to rely on physical contact to sleep, you cannot elect when to hold her and when to put her down. Well, you can, technically, but she's likely to get cranky if she's not provided with contact every time she needs to sleep. There are multiple situations, unique to our culture, which may make it impossible for a parent to hold their baby the entire time she needs to sleep. For example, you're legally required to secure your baby into an infant car seat whenever you drive. You may want to take a shower when there's no one else available to hold her. You might need to pick up and comfort your crying toddler, which is difficult with a baby in your arms. Or you might need to work to pay the bills. Trying to cook a meal with a baby in your arms or even in a sling can be dangerous, especially if heat is involved, not something with which mothers in these villages have to contend. It would be wonderful if mothers living in western societies also had the support of a village to assist them to raise their children. But the reality is that western families are often isolated from extended family members. The responsibility to provide for their children's daily needs often rests solely on the shoulders of parents, mothers in particular. From an anthropological perspective, this is far from a natural arrangement. Lack of support is why parents in western societies are at risk of becoming physically exhausted and often complain about infant sleep problems. While babies' needs have remained unchanged, our society has evolved. Our living environment and lifestyles differ dramatically from that of our ancestors and many other cultures today. Bed-sharing may indeed be a natural sleeping arrangement for some, but this does not mean it's going to fit within the context of our not-so-natural lifestyles. Depending on individual circumstances and support systems, some parents living in western societies find that bed-sharing works for them and their babies. For others, it could be likened to forcing a square peg into a round hole.

You could theorise on what's the best or most natural way for babies to sleep and even argue the point if you wanted to, or you could simply adapt your parenting practices to match your baby's needs within the context of your living environment and your family and social circumstances. That might include bed-sharing; it might not.

If bed-sharing is not working, most of us can choose to do something else. Admittedly, it's not always that simple for parents who come from cultures with firmly entrenched beliefs that babies should sleep with their parents.

Ching Lan

Ching Lan emigrated from China to Australia with her husband, Qiang, three years before becoming pregnant with her first child. Both her and Qiang's parents lived in China; the couple had no family in Australia. Ching Lan was raised with strong cultural beliefs that babies should sleep with their parents and should never be left to cry. The problem was that, because she shared her bed with four-month-old Cái, Ching Lan was severely sleep-deprived. She could not catch up on sleep during the day because Cái constantly demanded to be held in her arms. I explained the reasons for Cái's behaviour and suggested she have him sleep within arm's reach at night instead of cuddling him to sleep. Once he got used to this arrangement, I explained, he might not wake as often during the night to re-establish contact. Ching Lan would also be able to put him down to sleep during the day. I had warned her to expect Cái to fuss for few days and nights until he learned to sleep without physical contact, Ching Lan claimed she understood. As it turned out, Ching Lan was unable to ignore his fussing. She gave in as soon as he fussed, and cuddled him to sleep. The next day she lamented, 'My mother will think I am cruel if I don't cuddle Cái to sleep.' I suspect Ching Lan thought it was cruel, possibly due to her cultural beliefs that babies should never be left to cry. Although Cái had not cried, he had understandably fussed when Ching Lan tried to change the way she settled him to sleep.

Had Ching Lan been supported by her own mother (or mother-in-law) as is culturally the custom in China, she would not have suffered the degree of sleep deprivation that she did. And Cái's desire to be held while sleeping during the day would not have been a burden to Ching Lan if the responsibility to do so was shared by her mother or other family members.

Bed-sharing and breastfeeding

The Australian Breastfeeding Association, La Leche League International and many lactation consultants actively endorse bed-sharing as way to establish and maintain breastfeeding.[64] Dr McKenna claims bed-sharing promotes breastfeeding.[65] In a study published in 1997, McKenna and associates identified that babies who bed-share with their mothers breastfeed almost twice as often and three times as long per bout compared to babies who sleep alone.[66] These findings are often cited in support of bed-sharing. However, I would argue that an increased incidence and duration of night-time breastfeeds does not automatically equate to promoting breastfeeding.

While bed-sharing undoubtedly makes it easier for tired mothers to breastfeed at night there's a lack of conclusive evidence that bed-sharing helps to establish or maintain breastfeeding. After working for many years with both breastfeeding and bottle-feeding mothers I would even be so bold as to claim that bed-sharing does not, as a rule, support mothers living in western societies to successfully breastfeed over the long term. Some, yes; in particular, those who seek guidance from breastfeeding associations and lactation consultants, but not the majority of breastfeeding mothers.

McKenna's finding is not surprising. When a baby learns to associate falling asleep with having her mother's nipple in her mouth, she will fuss or cry until she's offered the breast to go to sleep. She may demand a breastfeed more frequently than expected. A breastfeeding-sleep association can also be why a baby might continue to demand night-time breastfeeds long after she's old enough to sleep through the night without feeding, generally six months for healthy, thriving, term babies.

Most babies are capable of self-regulating their milk intake to meet their nutritional needs. It's important to note that a baby doesn't necessarily receive more milk as a result of feeding twice as often. And suckling for a longer period of time does not guarantee increased milk intake. Not all the time a breast-fed baby spends suckling at her mother's breast is actual feeding. Breast-fed babies spend varying periods of time comfort sucking. A baby with a breastfeeding-sleep association may simply want to comfort suck as she drops off to sleep, because this is the way she has learned to fall asleep. Mia, aged eight weeks, would stay firmly attached to her mother's breast for up to two hours at a time. Most of this time was spent comfort sucking and dozing.

Breastfeeding rates in Australia and most other western societies can only be described as poor. Eighty-eight per cent of Australian babies are breast-fed on discharge from hospital, but less than one in four babies are breast-fed until the minimum recommended age of 12 months.[67] Why the drop? The most common reason mothers give for stopping is because they believe they're not producing enough milk to satisfy their baby's needs.[68] It is my belief that a major contributing factor to poor rates in western societies is that, by and large, breastfeeding mothers are unaware that breastfeeding their baby to sleep has the potential to cause increased wakefulness and give the appearance of extreme hunger. Contrary to being forewarned, breastfeeding mothers are encouraged by the Australian Breastfeeding Association, La Leche League International and lactation consultants in general to breastfeed their babies to sleep.[69]

Bed-sharing unquestionably makes night-time breastfeeding more convenient. However, bed-sharing encourages babies to learn to associate sleeping with breastfeeding. The confusion that mothers experience regarding the reasons for their baby's repeated awakenings, and the fussing or crying that can only be placated once their baby is returned to the breast, causes many mothers to doubt their milk supply. Owing to concern that their baby is not getting enough to eat, many mothers will take actions like giving baby infant formula or starting baby on solids too soon. But this won't provide a solution to wakefulness during the night owing to the loss of physical contact or baby's desire to have her mother's nipple in her mouth as a way to return to sleep. Exhausted from being woken multiple times during the night, confused by baby's behaviour, which is misinterpreted as hunger, and with no end in sight, it all becomes too hard for many mothers and so breastfeeding ends.

Admittedly, it's not only mothers who bed-share who fall into this trap, but any mother who breastfeeds her baby to sleep. It's just that, by bed-sharing, the potential for breastfeeding to become one of baby's sleep associations increases. Of course, not all mothers are troubled by their baby's frequent demands to breastfeed during the day or night, and many mothers successfully breastfeed over the long term while breastfeeding their babies to sleep. There is absolutely no reason why a breastfeeding mother cannot successfully breastfeed her baby long term while sleeping separately from her baby.

Bed-sharing and emotional development

Child development experts have pushed the importance of children's emotional development to the foreground over the past 10 years or so. This has prompted increased popularity of parenting models, such as Attachment Parenting, that promote childcare practices that include breastfeeding on demand, bed-sharing and 'baby wearing' (carrying baby in a sling) as a way to support babies' emotional development.[70] The reason these childcare practices are believed to help has to do with brain chemistry.

Our brains release a cocktail of chemicals, including oxytocin and endorphins, in response to pleasant touch. Oxytocin is best known for the physical effects it has on the body, for example, it causes a mother's uterus to contract during labour and after birth, and the release of milk from the milk ducts while breastfeeding. We all release oxytocin, males and females. Oxytocin affects us emotionally as well, generating feelings, including affection, love, caring, nurturing and emotional connection. This is why it's sometimes referred to as the 'hormone of love'. Oxytocin is believed to be important in pair bonding, including mother-infant, male-female, friendships and other types of one on one relationships. Endorphins are the body's natural painkillers. They produce feelings of wellbeing, relaxation, peace and security, and play a key role in relationships.

Hugging, kissing, stroking, patting, massage, skin-to-skin contact and breastfeeding are examples of ways in which oxytocin and endorphin release can be triggered in mothers and babies. Studies have shown that skin-to-skin contact between a mother and her baby following birth reduces infant crying, stabilises a baby's body temperature, assists the mother to breastfeed successfully, and enhances the bond mothers feel towards their babies.[71]

As a mother, I would say that there are few things more joyful than gazing at your beautiful newborn baby sleeping on your chest or cradled in your arms. However, the joy of cuddling your sleeping baby wears thin once you discover that you can't put her down. And after your baby has woken you for the sixth time that night to be helped back to sleep, it might take more than love hormone for you to generate warm, fuzzy feelings towards her.

A number of factors can inhibit oxytocin release, among them acute stress. So if you're sleep-deprived, hungry, anxious because the house is a mess, worried about the bills, upset over an argument with your spouse or partner, troubled that you haven't showered for two days because your baby cries every time you put her down, if it's getting late and you haven't prepared dinner for the family, if there's a mountain of laundry piling up, if your back is aching, if baby is screaming in your arms, or your toddler is throwing a tantrum while you're trying to feed your baby, the odds are you're not going to experience the glow of contentment that oxytocin and endorphins can elicit, at least not at the moment.

How much physical contact is necessary for a parent to connect emotionally with their child? That depends on the parent; it's not something that can be measured. And it's not simply a case of 'more is better'. An emotional connection is not solely dependent on physical contact. What's more important is how much you enjoy the contact you have. One mother may take pleasure in maintaining constant physical contact with her baby day and night, but another may find this too much. Bed-sharing will increase the time you have contact with your baby, but this does not guarantee that you will develop a stronger emotional connection with her, compared to sleeping alone.

What about from a baby's perspective: does maintaining touch during the night support a stronger emotional attachment? According to psychologist Mary Ainsworth, renowned for her work in developing the attachment theory, a secure emotional attachment is formed when a child learns to trust that her mother/main caregiver will provide for her needs in a nurturing and timely manner. If you want to encourage your baby to develop a secure emotional attachment to you, you must provide for her needs. Abraham Maslow, the psychologist acclaimed for his theory on the Hierarchy of Needs, identified that basic physical needs, like adequate food, warmth, shelter and sleep, must be satisfied before emotional needs can be met.[72] If your baby is malnourished, sleep-deprived, overheated or cold, then these must be addressed before worrying about meeting her emotional needs.

There's no disputing that spending time with your baby is essential to strengthening the special bond between you, and that touch is a fundamental component of providing nurturing childcare. However, increased physical contact with a parent does not automatically equate to a stronger emotional attachment to them. It's imperative that you or another responsible caregiver are available to your baby 24 hours a day, but it's not essential for you to remain in constant physical contact day and night in order to provide for her emotional needs.

In their book, A General Theory of Love, psychiatrists Thomas Lewis, Fari Amini and Richard Lannon state, 'What is important is that parents are responsive to the baby's cues when providing physical contact.' Emotionally secure babies are those who are held on the baby's terms, hugged when they want to be, and given freedom to move about. They are not necessarily, those who are held the most.[73]

The physical contact individual babies want and need varies. Your baby's temperament will influence this, as will your childcare practices, which also influence whether or not she gets enough sleep. Some babies are more cautious and reserved by nature, and may require the sense of security physical contact provides on a more frequent basis, compared to babies who are curious and outgoing. Babies who are sleep-deprived often appear clingy, wanting to be held constantly while awake, whether they bed-share or sleep alone. Babies who associate sleeping with physical contact will understandably want it every time they want to sleep because this is what they expect. Babies who have learned to fall asleep independent of others' help, although not requiring contact at the time of falling asleep, still enjoy being kissed, hugged or massaged and having physical contact with parents or caregivers at other times.

While physical contact is beneficial to babies' development, so, too, are periods of solitude. In her book, *The Call of Solitude: Alonetime in a world of attachment*, psychologist Ester Schaler Buchholz, PhD, describes alone time as a basic need. She claims that periods of solitude are an inherent biological and psychological need of humans.[74] According to Dr DW Winnicott, a British paediatrician and child psychiatrist, the capacity to be alone is one of the most important signs of maturity in emotional development.[75]

The bond between mother and baby is certainly extremely important to the emotional health of a child, but it takes two to form a relationship. What's more often overlooked is the emotional health of the mother.

happy mum = happy bub

Getting enough sleep and taking care of yourself will actually benefit your baby's emotional health. You cannot provide high quality care to your baby if you're sleep-deprived from being woken repeatedly throughout the night to re-establish contact with your baby. And, if you're severely sleep-deprived at present, it may be unsafe to share the bed with baby.

Bed-sharing and SIDS

There has been a lot of research into SIDS (Sudden Infant Death Syndrome), particularly over the past 20 years. Although SIDS is still not fully understood, numerous health professionals around the world continue to work tirelessly to solve the puzzle. Their combined efforts have yielded several recommendations on ways parents can minimise risks, the most significant being having sleeping babies lie on their backs.

Since the 'Back to Sleep' campaign was launched in 1994, the number of SIDS deaths in western societies has dropped by more than 50 per cent.[76]

Bed-sharing is not something that is included in current SIDS recommendations, and, yet, increasing numbers of parents choose to bed-share with their baby because they're advised it will reduce the risk of SIDS. Is there evidence to support this claim? Or is it an urban legend that has gained credibility through repetition?

Dr James McKenna leads the co-sleeping drive. He believes babies should never sleep alone.[77] Studies by McKenna and colleagues have revealed that bed-sharing infants have more awakenings and spend less time in deep sleep compared to babies who sleep alone.[78] McKenna believes this may offer protection from SIDS. In addition, because the adult sharing the bed with baby also has increased arousals and remains in close proximity to the baby, this may enable a quick response to rescue the baby from potentially dangerous situations during sleep.[79] However, McKenna himself acknowledges that his theories remain unproven.[80]

Although no sleeping arrangement can be 100 per cent safe, there are risks associated with bed-sharing that are not present when a baby sleeps alone. A UK study, published in the *British Journal of Medicine* in October 2009, identified that more than half of SIDS deaths in the UK during the study occurred while the baby was sleeping with someone else at the time.[81] However, the authors were quick to point out that most of these cases were believed to have occurred owing to 'hazardous co-sleeping environments and risk factors amenable to change'.[82] There are indeed unsafe co-sleeping environments. And there are factors, changeable ones, associated with co-sleeping that increase the risk of SIDS. These include:

- sharing a bed with someone who smokes[83]
- sharing a bed with someone under the influence of alcohol, sedatives, or who is overly tired[84]
- sharing a cramped or overcrowded bed, due to too small size or multiple bed-sharers[85]
- co-sleeping on a beanbag, sofa, waterbed or sagging mattress[86]
- if a baby's face becomes covered by pillow, doonas or heavy bed clothing[87]

- if baby sleeps on her tummy or side
- if other children or a pet are also on the bed when the baby is sleeping[88]
- the risks of a baby becoming trapped between a wall or bed rails and the bed.[89]
- bed-sharing with babies younger than four months of age as well as premature, low birth weight babies.[90]

Without these risk factors, bed-sharing is not generally considered to be hazardous.[91] Regarding the claim that bed-sharing reduces the risk of SIDS, again, this is unproven. Edwin Mitchell, Professor of Child Health Research Paediatrics at the University of Auckland, New Zealand, has done extensive research into risk factors associated with SIDS and states there is currently no documented evidence that bed-sharing reduces the risk of SIDS.[92] However, there is evidence that room-sharing reduces the risk of SIDS.[93]

SIDS and Kids recommends that a baby sleep in a cot next to the parents' bed for the first six to 12 months of life.[94] The American Academy of Pediatrics recommends against sharing a bed with a child under the age of two years, encouraging parents to have their baby sleep in a cot in the same room.[95] The majority of health professionals and health organisations promote room-sharing, especially for babies under the age of six months, but not bed-sharing, out of safety concerns.

It's not just SIDS you need to be concerned about. According to the Center for Disease Control and Prevention (CDC) in the US, bed-sharing is associated with an increased risk of infant death from suffocation and strangulation. In January 2009, the CDC reported the number of infant deaths in the US has quadrupled over the past 20 years, most apparently from parents sleeping with their babies.[96] The increase may correspond with the growing numbers of parents in the US who choose to bed-share. A national study published in 2003 found that, between 1993 and 2000, the number of babies seven months or younger who usually shared a bed with an adult rose from 5.5 per cent to 12.8 per cent. Forty-five per cent of babies had spent at least some time in their parent's bed at night in the previous two weeks.[97] A similar trend is seen in Australia. Australian forensic pathologist Professor Roger Byard states the number of children dying while sleeping with adults has 'increased dramatically' in the past few years. Byard believes there is no way to make bed-sharing completely safe.[98] When interviewed by the *Daily Telegraph* in 2009, Byard claimed western culture has turned co-sleeping into something dangerous. He added that in some cultures babies traditionally slept with their parents, but usually on firm bedding or the floor and without the weight of heavy coverings. In the west, adults are sharing soft, high beds with young babies and covering themselves with doonas or blankets.[99]

Valid points are made on both sides of the bed-sharing debate. Just as with sleep training, we're unlikely to get a consensus of opinion among health professionals or parents about the advantages and disadvantages. Providing an alternative perspective to the commonly claimed benefits of bed-sharing is not done to dissuade you from bed-sharing but, rather, to enable you to weigh the risks and benefits, which differ for each family. Choose to bed-share because it meets your baby's and your own sleep needs and not because someone tells you it's the natural way for babies to sleep, or that it will support you to successfully breastfeed, or enable you and your baby to have a closer relationship, or help you to prevent SIDS. Alternatively, choose for your baby to sleep on her own – within arm's reach from you, in the same room, or a separate room if she's six months or older – free from the burden of feeling that you might deprive her in some way by not bed-sharing.

While the proposed benefits of bed-sharing are speculative, the risks are real. The proclaimed benefits of bed-sharing can still be achieved when babies sleep in separate beds from parents. If you choose to bed-share with your baby it is imperative that you consistently provide a safe sleeping environment for her.

Safety recommendations while bed-sharing

Unlike a cot, an adult bed is not designed to meet the safety needs of a baby, so additional care needs to be taken if you choose to bed-share with your baby.

- Consider purchasing a larger bed if necessary to avoid overcrowding.

- Make sure head and foot boards are spaced no more than six centimetres (2½ inches) apart, which can trap your baby's head.
- Use a guardrail or move your mattress against the wall to prevent baby from rolling out of bed. Ensure there are no gaps between the mattress and the wall or bed rail where baby could become wedged.
- If you use a guardrail, purchase one with plastic mesh. Avoid those with slats.
- Avoid overdressing baby. Other warm bodies in the bed are an added heat source.
- Don't swaddle baby while bed-sharing; this restricts her movements, making it impossible for her to move away or let you know if you get too close.
- Keep pillows well away from baby. Don't use doonas; these can lead to overheating.
- Place baby on her back to sleep.
- Don't leave baby to sleep alone on an adult bed; she might roll off and injure herself or become entangled in bed clothing.
- Never let your baby bed-share with a smoker.
- Never sleep with baby if you or your partner is under the influence of alcohol, medications, or other substances that diminish your level of awareness.
- Babies under 12 months should not share the bed with older siblings.
- Don't wear lingerie with string ties longer than 20 cm (8 inches) and avoid wearing dangling jewellery, which can catch on your baby.
- If your hair length is at or approaching waist length, it should be pulled back and fastened. Your hair can wind around your baby's neck, posing a strangulation risk.
- If you have extremely large breasts or are obese, this can decrease your awareness of your baby's position. Consider using a sidecar cot arrangement instead.

Key points

- A baby who learns to associate sleeping with being in physical contact with others may require the same level of contact during the day and night.

- Many families find bed-sharing provides a solution to infant sleep problems. Alternatively, bed-sharing can cause sleep disturbance and subsequent sleep deprivation in babies and parents.

- Bed-sharing increases the likelihood of developing a breastfeeding-sleep association. An increased demand to breastfeed in order to go to sleep is commonly mistaken as hunger or low milk supply.

- There are both advantages and disadvantages to bed-sharing.

- No matter what sleeping arrangement you choose, some will support your choice, and others won't. Only you can decide what's best for your baby.

9
Gentle settling

Jack is eight weeks old. Since he was born, either his dad or I have cuddled him to sleep. Now we're finding he only wants to sleep in our arms. He wakes the moment we try to put him down. We have tried to get him to fall asleep in his cot but he keeps crying until we pick him up. We are both exhausted and can't keep doing this. How can we get him to fall asleep in his cot without leaving him to cry? – Irene

The bigger the change you make to your infant settling practices, the more upsetting it's likely to be for your baby. Trying to settle your baby to sleep in his cot once he has already learned to sleep in your arms, for example, represents a BIG change from his perspective. You must anticipate upsetting him by significantly changing his sleep associations if you do it in a short space of time. If it proves too upsetting, you can gradually encourage him to accept falling asleep in his cot if you're prepared to make a series of smaller changes over a longer period of time. You may find my 'gentle settling plan' a helpful guide.

My gentle settling plan uses a multi-step approach to changing a baby's sleep associations. It can be an effective way to gently encourage a baby who is already accustomed to falling asleep anywhere other than his bed, to learn to willingly accept falling asleep in his bed. It may not eliminate a baby's upset entirely during the learning phase, but it may minimise it.

Gentle settling plan

To effectively resolve a sleeping problem that occurs from learned dependence on negative sleep associations, you may need to achieve one, two, or as is often the case, all three of the Golden Rules of infant sleep self-regulation:

- withhold unreliable props at sleep time
- provide a suitable and consistent sleeping environment and
- promote independent settling.

A gentle settling plan is designed to achieve these three Golden Rules one at a time, through a series of steps. Each step supports your baby to slowly progress from parent-assisted settling to independent settling with the least amount of resistance. Whether you go as far as encouraging your baby to fall asleep independent of your help is up to you. You might be happy when he readily accepts falling asleep in his bed with just a little help.

The gentle settling plan involves a number of steps. These are grouped below under the Golden Rule they're designed to achieve. By achieving any one of these three Golden Rules, feel confident that you're supporting him to make progress. Achieve all three and you're doing all you can to support him to self-regulate his sleeping patterns.

Setting the scene for change

Steps 1 and 2 are about laying the groundwork to smooth the road ahead. By promoting positive sleep associations and encouraging your baby to learn to associate patting with settling, this prepares him to accept future changes to your settling practices.

Step 1: Promote positive sleep associations

Provide baby with as many positive sleep associations, such as swaddling, infant sleeping bag, security blanket or soft toy that you feel are appropriate at his current stage of development. (Turn to page 64 for more on these.) Once you recognise his behavioural cues indicating that he's tired and ready to sleep, prepare him by swaddling him or dressing him in an infant sleeping bag. By preparing him each time for sleep like this, he will begin to associate the swaddling or infant sleeping bag with sleeping.

Step 2: Encourage baby to associate patting with sleeping

Gently and rhythmically pat your baby with a cupped hand on his thigh or nappy area, about one pat per second, while cuddling him to sleep. It must be a pat versus a light tap so that he can feel the rhythm, while a cupped hand allows him to benefit from the sound patting makes. Once you're confident baby is deeply asleep, place him into his bed.

You might be wondering why you're introducing a negative sleep association. Patting your baby may help him to later accept other, more significant, changes in your settling practices. You may eventually need to stop patting if he continues to wake prematurely between sleep cycles, but you might find you can continue to pat him to sleep and have him sleep well, provided everything else is in place to support his sleep. Only time will tell.

You may be able to achieve steps 1 and 2 simultaneously. If not, one at a time is fine.

> **Tip:** It usually takes between five and twenty minutes for a baby to drop into a deep sleep.

Golden Rule No 1: Withhold unreliable props at sleep time

If your baby has learned to associate sucking on a pacifier, your breast or a bottle with falling asleep, then the next stage is to change this situation. While you continue to allow him to fall asleep with one of these props, his dependence on it to sleep is reinforced. Any sleep disturbance he experiences as a result of these negative sleep associations will continue. Remember, negative sleep associations include anything your baby learns to associate with sleeping that might change after he has fallen asleep, like a pacifier, breast or bottle, but also includes other things like lighting, movement or noise.

To discourage your baby's dependence on unreliable props you must prevent him from falling asleep while feeding or sucking on a pacifier or your finger, and ensure that everything in his sleeping environment remains the same throughout his entire sleep.

Step 3: Remove breast or bottle from baby's mouth before he falls asleep

If you're not sure when to remove your breast from baby's mouth see the box below.

If, after removing your breast or bottle from your baby's mouth, he cries, offer him a second chance to feed. If after doing so you observe that he wants to sleep rather than feed, remove your breast or bottle from his mouth again. Note: giving him a third chance to feed is unlikely to be productive. You can offer another feed when he wakes if you feel it's necessary. After sleeping, he will have more energy to feed effectively.

Aim to settle him to sleep in your arms by patting, but without your breast or bottle in his mouth. Once he's deeply asleep, place him into his bed. Continue this step at every sleep time for at least three full days and nights before trying to move to the next step. If your baby does not habitually fall asleep while feeding, skip this step.

Removing your baby from your breast

By closely observing your baby's feeding behaviour, you will learn to recognise his different sucking patterns and distinguish between active feeding (called nutritive feeding because he's receiving nourishment) and comfort sucking (non-nutritive feeding). Once he has finished active feeding and appears to be continuously comfort sucking to fall asleep, slip your finger into the corner of his mouth to break his suction. Don't remove him the moment he first starts to comfort suck as he may be waiting for another let-down. By consistently removing him before he falls asleep you will no longer reinforce his breastfeeding-sleep association. Once he no longer associates falling asleep with suckling at your breast, which could take a few days of you consistently removing him, he is likely to start to pull off himself once he has finished feeding.

Step 4: Remove your finger or pacifier from baby's mouth before he falls asleep

In general, babies under the age of five months have a strong desire to suck. They want to suck when they're hungry, tired, bored, overstimulated, experiencing discomfort and for pleasure. The desire to suck when tired is why many babies develop a sleep association with feeding or a pacifier during the early weeks of life. A newborn baby is not physically capable of satisfying his own sucking needs, unlike an older baby who has the ability to self-soothe by sucking on his thumb or fingers, should he choose to do so.

By all means allow your newborn to suck on his pacifier or your little finger, palm-side up, to satisfy his sucking needs. But aim to prevent him from falling asleep in this way. Closely observe his behaviour. Once you can see his sucking is decreasing, slip your finger or the pacifier out of his mouth. Encourage him to settle to sleep in your arms while patting him but without your finger or a pacifier in his mouth when he falls asleep. Once he's deeply asleep, place him into his bed.

Continue this every time you settle your baby to sleep for at least three days and nights before moving on to the next step. You can skip this step if he doesn't usually fall asleep while sucking on a prop. If he sucks on his own fist or fingers as he falls asleep, let him. This enables him to learn to self-soothe.

Golden Rule No 2: Provide a suitable and consistent sleeping environment

Once your baby has become familiar with the sensation of patting as he settles to sleep in your arms, and you have successfully discouraged his dependence on any unreliable props to fall asleep, the next step is to provide him with a suitable and consistent sleeping environment.

Step 5: Place baby to bed when drowsy but not asleep

Settle baby in your arms while patting him until he becomes drowsy, and attempt to place him into his bed *before* he's fully asleep. To help him accept this change, continue to pat his thigh or nappy area in a rhythmical pattern without missing a beat as you transfer him, and continue patting him until he appears to be relaxed in his bed.

If he lies quietly, you can ease off on patting him and leave him to fall asleep on his own. If he fusses or cries and is not soothed by patting him while in his bed, pick him up and calm him in your arms, and then, once he's again in a drowsy state, try placing him back into his bed. You may need to do this several times to soothe him before he finally accepts going into his bed while drowsy. If you persist in trying to soothe him in his bed with patting rather than automatically picking him up the moment he fusses, he will eventually accept this and it will get easier and easier for you to calm him in this way. If necessary, pat him to sleep. You might need to continue patting until he's in a deep sleep.

As with step 4, once you succeed, consistently do this for three days and nights before moving to the next step.

> **Tip:** If your baby's bed feels cold, he's more likely to object to being placed into it. Try pre-warming before placing him in it.

Step 6: Place baby into bed tired but awake

Spend a little time cuddling baby in your arms in the usual way until he relaxes. Don't forget to pat him at the same time. While his eyes are still open, gently place him into his bed. Try to continue patting him as you transfer him, as this will help him to accept going into his bed.

If he cries, try to calm him by patting him while he's in his bed. If that doesn't work, then pick him up to calm him. Once he's calm, try again to place him into his bed while his eyes are open. If he lies quietly in his bed, try leaving him to fall asleep on his own. But, if necessary, continue patting his thigh or bottom until he falls asleep.

If you have managed to regularly get baby to fall asleep on his own, in his bed, without any unreliable props, you may find his sleeping issues resolve over the next few days. If not, it's time to focus on independent settling techniques.

Golden Rule No 3: Promote independent settling

By the time you and your baby have reached this stage, you have already achieved two of the three Golden Rules of infant sleep self-regulation.

As long as your baby remains dependent on your help to fall asleep, he's at risk of waking up every time you remove your help. For him to self-regulate his sleeping patterns, and move from one sleep cycle to the next without others' help, he needs to relearn how to fall asleep on his own.

Step 7: Pat baby until drowsy but stop before he falls asleep
Place your baby into his bed while his eyes are open. If he cries, pat him until he stops crying, and continue patting until his little body relaxes and his eyes become heavy, then soften the patting and stop. Encourage him to settle from a drowsy state to sleep on his own. If he cries, pat him again until he becomes drowsy, and so on. If you find you often need to pick him up to soothe him, return to 6 before continuing.

Step 8: Pat baby until he's quiet but stop before he becomes drowsy
Place baby into his bed awake. If he lies there quietly, leave him. If he cries, pat him to calm him, but stop once he ceases crying. Rather than stopping abruptly, gradually soften your patting over 5–10 seconds and then stop. If he starts to cry again, pat him again until he is quiet, and so on.

Aim to stop patting him as soon as he's quiet but before he reaches the point of drowsiness. Once he's quiet, withdraw your support and leave him to settle from a quiet (but awake state) to asleep, independent of further help.

How to modify a gentle settling plan
The gentle settling plan is a set of guidelines that you can adapt as appropriate to your baby's circumstances. You can add more steps, if needed, or skip steps, depending on your baby's habits and how well he responds to change.

Be aware that adding additional steps might take the settling plan in another direction. If a step is not directed towards achieving at least one of the Golden Rules, that you're not already achieving, it may do little to improve his sleep. A sideways step, for example, would be re-offering your baby an unreliable prop, like a pacifier, to prevent him from crying as you withdraw your involvement as he settles to sleep. While a pacifier might successfully reduce fussiness at sleep-time, it has the potential to disrupt his sleep every time it falls out, and might hinder your efforts to improve the quality of his sleep in the long run. You might have spent weeks gradually progressing through all the steps of the gentle settling plan only to discover that the pacifier is disrupting his sleep. An example of a backwards step would be to use a baby hammock or a device that vibrates or rocks his bed as he falls asleep. Once the movement stops he's probably going to wake, either when it stops or the next time he enters a light sleep stage.

Skipping or combining necessary steps means the changes are likely to be greater and more readily recognisable to your baby, increasing the chance he will protest. Some parents are happy to accept a little crying for faster results. How quickly or how slowly you want to go is up to you.

Adding a step at the beginning could be helpful, depending on your baby's circumstances. For example, if he normally falls asleep in places other than your arms or his bed, say, in an infant swing, pram, rocker or elsewhere, you might first try to settle him to sleep in bed with patting. If this is too big a change for him, try to encourage him first to fall asleep in your arms and then progress with the gentle-settling plan as outlined to encourage him to fall asleep in his bed. If you currently jiggle or rock your baby to sleep in your arms, you might need to add another step to cease jiggling or rocking before getting to the stage where you will be able to put him into his bed to fall asleep.

What to expect

Don't expect your baby to suddenly start 'sleeping like a baby' in the early stages of this process. You might not witness any observable change in his sleeping patterns until you have been able to complete the steps that achieve all three of the Golden Rules for three to five consecutive days and nights. Although you're not seeing it, you are making progress by successfully completing each step.

During this process you must expect that your baby may continue to wake prematurely. If you suspect he has woken too soon, try to catch him as he begins to rouse between sleep cycles and repeat the settling strategies for your current step. This is the most effective way to help him return to sleep while providing the consistency required.

If you can't encourage him to return to sleep, he may have had enough and is ready to get up, or the edge has been taken off his tiredness. During the day, if you're unable to get him to return to sleep, get him up and try again later. At night, don't forget to ensure you have provided for all of his physical needs, that is, feeding, nappy changes, etc, before trying to settle him back to sleep.

As you can see, the time and effort required on your part to resolve an infant sleep problem related to negative sleep association dependence while minimising any upset is considerable, but is well worth the investment if his upset distresses you.

How long will the process take?

That depends. If you want to minimise crying when settling to sleep, you must take things very slowly. Depending upon how many steps you need to use and how quickly you can successfully progress through each step, it can take many weeks to get to where your baby settles to sleep in his bed independent of your help; sooner if you're happy to stop once he gets to the stage where he willingly settles to sleep in his bed with your help.

Will baby fuss or cry?

It would be unrealistic to expect your baby to accept changes to his associated sleep conditions without any protest whatsoever. When my gentle settling plan works well, baby does minimal to no crying as he settles to sleep. However, he may fuss a little or a lot initially with every new change to the way you settle him. If you persist, his fussing will decrease as he gets used to settling in the new way. Persistence and consistency are critical. You will need to follow the same strategies described in each step every time you settle him to sleep. This means day-time naps, evenings and overnight. By providing consistency, he gets the chance to become familiar with the changes and, as a consequence, any fussing associated with the change will decrease within a matter of days.

When you make any change to your settling practices, it will take your baby longer to fall asleep at first, compared to settling him in a way he's already familiar with, but he will settle quicker as he begins to accept the change. Resist the urge to help him fall asleep or return to sleep in a different way, as this is likely to confuse him and delay or inhibit his progress. Reverting to previous methods will probably help him to fall or return to sleep sooner, but it's not going to resolve his sleep problem over the long term.

Don't try to move through the steps too quickly. Ideally allow 72 hours or more for your baby to accept the change associated with each step. Wait until you can see signs of acceptance before moving forward. Watch his behavioural cues; once he's settling sooner and fussing less, then he's ready to progress to the next step.

Beginning each new step will require extra time and patience until your baby accepts the change. It's perfectly okay to wait until you feel you can provide the extra time and effort required before moving to the next step. Take as long as you feel both you and your baby need.

Why a gentle settling plan might fail

> I have been struggling with sleep issues since Ava was born. I tried your gentle settling method but it didn't work. I was not able to get her to stop crying. After she woke the fifth time the first night I knew I would not be able to keep doing this. – Dawn

Resolving a baby's sleep problem while avoiding crying is something that appeals to all parents, and is why many parents are attracted to 'no-cry' settling options. But, as stated before, not every method works in every case. A no-cry settling method might fail for a number of reasons, including:

- Baby is currently sleep-deprived. While a sleep-deprived baby's sleep habits can be changed using a gradual approach, sleep-deprived babies are typically irritable, and already crying from insufficient sleep. Until baby catches up on the sleep his little body needs, you cannot relieve his stress. And to achieve that you may need to first resolve the problem that's causing the sleep deprivation.
- Baby is over the age of four months. As a baby matures, his brain development and intellectual capacity expand; he becomes more aware of his surroundings and the care he receives. An older baby can often recognise and get upset by even subtle changes to the

way his parents settle him to sleep. That same baby might not have become as upset about these changes when he was younger, solely because he was less capable of perceiving changes then. Don't believe anyone who says it's easier to change a baby's sleep habits when he's older.

- Baby has a 'spirited' temperament. Babies in general don't like change. But some will be more accepting of change compared to others based on their temperament. 'Spirited' babies have a low frustration tolerance and don't readily accept change. A spirited baby may protest profusely if you attempt to make a change.

- If you're currently sleep-deprived, or physically or emotionally unwell, you may not have the stamina to maintain consistency over a period of weeks or months.

- If you're caring for other children as well, it's impossible to be in two places at the same time. An older child may become upset when your attention is focused on settling your baby for what may be long periods of time.

- If you're regularly separated from your baby because of work or other commitments, then you might not be available to provide the consistency he needs to change sleep associations gradually when using such an approach.

A gentle settling plan works best with babies under the age of four months who are not sleep-deprived, and who have an easy-going temperament. A stay-at-home mother of one, not currently suffering as a result of sleep deprivation, anxiety or depression, is the parent most able to follow a gentle settling plan with enough consistency to achieve a successful outcome. This narrows the field considerably. If you and/or your baby do not fall into this category, it may not be possible for you to change his sleep associations and resolve his sleeping problem without him crying.

As disappointing as it might be to discover that a no-cry option is either impractical or unachievable in yours or your baby's circumstances, this means you're getting closer to finding an effective solution to his sleeping problems. It may be time to consider some of the other sleep training options detailed in the following chapters.

Key points

- Babies in general resist change. You cannot make significant changes to a baby's sleep associations and avoid upsetting him. Minimising the upset means you must make a series of tiny changes over an extended period of time.

- Although you might succeed in avoiding crying when your baby settles to sleep, he might still fuss somewhat until the new way of settling becomes familiar to him.

- A multi-step approach requires considerable time, patience and consistency.

- A no-cry settling approach will not work for every baby or every parent.

10
Hands-on settling I and II

Topics

What does hands-on settling achieve?
Steps involved.
What to expect.
How effective is this method?
Why hands-on settling might not work.
How to use hands-on settling to promote independent settling.

Help. I am desperate. I'm due to go back to work in two weeks and the only way Tayla (aged 4 months) will go to sleep is lying on my chest. I realise this is not something they will be able to do at the childcare centre and I'm worried about how she's going to cope when we're separated. I know I need to do something to change the way she goes to sleep. I have tried to get her to fall asleep in her cot but she cries so hard I give in and cuddle her to sleep. I don't feel right leaving her crying. Please help! – Deirdre

Deirdre is right to worry in this situation. If it continues, Tayla is in for a big shock when she discovers the sleeping conditions at childcare are very different to those she has learned to expect. The clock is ticking and Deirdre needs a quick and effective solution. As she doesn't feel comfortable leaving Tayla to cry, she may find a hands-on settling method fits her criteria.

Hands-on settling involves helping a baby fall asleep while in her bed (cot, bassinette or cradle) by patting, stroking, rocking or shushing her. This strategy has the potential to improve the quality of sleep for babies accustomed to falling asleep in places other than their bed, and can be used by anyone caring for the baby.

Hands-on settling is a middle ground sleep training approach. It can resolve a baby's sleep problem much sooner than a multi-step approach, like my gentle settling plan, but not as quickly as with a one step settling method, like responsive settling, controlled crying or cry-it-out. Baby may protest cry for the first few days, until falling asleep in her bed becomes familiar to her, but parents can avoid the intense periods of crying that can occur with a one step method. Parents stay the entire time their baby learns that 'it's okay to fall asleep in my bed'.

Hands-on settling I

Settling a baby to sleep in her bed is effective, even impressive, in reducing the risk of wakefulness and improving sleep quality. One of the most common reasons for broken sleep is because the baby has been settled to sleep in one place and then moved into her bed once asleep. Remember, moving your baby after she has fallen asleep means you're changing her sleeping environment. This may threaten her sense of security. She's likely to feel even less secure if moving her has resulted in the loss of other familiar sleep associations as well.

The purpose of hands-on settling is to provide a suitable and consistent sleeping environment for your baby, and encourage her to associate her bed with sleeping and feel safe there. Settling baby to sleep while she's in her bed may make it possible to promote other positive sleep associations, such as swaddling, an infant sleeping bag or security blanket or soft toy as well.

The combination of a suitable, consistent sleeping environment plus positive sleep associations can go a long way to easing a baby's passage into sleep and decreasing the risk of her waking prematurely. Physical needs that require attention, such as hunger or a soaked nappy, will naturally awaken her, but the risk of her waking too soon owing to her noticing the absence of familiar sleep associations will be reduced.

Settling of your baby to sleep in her bed is an important step towards promoting independent settling. If you later decide that she might benefit from independent settling, this will be easier if she's already accustomed to falling asleep in her bed versus elsewhere.

Steps involved

- Choose a suitable, low-stimulus environment for your baby's bed, ideally a room that can be darkened and you can restrict noise levels. This could be your bedroom or a room that is close enough for you to hear her when she wakes.
- Once you have identified her early signs of tiredness, ensure all physical needs have been met and prepare her for sleep by swaddling or dressing her in an infant sleeping bag of fabric suitable for the temperature in the room she is to sleep.
- Let her know that bedtime is coming by using a consistent bedtime routine. For a day-time nap this might consist of a few minutes in your arms in a quiet, darkened bedroom as you sing her a lullaby.
- Place her into her bed *while her eyes are still open*. She needs to be aware that she's going into her bed.
- Now pat or rock her while she's in her bed until she falls asleep. You may need to do this until she reaches a deep sleep stage, which takes between five to twenty minutes after she's fallen asleep, but only if she wakes when you stop sooner.
- If necessary, pick her up for a brief cuddle to soothe her, but return her to bed as soon as she's quiet so that she gets the chance to fall asleep in her bed.

Deirdre said she didn't know how to calm Tayla other than to pick her up and cuddle her to sleep. There are a number of ways to soothe a baby while she's in her bed.

Soothing methods

- Patting her thigh or gently tapping her tummy. If she's not responding while on her back, try rolling her onto her side to pat her bottom. Newborn babies often calm more readily while on their side. But make sure you roll her back once she's calm so that she can safely sleep on her back.

- Body rocking, which involves placing your hands across her chest and hips and gently rocking her body from side to side.

- Jiggling or rocking her bed.

- Stroking her forehead.

- Making a shooshing sound.

Remember, the primary goal is for baby to fall asleep *while she's in her bed*. In order for this new way of settling to become familiar and acceptable, consistency on your part is vital. Provide her with the same sleeping environment and positive sleep associations each and every time she needs to sleep, day and night, whenever possible.

Baby Natalie

Brenda couldn't understand why Natalie (aged three months) would fall asleep in her cot in the evenings and sleep soundly all night but then refuse to fall asleep there during the day. It was because Natalie associated falling asleep with being cuddled in Brenda's arms, and that's what she wanted when tired. She would fall asleep in her cot in the evenings exhausted, because she wasn't getting enough sleep during the day. The large sleep debt she accumulated during the day as a result of her dependence on being cuddled to sleep, something which Brenda was unable to provide the entire time she slept, prevented her from waking during the night. Once Brenda persisted in getting Natalie to fall asleep in her cot during the day, within weeks she was settling to sleep sooner in her cot than she had ever done in Brenda's arms. Plus, she napped longer during the day.

What to expect

Learning new sleep habits takes time. The type of behaviour a baby will display during the learning phase is quite different to how she behaves once she has learned to associate her bed with sleeping.

During the learning phase

It is unrealistic to expect your baby to instantly accept being soothed in her bed if that's not what she's used to. Deirdre gave up and cuddled Tayla to sleep because she believed that was the only way she would calm. But had Deirdre persisted in soothing her while she was in her bed, Tayla would have eventually calmed, plus, it would become easier and quicker to calm her in her bed over the subsequent few days.

How quickly babies come to accept the change depends on how different hands-on settling is from the way they normally go to sleep.

Carmen learned to fall asleep while being rocked in a pram, while Jenah would fall asleep in her mother's arms, suckling at her breast. The change for Jenah using hands-on settling will be far more significant than for Carmen.

Changing to hands-on settling means it will likely take your baby longer to fall asleep initially, compared to how you usually settle her to sleep. However, as it becomes more familiar, she will not only soothe more quickly, but also settle to sleep sooner. If you persist in settling her to sleep in her bed, she gets to learn that her bed is a safe place to sleep, and recognise when she goes into her bed this means it's sleep time. You just need to be patient and give her the chance to learn. With consistency, the learning phase usually takes three to five days.

After the learning phase
Once the learning phase has passed, your baby now settles to sleep quickly in her bed, provided you get her into it before she becomes overtired. With a consistent sleeping environment and positive sleep associations, she will be less inclined to wake prematurely during her sleep and may sleep longer periods both day and night, thus, avoid overtiredness and sleep deprivation. However, other factors play a part.

How effective is hands-on settling?

> As you know I had gotten into the habit of letting Erica (aged eight weeks) fall asleep while breastfeeding and then discovered no one else was able to settle her but me. I was getting exhausted. It just didn't feel right to leave her to cry on her own. I needed to do something to try to help her. You recommended hands-on settling. I can't believe the difference this has made. Erica is sleeping for longer periods, her dad is able to settle her to sleep and feels good about being able to help out, and I am getting more sleep. So the whole family has benefited. I can't thank you enough for suggesting I try this method. – Rosemary

Rosemary succeeded, but not every parent who tries this settling method enjoys the same level of success, so don't be discouraged if it doesn't seem to be working for you. Hands-on settling will provide your baby with a consistent sleep environment and give her opportunities to learn positive sleep associations, but this may not be enough to prevent her from waking too soon from naps or repeatedly throughout the night.

In general, hands-on settling is more likely to resolve infant sleeping problems experienced by babies under the age of four months. It may not resolve an older baby's sleep problem as she's better able to perceive subtle differences in her surroundings and sleep associations. Babies, like us, develop multiple sleep associations. Even a change in one sleep association can be enough to cause broken sleep. So if you're helping her to fall asleep in her bed, and then remove your help once she has fallen asleep, she might notice at some point and wake.

While Rosemary found hands-on settling provided the solution to Erica's sleeping issues at eight weeks of age, six weeks down the track Erica's naps suddenly became shorter and she woke more often during the night. To resolve this problem Rosemary needed to take additional steps to enable Erica to self-regulate her sleeping patterns. This is because hands-on settling achieves only one of the three Golden Rules of infant sleep self-regulation: providing a consistent sleeping environment.

Again, the three Golden Rules to teach your baby to self-regulate her sleeping patterns and minimise premature awakenings are:

- **Provide baby with a suitable and consistent sleeping environment.** Hands-on settling achieves this Golden Rule. It can take a number of days for baby to learn to associate her bed with sleeping.
- **Withhold any unreliable props at sleep time.** Remember, learned dependence on just one negative sleep association can be enough to disturb sleep. If baby has a pacifier to fall asleep, her dependence can be enough to wake her when it falls out.
- **Promote independent settling.** Hands-on settling encourages parents to help their baby to fall asleep while in bed; it does not promote independent settling.

If your baby continues to be wakeful after a few days of consistently settling her to sleep in her bed, or, if like Erica, she starts to become wakeful when she's a little older, the most likely cause will be dependence on a negative sleep aid, your help to fall asleep, or both. In this case you might have to do more than provide her with a consistent sleeping environment.

Consider the three ways to support a baby to self-regulate her sleeping patterns. You can achieve these over a period of weeks or months by using my gentle settling plan (in Chapter 9), or in a matter of days using a one step settling method (see Chapter 11). Or you could take the middle ground and use hands-on settling II.

Hands-on settling II

Hands-on settling II is using hands-on settling as a stepping stone to self-settling. Three steps are involved, which match the three ways to support a baby to self-regulate her sleeping patterns.

Steps involved

Step 1: Provide a consistent sleeping environment

Encourage your baby to become accustomed to sleeping in her bed. To do this, she needs to fall asleep while she's in her bed. Start by using the steps previously described for hands-on settling I. You may want to continue using any sleep aids she's accustomed to, such as a pacifier, music or white noise, to help her to accept falling asleep in her bed.

Step 2: Discourage baby's reliance on negative sleep aids

Your baby is more likely to remain asleep if her sleep associations stay constant throughout. If she currently relies on any negative sleep aid, the next step is to stop giving it to her when she settles to sleep. During this stage, continue to pat or rock her to sleep while she's in her bed.

Step 3: Encourage independent settling

If you're helping your baby to fall asleep, by definition she's not settling independently. Soothe her when necessary, but not once she's calm. Ideally stop before she becomes drowsy.

What to expect

It may take three to five days for your baby to adjust to each step, and only if you settle her to sleep in the same way each time. Once she accepts the new conditions she will calm sooner and settle more quickly. You can decide when, or if, you want to take the next step. There's no need to take additional steps, as long as everything is working for you both. It's up to you to decide if you think taking the next step will help. Expect a new round of protest crying from your baby each time you make a change to the way you settle her to sleep.

Don't forget, there are alternatives. You might find you can resolve your baby's sleeping problem and minimise her upset by using my gentle settling plan. Admittedly, this will take considerably longer to resolve her sleeping issues. If you're feeling desperate, you can achieve all three Golden Rules at the same time by using a one step settling method, which includes responsive settling, controlled crying or cry-it-out. Just be aware that you can't change a baby's sleep associations quickly without upsetting her.

Key points

- Hands-on settling I promotes a consistent sleeping environment, a big step towards supporting baby to self-regulate her sleeping patterns.

- Hands-on settling II is a multi-step approach (three steps) to encourage independent settling.

- Hands-on settling will not provide a solution to every baby's sleep problem.

One step settling methods

Braydon hardly sleeps during the day and he wakes every hour or two at night. The only way I can get him back to sleep is to hold him and rock him in my arms. I am so sleep-deprived that I am afraid to drive the car. My husband and I are constantly bickering because we're not getting enough sleep. I feel so guilty that I am not giving my 2-year-old daughter enough attention but Braydon is so difficult to get to sleep and cranky when he's awake I just don't have time. I'm at my wits end! I can't keep doing this. What can I do to get him to sleep properly? – Jackie

Jackie's situation is far from an isolated one. Every week I meet families in crisis resulting from chronic sleep deprivation. If, like Jackie, you feel you can no longer live with your current situation, one solution is to use a one step sleep training method to encourage your baby to fall asleep independent of your help.

One step sleep training methods are the quickest way to resolve an infant sleep problem that develops because a baby has learned to rely on negative sleep associations. Improvements in baby's sleep can be seen in as little as three to five days, but babies tend to cry, often intensely, during the learning phase.

There are three one step settling methods: responsive settling, controlled crying and cry-it-out. I find many parents have preconceived ideas and mistaken assumptions about these methods, based on hearsay, preventing some from even considering possibly the only sleep training method that will effectively resolve their baby's sleep problem. Those with a lack of understanding about what's involved, what must be achieved, and what to expect, who do attempt these methods, may decrease their chance of success.

The more you understand about the various sleep training options available, the more likely you will find a method that suits your circumstances. How can you judge if you don't know what each method, including the one step sleep training method, involves?

Types of one step settling methods

To resolve a negative sleep association-based sleep problem, you must first change your infant settling practices. The one step method is designed to achieve all three of the Golden Rules of infant sleep self-regulation as baby falls asleep: provide a suitable and consistent sleeping environment; withhold any unreliable props at sleep time; and promote independent settling. 'One step' does not mean only one action is implemented, but, rather, that all the necessary changes to your infant settling practices are made simultaneously. Three settling methods use a one step approach:

- responsive settling
- controlled crying
- cry-it-out.

Each method is designed to enable a baby to self-regulate his sleeping patterns by promoting independent settling in his bed, ideally without any unreliable props.

When you make any significant change to how your baby falls asleep you can expect him to cry in protest. He has no desire to change his sleep associations. The main difference between the three one step settling methods is when you respond to your baby's cries.

Responsive settling

Responsive settling involves encouraging your baby to fall asleep on his own in his bed while at the same time supporting him to manage his emotions. It requires matching your response to your baby's behavioural cues.

When using responsive settling you can vary your response time depending on how he is coping.

- If baby is quiet, he's coping, so leave him to settle on his own.
- If baby is whining or fussing, a low to moderate level of crying that involves stopping and starting, he's not happy, but he's not overly upset either. Give him the chance to see if he can work things out on his own.
- If baby's cries sound distressed, eg, high-pitched screaming that continues without a break, give him a chance to see if he can calm on his own, but don't wait too long before responding.
- If baby's cries sound angry rather than distressed you might wait a little longer compared to a distressed cry before responding. From around three months of age, a baby can protest with an angry cry whenever he's feeling frustrated, like when he's tired and not being settled to sleep the way he wants. If you listen carefully, you can tell the difference.

The timing of your response has as much to do with your comfort as your baby's. When using responsive settling, you can respond to him as often as you deem necessary. Provided you achieve the three Golden Rules at the moment he falls asleep, it won't matter how often you respond to his cries.

Controlled crying

Controlled crying involves responding to your baby's cries at set intervals. Recommendations on when to respond vary depending on who you talk to or which baby sleep book you read.

- Many advocates for controlled crying recommend that parents first respond after five minutes. The next time, they wait 10 minutes, then 15, and then 20 minutes. They continue to respond every 20 minutes after that until their baby falls asleep.

- Some people suggest parents initially respond after two minutes. The next interval is four minutes, then six minutes, and then eight, until you reach 10 minutes, at which time you would respond every 10 minutes until your baby falls asleep.
- Another variation is to respond at a fixed-time interval, eg, every five minutes.
- Others endorse a more complex version in which the start time is extended each day.

Controlled crying is not a settling method I generally recommend, as it encourages parents to watch the clock rather than listen and respond to their baby's cues. Every baby's stress levels differ. By responding only at predetermined times, you could be ignoring your baby's distress and return at times when he's starting to soothe himself, escalating his cries once again. However, some parents feel more comfortable having set timeframes.

> I found the direct guidance, instead of the 'go with your instincts' or 'whenever you feel it is necessary' approach helped me because, when you're stressed, tired and don't know what you're doing, you feel like your instincts are not working correctly. Sometimes it's good to just be aware of how long it has been, because two minutes can feel like 10. – Sarah

Like Sarah, you might feel you cope better with a set time period in mind to respond to your baby's cries. If this is the case you might like to choose one of the timeframes listed. No particular timeframe is more effective than another. So, you needn't get too hung up about which set of times to use. The ultimate goal is to achieve the Golden Rules at the time your baby falls asleep. Achieve the Golden Rules and it won't matter whether you went to him five or 50 times, it will still work.

Cry-it-out

Cry-it-out is the most widely promoted of the three one step methods, possibly because it's the most basic. So when do you respond to baby's cries? You don't. You put him into his cot tired but awake, leave his room and don't return, except to attend to any safety and comfort needs. Renee found cry-it-out worked for her.

> I tried to get Aiden (aged 10 months) to calm down in his cot by patting him and rocking him but he would only calm down when I picked him up. He would then scream even louder as soon as I put him back into his cot. After doing this a few times I could tell we weren't going to get anywhere this way. In the end I decided to leave him to cry it out. It was the toughest thing I have had to do in my life, but it worked. Over the next two days he cried less. By the third night he slept through for the first time. Now he's happy to go into his cot to sleep and there's no crying and he sleeps through most nights. He's much happier now he's getting enough sleep, and so am I. – Renee

Leaving your baby to cry it out achieves the three Golden Rules, therefore, it is technically an effective sleep training method. But I don't recommend it myself. It can be very stressful and it's unnecessary to leave a baby to cry alone in order to resolve a baby's sleep problem. Renee left Aiden to cry it out because she found she could not soothe him while he was in his bed. She was not aware of other ways to support him to manage his emotions besides soothing him.

The only time I would encourage you to leave your baby to cry it out is if you were feeling frustrated and angry and there was a risk that you might harm him. In this situation, I suggest that you gently place him into the safety of his bed and leave him to cry it out. If you have thoughts of harming your baby, please seek help immediately. Call your spouse/partner, a family member or friend and ask them to care for baby while you take a break. See your doctor as soon as possible and tell him how you're feeling. You are by no means the only parent to experience such thoughts, so don't let feelings of embarrassment or shame prevent you from getting support.

Purpose of delaying your response

I can't see how ignoring my baby's crying will teach him to
sleep better. – Kerri-Lee

I questioned this concept myself when I first heard about these settling
methods. How can ignoring a baby's cries help him sleep better? It
turns out that crying doesn't help a baby to sleep better. But achieving
the Golden Rules does. So why leave your baby to cry? For one, it's not
always possible to a change a baby's sleep associations and avoid crying
at the same time. Another reason is because bedtime is an ideal time to
encourage a baby to develop self-soothing skills.

Consider the situation in terms of delaying your response to your
baby's crying rather than outright ignoring your baby's cries. The purpose
of delaying your response to baby's cries is to provide him opportunities
to learn and practise physical skills which will enable him to self-soothe.

Self-settling versus self-soothing

Self-settling: when baby goes from a quiet state to asleep
unaided.
Self-soothing: independently regaining a state of calmness
after crying.

Babies are born being able to self-settle, but they lose their willingness
to self-settle if we unknowingly teach them to rely on our help to fall
asleep. Sleep training gives a baby the chance to rediscover that it's okay
to sleep independently.

The ability to self-soothe is something that is learned. Of course,
there's no need for a baby to learn to self-soothe while his caregiver is
available to soothe him whenever he becomes upset. However, today's
busy lifestyles often preclude a parent or caregiver from accomplishing
this round-the-clock. There will be times when, although present, you
cannot stop to soothe your baby. If you're driving the car, attending to the

needs of another child, or tending to your own physical needs, and no one else is available, then it's an advantage if your baby can soothe himself.

One way to support your baby to learn self-soothing skills is to delay your response in situations where you feel confident he is safe, physically comfortable and his nutritional needs have been met. Another way is to provide positive sleep associations at bedtime; for example, giving him the chance to sleep in a low-stimulus environment, so that he's not irritated by noise or bright lights when he's tired. You might help your newborn to feel a womb-like sense of security and containment by swaddling him at sleep time, however, doing so once he reaches three to four months of age might prevent him from self-soothing. By three to four months, most babies have gained enough control of their arms to self-soothe by sucking on their hands or fingers. The ability to self-soothe is a learned skill that develops over time with practise. If, the moment your baby goes 'Wa-a-ah,' you rush in and sweep him up in your arms to soothe him, he doesn't get a chance to initiate or practise self-soothing skills.

As your baby gets older, and therefore more aware of his surroundings, increasingly more situations will frustrate him. According to paediatrician Ken Armstrong, babies who don't learn to self-soothe often become persistent criers by around nine months of age.[100]

Baby Griffin

Griffin, 11 months, only calms by suckling at his mother's breast. He hasn't developed self-soothing skills because his mother, Bronwyn, automatically offers her breast the moment he fusses. This would not be problematic if Bronwyn was happy to continue this, but she's not. 'I am so over it,' Bronwyn exclaims. 'The moment anything upsets him, he wants my breast. If I don't give it to him, he goes ballistic. I can't go back to work because I can't leave him with anyone, not even his dad. If I leave him for even an hour, his dad is ringing me up to come back because he can't calm him.'

When parents support their baby to master self-soothing skills at sleep time, oftentimes baby starts to activate these skills at other times as well. It may be because one step settling methods provide opportunities for baby to initiate, practise and eventually master self-soothing skills that they're the most effective of all sleep training methods. Not only does a baby get to sleep better, but he also gets the chance to learn how to self soothe.

Which method is best?

There's no one answer for everyone. The success of these methods is not based on how long you leave your baby to cry, but whether you consistently achieve the Golden Rules at the time he settles to sleep, often enough for him to learn new sleep associations. Therefore, responsive settling, controlled crying and cry-it-out have the potential to be equally effective.

Personally, I favour responsive settling because it considers the baby's emotional state. I find most parents choose this method when given the option because they can quickly resolve their baby's sleeping problem and yet respond to their baby as often as they feel is necessary. A major advantage of responsive settling is that it is suitable for every age group, unlike controlled crying and cry-it-out, which are not generally recommended for babies under the age of six months.

How to use responsive settling

Responsive settling enables you to change your baby's sleep associations in a way that promotes independent settling and supports him to manage his emotions at the same time. How best to support your baby largely depends on his physical capabilities, his memory and ability to understand. What you aim to achieve when responding to the cries of a newborn baby often differs from a response to an older baby. Let's examine how responsive settling might be adapted for various age groups. Read the information for all age groups as some of the tips might be relevant irrespective of your baby's age.

Birth to three months

If your baby is more than a few days old, he likely has already learned to rely on particular conditions, props or activities to fall asleep. In other words, he has developed sleep associations. If they're negative sleep associations, they can disturb his sleep, which, in turn, makes him vulnerable to sleep deprivation. Despite his young age, he's going to experience some level of stress if you change your settling practices to solve his sleep deprivation problem.

As a newborn, your baby's ability to self-soothe is limited. He may be unable yet to roll or change position on his own, or self-soothe by sucking on his hands or fingers. This does not mean he's incapable of calming independently. It just means you need to be aware of his limitations and realistic in your expectations.

How to support baby to manage emotions

You can support your baby by:

- identifying his tired signs early
- providing a consistent, low-stimulus sleeping environment
- swaddling him for sleep (if he loves to suck, swaddle him so that one fist is near his face).

If he starts to cry soon after you place him into his bed, provide him first with a brief opportunity to calm himself by delaying your response to his cries. Your challenge will be deciding when he needs your help to calm and when to allow him a little more time to see if he can work things out on his own. Listen to the tone and intensity of his cries to decide when to respond (see page 169). When you decide to return, try soothing him using a strategy of your choice outlined on pages 160–161.

What to expect

Don't expect your baby to immediately respond to a new calming method and drift off into peaceful sleep. The first few times you try it may take up to 30 minutes or more for him to finally fall asleep independently in his bed, even longer for an overtired baby. It will take many tries to soothe him before he eventually self-settles, going from a quiet state to asleep unaided.

If you're consistent in how you calm your baby, and work to achieve the Golden Rules every time he falls asleep, the intensity of his cries will lessen, he will calm more quickly, and the time it will take for him to fall asleep will generally decrease over the following few days. However, this improvement can only occur if you persist long enough for him to become familiar with the calming method and settling to sleep in his bed.

What to do when baby calms
The purpose of responding to this age group – when using this settling method – is to help your baby to calm, not fall asleep. Soothe him to the point where he's quiet and his body relaxes, but stop before he gets drowsy or falls asleep. As soon as he's calm, your job is done. Ease off your calming technique over the next five to 10 seconds so that he doesn't notice an abrupt stop. Then allow him to go from a quiet, but awake state, to asleep without further assistance from you, which means he gets to self-settle. You have now achieved all three Golden Rules.

If you had to return multiple times to calm your baby, you may be tempted to keep soothing him until he becomes drowsy or drops off to sleep. If you go this far, you have not achieved Golden Rule No 3. You might see some benefits as a result of providing him with a consistent sleeping environment but he might not get to the stage where he can self-regulate his sleeping patterns. Think long term. Helping your baby to fall asleep will get him to sleep quicker in the short term, but it might not solve his sleep problem. Your patience will be rewarded if you can persist with calming only. Repeatedly allowing your baby to go from a quiet, awake state to asleep unaided in his bed will enable him to self-regulate his sleeping patterns within a few days. This will result in better sleep for him and you in the long run.

What if baby doesn't calm
If your baby is not used to being calmed in his bed it may take time for him to learn to calm in this way. Don't assume that because he doesn't calm right away that he won't. He might just need more time for the new calming method to become familiar, and to learn that it's okay to spend a little quiet time in bed. If a calming method listed is similar to what you already use, I suggest you choose that one. If not, then choose

the calming method you can most comfortably provide. Swapping and changing between calming methods denies your baby the repetition he may need to respond to a method. In time, he will respond to whatever calming method you choose, and, as it becomes more familiar to him, he will respond faster. Within a few days you may find all it takes is a couple of pats or a brief rock in order for him to calm. Getting to that point, however, requires persistence.

Reassuring cuddle

If calming your baby while he's in his bed fails to quieten him, after five minutes, pick him up for a cuddle. (Five minutes is only a suggestion so that you give him a chance to respond to being soothed while he's in bed. Pick him up whenever you feel you need to.) The purpose of picking your baby up for a cuddle is not just to reassure him; it's also to reassure you that he's fine. If he calms quickly in your arms, you know there's nothing wrong. (See page 6 for more on assessing potential pain.) As soon as he's quiet and while his eyes are still open, return him to his bed. That way he gets the chance to learn to fall asleep in his bed and in time associate his bed with sleeping. If he starts to cry, give him a few moments to see if he will calm on his own. If he doesn't, return and try to calm him while he's in his bed. Try to avoid picking him up the moment he starts to cry as he won't get the chance to learn to calm while he's in his bed if you don't at least try to calm him while he's in his bed.

If your baby doesn't calm when in your arms, double-check that you have provided adequately for his physical needs: hygiene, nutrition etc. If you have, then try the Sanity Saver below.

Sanity Saver

Swaddle baby firmly, with his arms tucked in. Sit on a chair with your knees together and feet apart for stability. Lean forward slightly, to support his head in your hands, and lay him in a semi-side/semi-tummy position lengthwise along your thighs so that his feet are touching your stomach, his head is towards your knees, and his tummy is lying against one of your thighs. Then, while supporting his head so that it doesn't flop around, press your knees together and swing them together, from left to right and back, in wide sweeping movements. Swing at a rate of approximately one second each side. Dr Harvey Karp describes a very similar method in his book *The Happiest Baby*.

Diagram 11.1: Sanity Saver

The Sanity Saver can be a helpful way to soothe an overstimulated or overtired newborn baby. But try to avoid rocking your baby off to sleep this way. If he regularly falls asleep in this way it may become a parent-assisted sleep association, and as such can result in broken sleep every time you remove your help.

Soothing tip: A newborn baby is especially vulnerable to overstimulation, more so if he becomes overtired, because his nervous system is still immature. To reduce the risk of overstimulation, remain in a low-stimulus environment while calming baby.

What if baby takes a long time to fall asleep?

If your baby remains unsettled, every 15 minutes ask yourself the following questions:

Diagram 11.2: What's wrong baby?

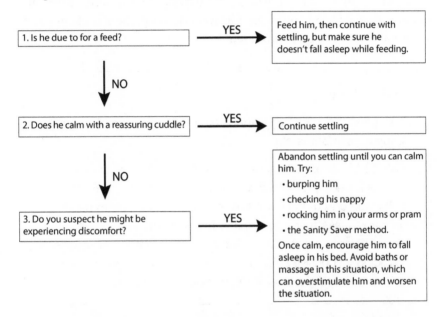

Soothing tip: Most babies have a strong desire to suck until five to six months of age, whether they're hungry, tired, bored, experiencing discomfort or seeking pleasure. Their desire to suck is often misinterpreted as hunger. If baby has fed recently, offer your little finger palm-side up instead. As your finger curls slightly and the tip of your finger touches the roof of his mouth, it may stimulate his suck reflex. Make sure your nails are clean and neatly trimmed first.

What to do at night

Most babies under four months require night-time feeds, on an average of between one and three feeds each night. Feed your baby as often as necessary, but avoid letting him fall asleep while feeding, to discourage a feeding-sleep association. Return him to his bed while his eyes are still open and follow the same settling strategies used during the day. The more consistent you are in the way you settle him to sleep, the faster he will learn.

If your baby wakes at times unrelated to his need to feed, ensure his comfort by picking him up to see if he wants to burp, check his nappy and re-swaddle him, and then return him to his bed to self-settle.

True or false?

You cannot do anything about an infant sleep problem until baby is six months old.

FALSE: Many people mistakenly believe the only way to solve an infant sleep problem is to leave baby to cry it out. Because controlled crying and cry-it-out are *not* methods recommended for babies less than six months, they assume nothing can be done before that point. However, a number of strategies, including responsive settling, can be used to manage or resolve an infant sleeping problem, irrespective of baby's age.

What to keep in mind

Newborn babies are vulnerable to suffering abdominal discomfort resulting from feeding-related problems, such as oversupply syndrome when breast-fed and overfeeding when bottle-fed (see pages 11–14). Some newborn babies will underfeed for various reasons. You need to assess the possibility of these problems, and take effective steps to resolve or manage them before attempting sleep training.

Another problem common in this age group is that many newborns sleep for long periods during the day and want to be awake for long periods during the night. Sleep training is not appropriate for this type of problem. We will discuss babies' internal body clocks in Chapters 13, 14 and 15.

Babies aged four to six months

By this age, your baby's physical capabilities and memory have advanced considerably compared to when he was a newborn. Each day he gains more control over his limbs and body movements. He will begin rolling sometime during these months. You might see him frequently sucking or chewing on his fists or fingers to satisfy his sucking urge and self-soothe.

Not only is your baby physically more capable than he was at a younger age, his ability to think and remember has expanded, and continues to expand at a rapid rate. He now can link a simple sequence of events. He's learning to recognise when he is about to get what he wants, such as when he's going to be fed, and will quieten even before he receives the feed. He might stop fussing or crying as soon as he sees you or when you pick him up, or once he sees his bottle or his mother unbuttoning her blouse. Alternatively, if he's not getting what he wants, his cries will escalate as his frustration builds. You may notice a new, more intense tone to his cries, as he begins to convey anger, an expression of extreme frustration.

How to support baby to manage emotions

When using responsive settling with a baby of this age, know that he has a greater ability to soothe himself compared to a few months ago. As long as you feel confident that you have satisfied your baby's physical needs, you needn't respond now to his cries as quickly at sleep times as you did when he was younger. Delay your response depending on the level and intensity of his cries. When you decide it's time to return, aim to calm him while he's in his bed using one of the calming methods described on pages 160–161.

If you see baby frequently sucking or chewing on his fists, you might want to stop swaddling him with his arms tucked inside for sleep. His own hands and fingers are the best tools he has to enable him to self-soothe. Instead, swaddle him with one or both arms out, or switch to an infant sleeping bag. You might also consider leaving him just a little longer at sleep times before responding to his cries to give him the chance to figure out that now is a good time to suck on his fist or fingers.

What to expect

Your baby wants you to help him fall asleep in the way he has learned to expect. If you suddenly change your infant settling practices, he's going to feel confused, frustrated or angry until the new way becomes familiar. During the learning phase, he's going to cry; possibly intensely.

Because your baby knows what he wants – for you to help him fall asleep in the usual way – it's going to be challenging to soothe him in a different way. Babies of this age generally don't accept an unfamiliar calming method straight away, and many parents give up mistakenly believing it's a futile exercise. Although you might not witness immediate results when you first attempt to calm him in a new way, provided you persist, your efforts will be rewarded over the long term. He will eventually learn to calm in his bed. Once he accepts being calmed in his bed, he will begin to soothe more and more quickly over the coming days as the new calming method becomes familiar. Within days, you will likely need to return only briefly to give him a few of his customary quick pats or momentary rock or stroke him before he quietens. The need to return to soothe him will also decrease over time as you encourage him to self-soothe and give him opportunities to become familiar with falling asleep while he's in his bed.

Generally, the older the baby the longer it will take him to self-settle, to go from a quiet state to asleep unaided, when you first change settling practices. As he gets older, he becomes stronger and physically better equipped to protest for longer periods of time. The time it takes for four- to six-month-olds to self-settle on their first attempt could range from 20 minutes to an hour or more. Once your baby has had many opportunities to fall asleep in his bed, he will learn to associate it with sleeping. He also learns that his bed is a safe place to sleep and will calm more quickly and settle to sleep sooner.

Babies respond differently depending on their temperament and level of tiredness. Some babies by their nature are more sensitive to change, more easily frustrated, and more determined than others. Overtired babies often find it difficult to fall asleep. Exhausted babies cave in quickly.

What to do when baby calms

The purpose of returning when using responsive settling with this age group is to help your baby to calm; it's not to help him to fall asleep. Once baby is quiet, ease off and step back or leave the room, leaving him to go from a quiet state to asleep on his own.

> **Soothing tip:** Help until quiet, not drowsy and not asleep. It's a very fine line between drowsiness and falling asleep. If you frequently help baby to a drowsy state or to fall asleep you may find you achieve nothing more than to replace one negative sleep association with another.

What if baby doesn't calm?

Be patient. It takes time. If you cannot calm him in his bed by patting, rocking, stroking or shooshing, after a few minutes leave and see if he calms on his own. If he doesn't self-soothe, return and try again to calm him in his bed. The reason for leaving is because I have seen babies of this age often respond more quickly to being calmed in their beds if they're given a little time on their own. You may need to do this a number of times before your baby responds to being calmed in his bed for the first time. Whether you leave him crying for a little while longer or continue trying to calm him in his bed despite his protests, he will eventually respond either way.

Pick your baby up for a reassuring cuddle whenever you feel it's necessary, but I recommend you first make a reasonable attempt, say, for 10 minutes or so, to encourage him to calm while he's in his bed, either on his own or with your help. So long as you achieve the three Golden Rules at the time he falls asleep, you can resolve his sleeping problem irrespective of how often you pick him up. Bear in mind that he's likely to become just as upset every time you try to put him back to bed awake. And if you're constantly picking him up to soothe him instead of doing it while he's in his bed, it will likely take longer for him to accept being calmed in his bed. Repeatedly encouraging your baby to accept being calmed in his bed provides better results over the long term.

What if baby takes a long time to fall asleep?

If your baby remains unsettled for 30 minutes, it's time for a quick comfort break, a time to assess if any physical needs require attention. Check his nappy and whether he is due for a feed. Make sure he doesn't fall asleep while feeding. Once all of his physical needs are cared for, encourage him again to self-settle in his bed.

What to do at night

Most babies this age require one or two feeds during the night; just try to avoid letting him fall asleep while feeding. Return him to his bed while his eyes are still open and encourage him to self-settle in his bed using the same strategies as you use during the day.

If your baby wakes at times unrelated to hunger, check his physical needs and return him bed while his eyes are still open and support him to self-settle in same way as you do during the day.

What to keep in mind

Babies of this age are particularly vulnerable to circadian rhythm sleep problems, where their internal body clock gets out of sync with a normal day-night pattern. It's possible for a baby's sleep issues to be due to both negative sleep associations and a circadian rhythm sleep problem. If your baby's internal body clock is out of sync, you could be attempting to settle him to sleep at times when he's not tired. This is discussed in greater detail in Chapters 13 and 14.

If you suspect these two different types of infant sleep problems are troubling your baby, I recommend you first resolve the negative sleep associations before attempting to adjust his day/night sleeping patterns. He's not going to self-settle if he's not actually tired.

Babies over six months

By this age, your baby has made significant advances in his physical, intellectual and emotional development, and you may need to adapt your infant settling practices accordingly. Awareness of what your baby is capable of understanding and achieving now may assist in adapting your settling practices to match his needs.

By six months, your baby is literally older and wiser than ever before. He has learned what he wants and what to expect from you regarding the way you feed and settle him to sleep. Through his past experiences he has learned that crying gets him what he wants.

A normal, healthy baby is now physically capable of self-soothing in familiar, safe situations like going to bed, provided all physical needs have been satisfied, but he will only self-soothe when he chooses to do so. If a baby of this age is never self-soothing, it's often because he has not had sufficient opportunity to practise.

How to support baby to manage emotions

All babies are comforted when the care they receive is consistent, namely that it's familiar and predictable. Your baby will become upset, frustrated, angry or distressed when you suddenly change the way you settle him to sleep. Supporting him to manage these emotions does not mean you must placate his cries by physically soothing him. Support can also include guidance, reassurance and encouragement without soothing.

Responsive settling is about responding in a way that matches your baby's needs. What he needs from you at this age differs from what he needed when younger. He's bigger, stronger and smarter now, and physically capable of self-soothing in safe situations, like going to bed. So, from six months onwards, the purpose of responding to his cries at sleep times gradually shifts from physically helping him calm to supporting and encouraging him to activate self-soothing skills.

True or false?

It's easier to resolve a sleep problem once a child is capable of understanding.

FALSE: No one likes to change conditions already associated with sleeping, no matter how old. A baby or child can't understand why you're doing this. It's by no means easier to resolve a sleeping issue when a child gets older. In fact, it becomes more challenging because the older your child, the longer and more intensely he's likely to protest when you first change your settling practices.

What to expect

Your baby wants you to settle him to sleep in the way that has he has learned to expect. If you don't, he's going to cry, he's not going to suddenly attempt to self-soothe. And if his cries don't get him what he wants, he's going to cry louder. He will not readily accept being calmed in his bed if this is not already familiar to him. You may find that the only way you can appease your baby's cries is to fool him into thinking he's about to be helped to fall asleep in his usual way. For example, if he's accustomed to falling asleep while being breast-fed or cuddled, he'll probably quieten as soon as he's picked up, but this is only because he thinks your next move will be to breastfeed or cuddle him to sleep, as you have done in the past. If you don't offer him your breast or a cuddle, or if you put him back into his bed, he will cry again with as much if not greater intensity than before. And once he catches on that picking him up does not necessarily mean he's going to get what he wants, he will no longer quieten when you pick him up.

Babies over six months can easily continue to protest for an hour or longer before finally falling asleep in a new way for the first time; some will settle sooner. Provided you successfully follow the three Golden Rules when you settle your baby to sleep, he will learn that falling asleep in his bed is not so bad after all, and the time it takes for him to settle to sleep lessens. This will fluctuate, so don't be alarmed if he takes longer to settle for some sleeps than others.

Things don't always steadily progress towards acceptance. With some babies, it may get worse before it gets better. Many parents give up by the second day thinking their baby has become fearful of going into his bed, because he starts to cling to his parent and scream as soon as he is taken into his room or laid in his bed. This is common behaviour for a child this age unaccustomed to falling asleep in his own bed. In psychology terms, a baby's behaviour in this situation is called a 'post extinction response burst' (PERB). An escalation in a baby's behaviour is an expected part of this learning process, an indication that he has already learned what's going to happen when you take him into his room or place him into his bed. But at this point in the process, it's too soon to have learned new sleep associations and willingly accept going into his bed. By day two, your baby is getting fed up with the whole business of you trying to get him to sleep in a place and way that he doesn't want. You're not doing what you would usually do. As his confusion, frustration and anger escalate, so too do his cries and his behaviour. He may cling to you and scream. He's not doing this to manipulate you – babies are not capable of manipulation – he simply wants what's familiar to him, you to settle him to sleep in the way he has learned to expect. If you give in and help him to fall asleep, then nothing changes. If you persist in getting him to fall asleep in the new way, this PERB will pass. And once he gets the chance to learn to associate his bed with sleeping, he will long for bed when he's tired, just like we do.

Not only may your baby's crying appear to escalate, but, in some cases, a baby's sleeping patterns may deteriorate in the early stages of learning new sleep associations. Susan experienced this with her baby, Parker.

Baby Parker

Parker had been breast-fed to sleep since birth. Breastfeeding had become his sleep association. By eight months, he still awoke six or more times a night wanting to be breast-fed back to sleep. Susan explained that she had long ago resorted to co-sleeping, not because she wanted to but it was the only way she could get any sleep. During the day, she was forced to cuddle him the entire time he slept or he would awaken either as soon as she put him down or within 40 minutes.

The months of broken sleep and days spent holding Parker had taken its toll on Susan's physical and emotional health, as well as her relationship with her partner, David. She decided to use responsive settling to support Parker to learn to sleep independently in his bed. I warned Susan to expect things to get worse before they got better. Susan would have to sacrifice even more of her precious sleep for the first few nights in order to get up and respond to Parker, who would very likely wake multiple times due to the absence of his familiar sleep associations. After feeding him to rule out hunger, she would no longer breastfeed him to sleep. During the day, Parker might wake after only one 40-minute average sleep cycle because he was sleeping in his bed rather than her arms. But this perceived deterioration in Parker's sleep patterns would only be temporary, I assured her, if Susan persisted.

It took three days and nights but, once Parker learned to associate his bed with sleeping, he began to settle to sleep quickly and nap between one and two hours, twice a day, in his bed. By the fourth night, Parker slept through the night without disturbing his parents' sleep. Susan later said that, had she not been prepared for things to get worse before they got better, she would have likely given up when Parker became more wakeful, thinking that sleep training was not working.

An escalation in a baby's crying and a deterioration in sleeping patterns is not restricted to babies in this age group; it can occur at any age during the learning phase. However, an escalation in crying is generally more noticeable with babies over the age of three months owing to their ability to express anger when they don't get what they want. This type of behaviour is not exclusive to one step methods, but occurs in varying degrees with all sleep training methods.

I like to prepare parents for worst-case scenarios so they are not caught unawares. But many times things run far more smoothly than they did for Susan. Every so often I am pleasantly surprised when a baby emits only a brief protest before sticking his fingers in his mouth or rolling over and peacefully drifting off to sleep in his bed. That is the other end of the spectrum. Expect resistance, and lots of it, and you may be pleasantly surprised that it's not as hard as you anticipate.

What to do when baby calms

If your baby is already familiar with being soothed in his bed, you can continue doing so, but not to the point where he becomes drowsy or falls asleep. Expect that he will cry just as intensely once you stop. Leave him for a period of time to give him the chance to initiate and practise his self-soothing skills before returning to soothe him.

Pick up/put down method

Some people recommend that parents repeatedly pick their baby up to soothe him and then put him back to bed once he's calm. While it's fine to pick your baby up if you feel you need to, I don't recommend this strategy as soothing method for babies over the age of six months because of the message it sends. The message this method may inadvertently send is 'I am about to give you what you want', followed by 'No I won't' when you put him back to bed. Imagine how frustrating that would be from your baby's perspective to repeat this over and over.

As a parent, you will understandably feel better if you have been able to calm your baby, even briefly, as this may lessen your anxiety, slightly. However, if the only reason your baby calms is because he's been tricked into thinking you're about to give him what he wants, it's probably not helpful from his perspective. He will cry just as intensely if not more when you return him to his bed. Ask yourself: are you soothing him? ... or teasing him?

What if baby doesn't calm?

Bear in mind that a normal, healthy baby over the age of six months is physically capable of self-soothing in non-threatening situations where all of his comfort and nutritional needs have been attended to, and provided his body movements are not restricted in some way, preventing him from moving or self-soothing by sucking on his hands or fingers. This means that, if your baby does not readily calm when in his bed when you pat or rock him, you have two choices:

1. continue trying to calm him in his bed despite his protests or
2. stop trying.

If you continue for long enough, he will eventually calm, but it may take 30 minutes or more if he's not yet used to being calmed in his bed, because it's not what he wants. Once he finally responds to being soothed while he's in his bed he might then expect you to continue until he falls asleep. If he does, then expect that he'll likely cry just as intensely once you stop to allow him to fall asleep independently.

Some parents choose not to continue calming their baby because it's not working or because they feel it's not helpful. Others say they don't feel right if they don't keep trying to calm their baby. The choice is yours. Either way will work provided you achieve the three Golden Rules as he falls asleep. If you decide not to continue trying to physically soothe baby, at least return to him regularly.

Reasons to return

If you find your baby does not calm when you return, or he cries more intensely when you do, you might start to question whether doing so is a good idea. It is. While your baby might not need your help to calm, your guidance and support will help him cope with this new and confusing situation. You can provide guidance and support in the following ways.

- **Check his safety and comfort:** Babies of this age are mobile and they can get stuck in positions they're unable to alter and need help to reposition. Some babies vomit if they get upset with a tummy full of milk. Your baby might need his nappy, clothing or sheets changed.
- **Reassure him by your presence:** Separation anxiety begins around seven months of age and peaks at 12 to 18 months. So your baby needs to know you're around. Babies of this age will observe their parent's behaviour to decide if a new situation is threatening or not. So if you're anxious, teary, clinging and emotional, he probably will be, too. In a calm, relaxed voice, reassure him that, 'It's okay' and tell him it's time for sleep before leaving the room or sitting in a chair in his room.
- **Tell him and show him what to do:** Your baby will feel confused when you suddenly change your settling practices. Initially, he won't know what he needs to do in order to fall asleep without

your help. You can help him through your words and actions to learn what to do. First tell him and then follow this up with matching actions. For example, if he's sitting or standing, tell him, 'Lie down.' If he doesn't lie down, and he probably won't to start with, then lay him down while repeating your words, linking your actions to the words. He will probably get up again as soon as he can. Lay him down only once and leave. Next time you return, repeat the same. With responsive settling it's your role to guide your baby, not to dominate by holding him down or engage in a battle of wills by repeatedly laying him down the moment he gets up. Before you leave remind him 'It's time for sleep.'

Remember, this is all new to your baby. Be consistent, persistent and patient as you support and guide him. In this way, he will learn that it is okay to fall asleep in his bed on his own.

What if baby takes a long time to fall asleep?

If your baby has not settled to sleep in one hour, it's time for a comfort break. Check his nappy and offer a drink or food if appropriate. Observe his behaviour for signs of tiredness. (You might have misinterpreted his behavioural cues as tiredness earlier). Once you recognise his tired signs, return him to his bed and encourage him to self-settle.

Settling tip: Avoid taking your baby for outings during the learning phase if you suspect he might fall asleep in his stroller or car seat. The goal is to learn to fall asleep in his bed. It may confuse him if he's allowed to fall asleep in different places during the learning phase. If it's not possible to avoid outings or the possibility that your baby might fall asleep elsewhere during the learning phase, this doesn't necessarily mean it's going to be impossible to change his sleep associations. What it might mean is that you're inadvertently using gradual extinction. Gradual extinction can still work, but it takes longer and has a higher failure rate compared to extinction and modified extinction.

(See pages 85–86 for more on extinction.) After the learning phase, it probably won't matter if he occasionally falls asleep in his stroller or car during outings, provided most of his sleeps are in his bed.

What to do at night

Normal, healthy, thriving babies over the age of six months no longer require night-time feeds. This does not extend to babies born preterm or who struggle to gain sufficient weight; they may still require night-time feeds. If a healthy baby continues to demand night-time feeds beyond this age, it's usually as a result of a feeding-sleep association; or he may have developed a dysrhythmic day-night feeding pattern where, because he feeds during the night, his appetite the next day is reduced, which will perpetuate until corrected. See pages 255–259 for more strategies on how to manage a dysrhythmic day-night feeding pattern.

If you choose to continue to feed your baby at night beyond the age of six months, this will cause him no harm. It just means he probably won't need to eat as much the next day. It's possible to continue night-time feeds and still successfully minimise excessive night-time wakefulness due to negative sleep associations, but you must withhold *all* negative sleep associations, including letting him fall asleep while feeding.

If your baby is no longer feeding during the night, and wakes, which is likely during the sleep training learning phase, check his comfort needs and that he's not overheated or chilled. Keep the lights low and avoid stimulating him through conversation when you attend to him. Once you're sure he's comfortable, encourage him to self-settle in his bed using the same strategies as you use during the day.

What to keep in mind

Beginning at about seven months, babies can experience separation anxiety, one reason I believe leaving a baby to cry it out is ill-advised. However, don't automatically assume the reason for your baby's cries is due to separation anxiety. Observe how he responds to brief separations during the day to identify any separation anxiety issues. If he's not upset when his main caregiver, typically his mother, leaves the room during the day, he's probably not experiencing separation anxiety at night either. If you're concerned that your baby could be experiencing separation anxiety, you can successfully resolve his sleeping problems while remaining in the room with him, or return frequently. For more details on separation anxiety see pages 22–24.

Staying versus leaving

It's possible to achieve the three Golden Rules and resolve a baby's sleep problems while staying within his line of sight as he's settles to sleep. If you think your presence will help, then by all means stay with your baby, but assess how he responds. Some babies are reassured by a parent's presence and will settle to sleep sooner. Others can become distracted or stimulated by a parent's presence and take longer to settle to sleep. Others may become even more frustrated or angry when their parent is present but not helping them to fall asleep. You may also have no choice but to leave the room while your baby settles if you have older children to supervise.

If you decide to stay with your baby while he settles to sleep, apart from the times where you're checking on his comfort, and telling him what he needs to do, sit in a chair in his room and be as boring as possible. Avoid eye contact and talking to him other than periodically telling him it's time to lie down and go to sleep. Try to avoid repeatedly telling him what to do. It won't make him fall asleep any sooner.

How to measure success

> If my baby's crying is expected to get worse before it gets better, how will I know if I am doing it right? – Barbara

This is a good point. But it's not only your baby's crying that might escalate before subsiding. In some cases, the baby's sleep patterns may appear to deteriorate before they improve. Your baby might have shorter naps and become even more wakeful during the night when you first make changes. Such behaviour can be exhibited irrespective of your baby's age. This is a completely normal response to changes in settling practices yet seldom expected by parents and mistakenly interpreted as the problem worsening. So how can you tell that you're doing things right? By identifying that the three Golden Rules have been achieved when your baby falls asleep. By doing so, you're supporting him to regain the ability to self-regulate his sleeping patterns. Each time you settle your baby to sleep, ask yourself the following questions:

1. Did I place my baby into his bed while his eyes were open?
2. Did I withhold any unreliable props? Anything that can change after he falls asleep?
3. Did I allow my baby to go from a quiet state to asleep unaided?

If you answer 'yes' to all these questions, you're on track. It simply requires repetition to learn new sleep associations. Don't give up just because there's no dramatic improvement in the first few days. Watch for subtle signs of progress during the learning phase, like your baby responding to being calmed in his bed or settling to sleep a little sooner. It will take at least three to five days to spot any significant improvement in his sleeping patterns. If you observe improvement before that time, consider it a bonus. Stay confident. Follow the Golden Rules. Be consistent and persistent.

If, after 72 hours, you observe not a single sign of improvement in your baby's sleeping patterns or behaviour, then it's time to consider other possibilities.

1. Check that you and all caregivers have adhered to the three Golden Rules each time your baby needed to sleep. If there have been inconsistencies, then you cannot expect his sleeping patterns and behaviour to change in a positive way.
2. If the Golden rules have been followed consistently, then there may be another reason for his sleeping problem that has not yet been addressed. Revisit Chapter 1 to identify any physical problems, and read Chapters 13, 14 and 15 which cover circadian rhythm sleeping and feeding problems.
3. Are you being realistic in what you're expecting your baby to achieve? Talk to your healthcare provider and parents of babies of a similar age to yours. Bear in mind that just because your friend's baby is able to achieve something at a certain age, it doesn't mean yours is yet ready.

What if responsive settling is too difficult?

Unfortunately, you don't win points just for trying. By not following the Golden Rules consistently, your baby might not get the chance to learn new sleep associations to enable him to self-regulate his sleeping patterns. If you don't adhere to the Golden Rules each time he falls asleep, then the estimated learning phase of three to five days does not apply.

While it's not always possible to be 100 per cent consistent, and you may still see improvements without it, by means of gradual extinction, if the scales are tipped too far towards inconsistency all that happens is that your baby becomes even more confused and frustrated. He doesn't get to learn new sleep associations and his sleep problem continues.

If, for some reason, you can't follow the three Golden Rules consistently, then don't persist, as you may make the situation worse. If you attempt to encourage your baby to self-settle but then give up and help him to fall asleep in his usual way after a period of crying, you may be teaching him to cry longer. In this situation, it would be kinder to help your baby fall asleep in the first place rather than yo-yo, upsetting him by withholding his familiar sleep associations only to give them back after a long crying session.

If it's too difficult to wait until you can be consistent, get someone to help you or consider using a multi-step approach such as my gentle settling plan or hands-on settling II.

Choosing the right method

One step sleep training methods are the final frontier as far as changing a baby's sleep associations go. In my experience, parents generally choose a one step method only after all other means have been exhausted. No parent enjoys doing something that will upset their baby, not even when it's temporary. But many are prepared to use a one step approach if they believe the long-term benefits outweigh a few days of upset.

Unfortunately, there's no magic cure to an infant sleep problem that develops from negative sleep associations, but, once learned, your baby's sleep associations can be changed gradually using a multi-step approach or quickly by a one step approach. Only you can weigh the benefits of minimising your baby's upset with gradual changes to your settling practices against those to be gained by resolving the problem as quickly as possible. In some cases, it's simply not possible to change a baby's sleep associations and avoid crying at the same time. Or you might not be in a position to change your baby's sleep associations gradually, perhaps because of your responsibilities to care for other children or because you're working.

Key points

- No matter how often you respond to your baby's cries, provided you achieve the three Golden Rules at the time he falls asleep, you can successfully resolve a negative sleep association-related problem.

- The older your baby, the more difficult it is to soothe him without tricking him into thinking he's about to get what he wants.

- Supporting your baby to manage his emotions doesn't mean you must stop him from crying. It might involve reassurance or support and encouragement to activate his self-soothing skills.

- Bedtime is an ideal time to allow your baby opportunities to practise his self-soothing skills.

- If you have not witnessed an improvement using a one step sleep training method after 72 hours, stop and reassess to see what else might be the problem.

12

Tried it – didn't work

Topics

Why sleep training might appear to fail.
What you can do to improve your chances of success.

Not everyone who attempts sleep training with their baby will succeed. Parenting books that oppose sleep training share many a horror story of failed attempts. Most parents I meet regarding an infant sleep problem have at some stage attempted sleep training, or so they thought, without achieving the results they hoped for. There are reasons for the lack of success.

Sleep training is not a fail-safe way to fix every sleep problem. It involves the use of behavioural learning techniques directed towards changing a baby's or child's sleep associations. The most common reason sleep training methods appear to fail is that parents give up before giving it sufficient chance to work. Parents also often use strategies based on flawed advice, thereby doomed to fail before even starting.

Even if you have yet to attempt sleep training, reading about the potential pitfalls may save you both time and anguish.

Common reasons for lack of success

Sleep training might appear to fail for many reasons:

- parental anxiety
- unrealistic expectations
- insufficient advice
- flawed strategies
- gradual extinction methods

- inconsistency
- inappropriate use of sleep training.

Parental anxiety

Parents who have a previous history of, or suffer from anxiety as a result of caring for a constantly crying baby for months on end, and parents who suffer from depression may find sleep training especially difficult. Some parents are emotionally unable to undertake sleep training because it can intensify feelings of anxiety. Anxiety will make us hypersensitive to infant crying. The combination of the baby's crying due to changes in settling practices and uncertainty about what to expect can escalate anxiety to an unbearable level. To defuse our anxiety, we revert to the old ways, even though we might know we are reinforcing baby's behaviour and hence her sleep problem by doing so. Anxiety can make us feel like we're powerless to change the situation.

If you're currently suffering as a result of anxiety or depression you might find a multi-step method like gentle settling or hands-on settling II better, as they involve a series of changes potentially less upsetting to your baby and therefore less stressful for you. Doing so, however, will take longer to resolve your baby's sleep issues. Perhaps you might allow another trusted person to use a one step settling method like responsive settling with your baby for faster results. I have worked with a number of fathers and grandmothers who have undertaken baby's sleep training during the learning phase and then handed over responsibility to the baby's mother once there's minimal resistance from the baby, who has now learned to fall asleep in the new way.

Baby Daniela

Daniela, aged five months, was accustomed to falling asleep while held upright in her mother's arms and sucking on a pacifier. Milly decided to encourage Daniela to learn to self-settle using a responsive settling method. However, a week after she started, Milly contacted me, frustrated at the lack of improvement in Daniela's sleeping patterns and settling behaviour. When I questioned if she had followed the Golden Rules, she confessed

---

that, although she tried hard, she had not been successful. Once she stopping giving Daniela her pacifier, the only way she could calm her was to pick her up for a cuddle. Daniela would calm almost instantly, but would cry again as soon as she was returned to her cot. Her cries sounded so desperate that Milly picked her up constantly. Although she tried to put Daniela back into her cot while her eyes were open, after numerous attempts, Daniela would fall asleep in Milly's arms, exhausted. By this stage, Milly felt so exhausted that, not wanting to wake Daniela, she would place her into her cot asleep.

Despite her efforts, Milly had not managed to make all the changes in settling practices that she had planned. She had succeeded in encouraging Daniela to fall sleep without her pacifier, but Daniela was still falling asleep in Milly's arms, and still waking every 30 minutes or sooner. Milly asked if reflux could be causing Daniela's tears. I shook my head. The fact that Daniela would calm so quickly when she was picked up indicated that she was not in any pain. Daniela had learned to sleep without a pacifier but she cried because she wanted to sleep in Milly's arms as this is where she had always slept. In Daniela's situation, picking her up was not helpful. It calmed her because she believed, rightly so in this case, that she was going to be cuddled to sleep. Milly needed to persist in comforting Daniela longer while she was in her cot. Daniela would eventually quieten in response to a calming method. If she did not calm within five minutes, Milly could either continue to calm her or leave her for a short time, return and try again. If, for her own sake, Milly wanted to pick Daniela up to reassure herself that she was fine, she could do so at any point. However, it was imperative that she return Daniela to her cot as soon as she was quiet if she wanted her to learn to sleep well in her cot. Once Milly followed the Golden Rules consistently, it took only three days for Daniela to learn to self-settle in her cot. The quality of her sleep improved and irritability due to sleep deprivation resolved.

Unrealistic expectations

'I tried controlled crying and it didn't work!' exclaimed Melanie.

'What exactly did you do?' I asked, knowing that people often have different interpretations of what controlled crying and other settling methods involve. 'I put Halley in her cot awake. She cried. I went back to calm her down after two minutes, then four minutes, and then six minutes. She would calm as soon as I stepped into her room, but screamed as soon as I left. I knew it was not going to work, so I picked her up and rocked her to sleep.'

I meet many parents like Melanie who attempt sleep training but give up before the process has a chance to work. Usually it's because they don't expect their baby to protest as vigorously or for as long as she does. So, after a brief attempt, they think, 'This is never going to work,' and return to the old ways. Melanie gave up after 12 minutes. Some parents last longer than this before giving up, others less. I met one mother who claimed sleep training didn't work after she'd tried it for two minutes.

Let's be practical. We're talking about changing habits, something that is not learned in a matter of minutes and therefore not unlearned in a few minutes. Imagine how long it would take you to learn to fall asleep without a pillow or in a sleeping position different to what you now enjoy. It would probably take you weeks. Babies are quick learners, but don't expect that when you've been helping your baby to fall asleep her entire life that she will fall asleep on her own in a matter of minutes, or that her sleep issues will be resolved after she manages to fall asleep on her own once or twice. She needs to psychologically associate the new conditions with sleeping before her sleeping patterns and behaviour will change. This requires consistent repetition. It could take days, weeks or months, depending on whether you chose to use a one step or multi-step approach to changing her sleep associations, for her to be able to self-settle and as a result self-regulate her sleeping patterns. You will need to be patient.

Janelle's baby, Jemma, became even more wakeful once she changed from cuddling her to sleep to settling her in her bed. Janelle gave up on sleep training as a result. Janelle had not been informed that this is to be expected during the learning phase and she mistakenly thought that sleep training had made the situation worse instead of better. So, she reverted to cuddling Jemma to sleep in her arms.

Even when change occurs, sleep training requires maintenance. Chris claimed sleep training didn't last with her 11-month-old daughter, Winona. Chris had shared her bed with Winona and breast-fed her to sleep since birth, not because she had planned or wanted to, but because she didn't want Winona's crying to wake her older son or husband. Chris had tried multiple times to change this situation. Eventually Chris's mother stepped in and stayed with the family to help resolve Winona sleep issues. Grandma encouraged her to fall asleep in a cot. Winona complained about going into her cot initially but after three days and nights she was going down easily, napped well during the day and slept through the night. The next day Grandma returned to her home. That night Chris settled Winona to sleep in her cot. But, when Winona woke during the night and had not settled back to sleep after 15 minutes, Chris made the mistake of taking her into her bed. (This was only a mistake because it was a practice that Chris claimed she wanted to stop.) She cuddled her to sleep instead of breastfeeding her. By the second night, she was back to breastfeeding her during the night. Chris claimed sleep training didn't last, but it wasn't that sleep training that didn't last; it was because Chris didn't last. She didn't maintain what her mother had started. Had she persisted, Winona would have accepted the new way of sleeping that Grandma had encouraged her to learn in just three nights.

If you return the negative sleep associations that previously caused your baby's disrupted sleep, she will become wakeful once again. Your actions either encourage or discourage your baby's dependence on certain sleep associations.

Flawed strategies

Changing your infant settling practices does not necessarily mean you will resolve your baby's sleep problems. Without an effective plan, you could change your baby's sleep associations and yet make no difference to her sleeping patterns or behaviour.

Many parents have attempted what they thought was sleep training, making multiple changes to their infant settling practices, but all they managed was to switch their baby's dependence from one negative sleep association to another. Baxter's story is a good example.

Baby Baxter

Baxter's mother, Anne, had from an early age encouraged him to fall asleep in his cot on his own, while relying on a pacifier. This worked well as a newborn, but later it became problematic. By four months of age Baxter was waking Anne and her husband five to seven times a night, because his pacifier had fallen out and he wanted it back in order to return to sleep. After two months of this, Anne was exhausted. The pacifier had to go, she decided. Without it, the first time, Baxter cried intensely. To help him adjust, Anne decided to pat him to sleep. Within a few days Baxter adjusted to sleeping without a pacifier, but he awoke just as many times each night, now he cried to be patted back to sleep. Anne had inadvertently made the situation worse. Before, she could return Baxter's pacifier and go back to bed. Now she needed to stand by his cot for 10 minutes or longer patting him until he had fallen asleep. She decided to return to giving him the pacifier as she felt it was easier to get up and replace his pacifier than to stand and pat him. Baxter willingly accepted his pacifier, but now, in addition, he wanted to be patted back to sleep. He had learned to associate patting with falling asleep.

Anne didn't realise that she had simply replaced one negative sleep association with another. Neither would remain consistent throughout Baxter's sleep. Coupled with Baxter's increased level of awareness as he matured and his ability to recognise when his sleep associations were missing meant he would cry and wake his parents frequently during the night. This was not going to change while Anne provided him with negative sleep associations at the time he fell asleep.

The goal of sleep training is to provide the right conditions and opportunities to support your baby to change her sleep associations in a way that will enable her to self-regulate her sleeping patterns. Therefore, sleep training is most effective when each of the three Golden Rules of infant sleep self-regulation is followed: provide a suitable and consistent sleeping environment; withhold any unreliable props at sleep time; and promote independent settling. It's up to you whether you aim to achieve this quickly, using a one step approach, or gradually, using a multi-step approach. If the strategies you're using don't achieve at least one or more of the Golden Rules, you probably won't make any progress resolving your baby's sleeping problem.

Insufficient advice

To increase your chances of success, you need to know what to achieve when using sleep training, within what timeframe you can expect your baby to fall asleep, what to do if she doesn't fall asleep within this time, and when to expect to see a change in her sleeping patterns. Without this, you might not have the confidence to continue for long enough to successfully change your baby's sleep associations.

Most parents quit prematurely when they see no immediate signs of improvement. On the other hand, some parents persist too long with faulty methods. Narelle had no idea what to expect and so she continued to follow flawed sleep training advice for weeks despite no signs of improvement.

Narelle's story

When Layla was eight months old, Narelle wanted to encourage her to sleep through the night. She had been doing sleep training with her a month, and had witnessed a glimmer of improvement when Layla slept through the night for two nights. Prior to sleep training, Narelle had been cuddling Layla to sleep but understandably found it tiring to be woken three or four times during the night to cuddle her back to sleep. Her child health nurse advised her to settle Layla in her cot by patting her for five minutes and then leaving her to cry for five minutes before patting for another five minutes, and so on.

204 I Your Sleepless Baby

'Did the nurse tell you to pat Layla only until she was quiet and avoid patting her to sleep?' I asked. Narelle couldn't remember. Because she hadn't gotten enough information, Narelle patted Layla to sleep during one of these five-minute sessions. Technically, sleep training succeeded because Layla had learned a new way to fall asleep, but, because Narelle had simply replaced one negative sleep association (cuddling) with another (patting), Layla's sleeping patterns improved only briefly. Once Layla learned to associate patting with falling asleep, her sleeping patterns deteriorated again.

Narelle would need to withhold all negative sleep associations when Layla fell asleep. Once Narelle had been provided with comprehensive details on what to do if Layla cried, what to expect and how she would know if she was on track, she succeeded in supporting Layla to learn to self-settle. Within a few days, Layla began sleeping through the night.

Gradual extinction

Some health professionals and authors recommend settling methods based on the principle of gradual extinction because they believe these to be kinder to the baby and easier for parents to manage. Following are examples of the use of gradual extinction:

- You withhold baby's negative sleep associations and encourage her to fall asleep independently when she first falls asleep in the evenings. If she wakes during the night, you help her back to sleep in the usual way. Or
- You settle baby to sleep in her normal way during the day but withhold negative sleep associations during the night, or vice versa.

Gradual extinction is *not* something I recommend because it sends the baby mixed messages, adding to her confusion and frustration. You may think you're being consistent because you do the same thing at certain times, but gradual extinction involves inconsistency. Sometimes you will reinforce your baby's dependence on negative sleep associations by providing these and sometimes you won't. How can your baby understand your willingness to help her to fall asleep sometimes but then not other times? Gradual extinction has a higher failure rate compared to extinction (cry it out) and modified extinction (controlled crying and responsive settling) settling methods because of the inconsistencies in the way baby is settled to sleep. It might work, it might not. Why put your baby through the stress associated with sleep training if you're not resolving her sleep problem? It's far more effective and less confusing to do the same thing every time she goes to sleep.

Another problem is that the learning phase is longer with gradual extinction compared to extinction or modified extinction, due to the inherent inconsistency. And, if your baby is already distressed due to sleep deprivation, prolonging the learning phase might not be kinder to your baby or easier for you, especially if it doesn't work.

Baby Fleur

Dianne tried to encourage Fleur, aged nine months, to sleep through the night without a pacifier. When she woke during the night, Dianne left her to cry it out. After crying for an hour or so she would eventually fall back to sleep, exhausted. After two weeks, Fleur was still crying as much and for as long, and so Dianne assumed the sleep training had failed. The problem, however, was that Dianne was inconsistent in her settling practices. Only Fleur's night-time awakenings bothered Dianne. She would give Fleur a pacifier during day-time naps and in the evening when she settled to sleep, but during the night she left Fleur to cry it out. By giving Fleur a pacifier to fall asleep during the day, Dianne continued to reinforce Fleur's dependence on a pacifier as a way to fall asleep, and that's why the situation didn't improve.

Another gradual extinction technique is to advise you to leave your baby crying for a specified time period, say, 20 minutes or an hour, and if after that time she has not fallen asleep, you help her to do so. If you find you're repeatedly helping her to fall asleep, then this is unlikely to resolve her sleep problem because helping her to fall asleep encourages her dependence on your help to fall asleep. Also, repeatedly allowing your baby to cry before helping her to fall asleep could teach her to cry for longer periods of time. Your actions will send the message 'You need to cry for a long time to get what you want.'

Inconsistency

Mikayla showed no signs of the expected improvement by day four of sleep training. Her mother, Norma, said that Mikayla was taking longer than expected to fall asleep and was still waking after only one sleep cycle. Norma assured me of her consistency in following the Golden Rules each time Mikayla fell asleep. The next day Norma emailed me to tell me she discovered the reason why Mikayla's ability to self-settle had not progressed. Her husband, who had been sharing responsibility for sleep training with her, had been patting Mikayla to sleep, mistakenly believing he was making it easier for her.

Babies cope better when the care they receive is consistent. It's important that every caregiver does the same things when settling your baby to sleep. During the learning phase it may be wise to avoid leaving your baby in the care of others so that you can ensure consistency. Consistency is vital to learning.

Once the learning phase has passed, most babies can tolerate a little inconsistency from time to time, so, if Grandma cuddles your baby to sleep once in a while, it will probably make little difference. Just avoid letting it happen too often.

Inappropriate use of sleep training

Sleep training will only fix infant sleep problems related to negative sleep associations. However, it's important to note that there are other types of infant sleep problems for which sleep training will have little or no effect.

Reasons for infant sleep problems:

- Physical or developmental reasons (described in Chapter 1).
- Behavioural reasons, the most common reason for physically well babies to experience ongoing sleep problems, include missing infant tiredness behavioural cues (see Chapter 3), learned dependence on negative sleep associations (Chapter 5), and circadian rhythm problems (Chapters 13 and 14).

Key points

- Sleep training is not a fool-proof way to resolve infant sleep problems.

- Sleep training will not solve every sleep problem.

- Most parents who claim sleep training failed either did not effectively implement the strategies or used sleep training for an infant sleep problem caused by problems other than negative sleep associations.

- If you don't allow your baby to fall asleep independently, you cannot expect her to learn to sleep independently.

- The greater your understanding of sleep training, the more likely you will use settling strategies successfully.

13
Circadian rhythms

For the past two months Henry has woken at around 1 am every night. He then wants to stay up for two hours before he's ready to go back to sleep. At first I thought he was teething but he's fine during the day and he's happy when I pick him up, so I figure that's not the problem. He wakes at the same time every night. I can almost set my clock by him. It's like he has an alarm clock in his head that keeps waking him. We have tried leaving him to cry but he doesn't go back to sleep any sooner. It's driving me batty. What can we do to get him to stop him waking at that time? – Cathy

Cathy is close to the mark when she says it's like Henry has an alarm clock in his head. He does. Everyone has an internal body clock controlled by their brain. Many of our physical functions follow a 24-hour cycle called our circadian rhythms, which, among other things, influence our ability to fall and stay asleep at certain times of the day or night. Henry's pattern of wakefulness in the middle of the night might point to a circadian rhythm sleep problem. But it's not just a baby's sleep that can get out of kilter with a normal day-night pattern; feeding can be affected also. If your baby wants to eat during the night more often than you would expect, this too could be linked to his circadian rhythms.

Because circadian rhythm sleep problems relate to the timing of a baby's sleeping patterns, they cannot be resolved by sleep training.

What are circadian rhythms?

The word circadian is Latin in origin from the word *circa* meaning 'approximately' and *dian* meaning 'day'. Circadian rhythms are our natural biological rhythms, more commonly known as our internal or 24-hour body clock, because they repeat about every 24 hours.

Circadian rhythms regulate the timing, quantity and quality of hormones produced by your endocrine system, and neurotransmitters, chemicals produced by your brain. These play a crucial role in coordinating physical functions, including:

- hunger cravings
- energy levels
- sleeping patterns
- mood swings
- stress response
- growth stimulation
- immune system activation and
- other bodily processes that maintain homeostasis.

The more stable your circadian rhythms, the more efficiently your body works. The more stable your baby's circadian rhythms, the better he eats and sleeps, the fewer digestive and elimination problems he experiences, and the greater his general level of contentment. Anything that changes the timing of your circadian rhythms has the potential to alter the production of hormones and neurotransmitters, affecting how your body functions, and how you feel. This also applies to your baby.

Infant feeding and sleeping patterns

In the womb, your baby's biological functions are synchronised with his mother's circadian rhythms via the placenta. After birth, his circadian rhythms develop in the early months of life and continue to evolve throughout his entire life. Consequently, your baby's feeding and sleeping patterns will continue to adjust. This is especially obvious during his first

12 months of life, a time when he develops physically at a mind-blowing rate. Your baby's feeding and sleeping patterns will change so often during these first 12 months that it can be a challenge for you to keep pace if you don't know what to expect.

If you know what changes to expect, you will worry less if his changing cycles are normal and spare your baby from any upset were you to attempt to make him stick to a feeding or sleeping pattern that he has outgrown.

Normal, healthy babies tend to follow a similar progression in their feeding and sleep-wake patterns. Over time, as your baby's stomach increases in size and his rate of growth naturally declines, he will demand fewer feeds. He will go for longer stretches between feeds during the day. He will gradually drop feeds during the night and eventually eliminate night-time feeds altogether between the ages six to nine months, maybe earlier. The number of naps required during the day decline as your baby's day-night sleeping pattern evolves. He will start to have bigger blocks of sleep during the night and will be able to comfortably remain awake for progressively longer periods of time during the day.

Table 13.1 depicts the typical pattern for the average baby at different ages. If your baby was born preterm, then you need to make allowances for this.

This is only a guideline. It's important to remember that, if your baby is healthy, thriving and content, then it doesn't matter how many feeds or naps he has; whatever he's getting is fine.

If your baby is not thriving or content, and exhibits feeding and sleeping patterns starkly different to the averages shown in the following table, there may be steps you can take to improve the situation.

Table 13.1:   Average sleeps and feeds, 2 weeks–12 months

Approximate number	2 weeks	3 months	6 months	9 months	12 months
Hours of sleep in 24-hour period	16–18	14–15	14.2	13.9	13.9
Hours of sleep overnight	8–9 with 2 or 3 feeds during the night	10–12 with 1–2 feeds during the night	10–12 with 1 feed during the night	10–12	10–12
Hours of sleep during the day	7–9	3.5–4.5	3–4	2.5–3.5	2–3
Day-time naps	4–5	3–4	3	2	1–2
Hours awake between naps	1–1.5	1–2	1.5–2.5	2–3.5	3–5
Bottle-feeds	6–8	5	4	3	3
Breastfeeds	8–12	5–8	4–6	3–5	3–5
Solid feeds	0	0	1–3	3 main meals plus 1 or 2 snacks	3 main meals plus 2 snacks

How care-giving influences baby's circadian rhythms

In addition to internal factors, like hormones and neurotransmitters that influence circadian rhythms, external sensory cues shape a baby's circadian rhythms into a 24-hour pattern. As your baby's parent or caregiver, you control the external sensory cues, such as light and noise, that enable him to establish and maintain his circadian rhythms in a 24-hour pattern, helping him distinguish between day and night. You also control other sensory stimulation that he receives, as well as the timing and types of activities he's involved in. When you feed your baby and provide him with opportunities to sleep will influence when he wants to eat and sleep. You will support him to stabilise his circadian rhythms by providing care that is consistent with his biological needs, for example, feeding him when he's hungry (not every time he cries or wants to suck). He also needs to be provided with opportunities to sleep in a quiet non-stimulating environment when he's tired, and he needs support to fall asleep by means of his familiar, ideally positive, sleep associations. The care and activities you provide like bathing, talking, playing, taking a walk in his stroller and his bedtime routine all help to establish and maintain his circadian rhythms, especially when repeated at a similar time each day.

How to support baby to stabilise circadian rhythms

Health professionals and parenting educators agree that the most effective way to promote a baby's contentment is to provide care in harmony with his biological needs. However, opinions differ on how parents can best achieve this. The various methods recommended to parents include being guided by:

- your baby's lead
- a cyclical pattern
- a flexible daily routine
- a pre-determined feeding and sleeping schedule.

These methods differ in the amount of guidance baby receives.

less ← Guidance → more			
following your baby's lead	cyclical pattern	flexible routine	feeding and sleeping schedule

As in all aspects of parenting, each method has potential advantages and disadvantages that differ depending on individual circumstances, as shown on the table over the page.

Table 13.2: Options – when to provide baby's cares

	Following baby's lead	Cyclical pattern	Flexible daily routine	Feeding and sleeping schedule
Description	Baby's behavioural cues guide the parent as to what baby needs at any given time.	Activities are performed on a regular cycle, eg, feed – play – sleep, and are repeated throughout the day, following both baby's behavioural cues and timeframes for feeding, awake time and sleeping.	Activities are performed at similar but not necessarily exact times each day, depending on baby's behavioural cues.	Activities are scheduled according to a set plan, consistent and unvarying.
Goals	Support baby to self-regulate his feeding and sleeping patterns.	Support baby to self-regulate his feeding and sleeping patterns. Assist parent to gain accuracy in interpreting baby's behavioural cues.	Support baby to stabilise his circadian rhythms. Assist parent to gain accuracy in interpreting baby's behavioural cues.	Support baby to stabilise his circadian rhythms in a 24-hour pattern. Guide parent on when to provide baby care.

	Following baby's lead	Cyclical pattern	Flexible daily routine	Feeding and sleeping schedule
How it works	Care is provided depending on how parent interprets baby's behavioural cues. Relies on baby's ability to signal needs and parent's ability to accurately interpret baby's behavioural cues.	Does not rely on parent's ability to accurately interpret baby's behavioural cues. Timeframes help parent to determine most likely reason for baby's behavioural cues.	Does not rely parent's ability to accurately interpret baby's behavioural cues. Timeframes help parent to anticipate baby's needs and determine most likely reason for baby's behavioural cues.	Does not rely on baby's ability to signal needs or parent's ability to accurately interpret baby's behavioural cues. Baby care is provided at predetermined times irrespective of baby's behavioural cues.
Advantages	Accurate interpretation of baby's behavioural cues combined with the appropriate response from parent provides care that harmonises with baby's biological needs and supports him to self-regulate his feeding and sleeping patterns.	Timeframes support baby to regulate feeding and sleeping patterns in harmony with biological needs. Flexible to accommodate variations in baby's appetite and energy levels. Parent is able to anticipate baby's needs. Enhances parent's confidence in interpreting baby's behavioural cues.	Timeframes provide consistency and predictability which support baby to stabilise his circadian rhythms. Flexible to accommodate day-to-day variations in baby's appetite and energy levels. Parent is able to anticipate baby's needs. Enhances parent's confidence in interpreting baby's behavioural cues. Parent can plan their day around baby's cares.	Set times guide parent on when to provide care. Provided care matches baby's biological needs and circadian rhythms, he will be relatively content. Parent can plan their day around baby's cares.

	Following baby's lead	Cyclical pattern	Flexible daily routine	Feeding and sleeping schedule
Disadvantages	Stressful for baby and parent if parent misinterprets infant behavioural cues, in which case care will not harmonise with baby's biological needs and could destabilise his circadian rhythms. Overfeeding can occur in the newborn period if behavioural cues are misinterpreted as hunger.	Stressful for baby if parent ignores baby's behavioural cues in an attempt to rigidly adhere to timeframe guidelines.	Stressful for baby if parent ignores baby's behavioural cues in an attempt to rigidly adhere to timeframe guidelines, or if routine does not match baby's biological needs.	No flexibility. Does not allow for day-to-day variations in baby's appetite or energy levels. Stressful for baby if parent ignores baby's behavioural cues while rigidly adhering to predetermined timeframes or if schedule does not match baby's biological needs. Underfeeding and even low breast milk supply can result.

	Following baby's lead	Cyclical pattern	Flexible daily routine	Feeding and sleeping schedule
Parents who may benefit	Experienced parents; parents who feel confident in interpreting their baby's behavioural cues; and parents who prefer to 'go with the flow' when providing baby's care.	Parents who lack confidence in interpreting infant behavioural cues.	Parents who lack confidence in interpreting infant behavioural cues; parents who enjoy some degree of predictability to their day; parents caring for multiple birth babies.	Parents who lack confidence in interpreting infant behavioural cues; parents with intellectual disabilities; parents caring for multiple babies.
Babies who may benefit	Babies who rely on negative sleep associations, in particular, a breast or bottle feeding-sleep association.	Newborns who over- or underfeed. Babies who rely on negative sleep associations other than a feeding-sleep association.	Babies over four months, able to self-regulate their sleeping patterns but lacking support from parents to stabilise their circadian rhythms.	Physically weak or babies with disabilities who are unable to signal their needs, such as babies with neurological impairment and preterm babies until more fully developed.

Each of these methods has advantages and disadvantages. Any method will work if it provides for a baby's biological needs in a way that harmonises with his circadian rhythms.

Why things go astray

Because they depend on others to provide for their needs, and lack the ability to verbally communicate their wants and needs, babies are far more vulnerable to developing circadian rhythm problems than any other age group. Without the necessary external cues from parents or caregivers, a baby cannot instinctively adjust his feeding and sleeping patterns to harmonise with a 24-hour cycle.

It's easier than you might think for a baby's circadian rhythms to become destabilised. If you were to overlook or misinterpret your baby's signs of tiredness and not provide the opportunity to sleep, this will move his sleep time back. If you don't provide his familiar sleep associations, he will resist falling asleep, also moving his sleep time back. If his sleep associations don't remain consistent throughout his entire sleep and he wakes prematurely, then it won't be long before he's tired and ready to sleep again, moving his sleep time forward. Misinterpreting infant hunger cues, overfeeding or underfeeding can affect feeding patterns in much the same way.

Inadvertently allowing a baby to develop a feeding-sleep association may also destabilise his circadian rhythms. As a result he may experience broken sleep, want to feed when he's tired as well as when hungry, overfeed while his suck reflex is active, he may continue to demand feeding at night well beyond the age he needs to do so. As well, extended night-time feeds may then decrease his appetite during the day. You might think you're following your baby's lead, but if the care you provide does not align with his biological needs or circadian rhythms you could end up with an upset little baby, sleep-deprived and with tummy discomfort, who feeds and sleeps erratically.

Often, rather than developing semi-predictable feeding and sleeping patterns in the early weeks of life, many newborns develop erratic feeding and sleeping patterns with marked daily fluctuations in their appetite and energy levels. This is not necessarily problematic. If baby is happy, healthy and thriving, then the unpredictability of his feeding and sleeping patterns may only be problematic for the parent. Many babies who feed and sleep erratically, however, are not content, suffer under the strain of sleep deprivation, gain insufficient or excessive weight, or are diagnosed with digestive disorders. These problems can occur for many different reasons, but wouldn't you want to rule out the possible destabilisation of baby's circadian rhythms first?

A baby's circadian rhythms can also get out of sync with a normal day-night pattern, when he sleeps for long periods during the day and is awake for long periods at night; or he eats very little during the day but then wants to feed excessively during the night, often well beyond an age when night feedings are necessary. These types of circadian rhythm problems don't cause a baby any physical harm, but they can cause a lot of needless stress for parents.

Diagram 13.1: Irregular feeding and sleeping patterns fuelled by parenting mistakes

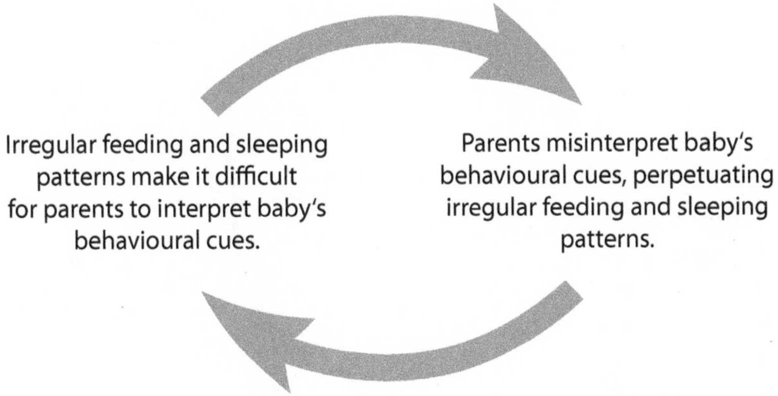

Irregular feeding and sleeping patterns make it difficult for parents to interpret baby's behavioural cues.

Parents misinterpret baby's behavioural cues, perpetuating irregular feeding and sleeping patterns.

Many parents who experience infant feeding or sleeping problems lose confidence in their ability to accurately interpret their baby's behavioural cues and seek a routine or schedule to use as a guide. Provided the care given matches their baby's biological needs, a routine or schedule could prove beneficial. However, attempting to follow a routine or schedule that does not match baby's needs has the potential to destabilise his circadian rhythms.

Simplistic advice to follow a baby's lead or to provide care at specified times, is not an effective replacement for education about babies' changing developmental needs.

Physical and emotional effects

A happy baby is one who receives care in harmony with his biological needs, which has a stabilising effect on circadian rhythms. What is not fully understood are the physical effects that any destabilisation can have on a baby. The only gauge we have is how it affects adults.

If you have ever been a shift worker or experienced jet lag, you know what it feels like when your circadian rhythms are out of sync. Jet lag, medically referred to as desynchronosis, is a physiological condition that results from alterations to the body's circadian rhythms when travelling across time zones. Symptoms of jet lag can include:

- headaches
- fatigue
- irregular sleep patterns and insomnia
- disorientation
- grogginess
- irritability
- mild depression
- nausea
- constipation or diarrhoea.

The combined effect of circadian de-synchronisation and lack of sleep can depress our *immune systems, making us pr*one to more colds, flu and other health problems.[101] Gastrointestinal and digestive problems such as indigestion, heartburn, stomach ache and loss of appetite are common problems experienced by shift workers, as are overeating and obesity.[102]

When our circadian rhythms are out of sync with a normal day-night pattern, our body is not functioning at optimal capacity and life is not as pleasurable as it could be. Although we don't know how instability of babies' circadian rhythms affects them, it is reasonable to assume that the effects are not pleasant ones.

Guiding baby towards contentment

Parents generally seek help when what they're doing is not working. In many cases, baby is irritable and feeding and sleeping either erratically or at unusual times of the day and night, or he's suffering from tummy troubles or displays poor growth. I find many parents unsuccessfully attempt to correct this situation by following rigid feeding and sleeping schedules. This is because they're putting the cart before the horse. In order for a baby to follow an age-appropriate routine, he needs to first be supported to self-regulate his sleeping patterns and dietary intake.

The first most effective way you can help your baby stabilise his circadian rhythms is to change your infant settling practices in a way that will support him to self-regulate his sleeping patterns, by following the three Golden Rules (see page 112). Most (but not all) babies will naturally fall into a semi-predictable sleeping pattern within a matter of weeks once they're supported to self-regulate their sleeping patterns. Sleeping patterns influence feeding patterns. Once a baby's sleeping patterns stabilise, so too does his feeding. It then becomes easier to follow baby's lead. But this depends upon the individual baby's ability to give clear signals and on the parent's ability to accurately decipher the meaning of baby's behavioural cues. This is where a cyclical pattern or daily routine comes in. It can help parents to gain confidence in accurately interpreting their baby's behavioural cues. If a routine is something you think might be helpful, start by taking a middle-ground approach, such as a cyclical pattern or flexible daily routine, whichever is more appropriate for your baby's age and circumstances, rather than adopting a schedule with predetermined times for feeding and sleeping. A cyclical pattern or flexible daily routine can help to stabilise your baby's circadian rhythms while offering enough flexibility to accommodate subtle, day-to-day, normal variations in his appetite and energy levels and assist you to anticipate his needs and gain more confidence in reading his cues. As your confidence builds, you will figure out just how flexible or structured you need to be while providing your baby's cares in order to promote his contentment.

The type of routine I recommend varies depending on a baby's age and ability to self-regulate his feeding and sleeping patterns.

Table 13.3:   Recommended routines

Age and ability to self-regulate	Cyclical pattern	Age-appropriate daily routine
Two weeks to four months.	yes	no
Babies over four months who can fall asleep independently.	yes	yes
Babies who rely on negative sleep associations.	yes	no
Babies who rely on feeding as a way to fall asleep.	no	no

Chapters 16 and 17 provide more details on cyclical patterns and flexible daily routines. However, you may need to use other strategies to fix existing circadian rhythm sleeping or feeding problems before your baby is ready for a routine. The various sleeping and feeding problems related to circadian rhythms are discussed in Chapters 14 and 15.

Key points

- Babies feel and cope better when they receive support to maintain their circadian rhythms in harmony with their biological needs.

- Babies differ in the amount of support they require from parents to maintain their circadian rhythms.

- Dependence on others to provide the necessary external cues makes a baby vulnerable to circadian rhythm problems.

- Too little support, which occurs when a baby's behavioural cues are misinterpreted, can be just as problematic as exerting too much control over when a baby eats and sleeps.

14
Circadian rhythm sleep problems

My 7-month-old baby girl, Grace, thinks a good time for bed is 11 pm. The problem is I have a toddler who gets up at the crack of dawn. Needless to say I'm exhausted. I need Grace to go to bed earlier but no matter what I do I can't get her to go to sleep at a reasonable time. How do I make a child go to sleep when she doesn't want to? – Kerry

You can't make a child sleep if she's not tired. However, there are ways you can influence her day-night sleeping pattern to encourage her to become tired earlier and ready for a good night's sleep.

What Kerry describes sounds like a circadian rhythm sleep problem. Such problems can present in a number of different ways. The good news is this type of infant sleep problem is usually easy to correct once you know how.

What's normal?

We all know that babies wake during the night. But how many times is normal? How long is a baby expected to be awake for? When is a baby expected to sleep through the night, or more accurately, return to sleep independently following normal arousals between sleep cycles?

A normal healthy baby's sleeping patterns will change multiple times as she matures. To distinguish a circadian rhythm sleep problem, which can be resolved, from a normal sleeping pattern based upon a baby's stage of development, which cannot be changed, you need to be aware of the normal sleeping patterns at each stage of development. The following applies to healthy full-term babies.

Birth to one month

The average amount of sleep in a 24-hour period required by a newborn baby is 16 to 18 hours. This generally drops to 14–16 hours by around four weeks. A baby's nervous, digestive and endocrine systems are immature during the first few weeks of life, so feeding, sleeping and waking times will be irregular day and night, with as many as seven to eight sleep periods, ranging from 20 minutes to three hours, every 24 hours, and awake periods ranging from only a few moments to an hour or so.

Newborn babies typically exhibit at least one wakeful period during the night, often involving some fussiness, mainly because baby wants to be held at a time when you want to be sleeping. As a baby's circadian rhythms develop, she begins to stay awake more during the day and less at night, and the period of fussiness typically moves to the evening instead.

> **Tip**: Swaddling your newborn baby for sleep can help to provide her with the sense of containment that she experienced in the womb.

One to three months

By four to six weeks of age, a baby's feeding and sleep-wake patterns tend to become more predictable. Her wakeful periods during the night continue to shorten and lengthen during the day. By six weeks or earlier, her circadian rhythms will develop to where she can differentiate between day and night. When this happens, her night-time awakenings are generally only long enough to feed.

Most babies cannot yet sleep for five hours or longer without feeding until between six and 10 weeks of age. As a baby's endocrine system matures, it releases hormones, such as melatonin, a sleep-inducing hormone, and leptin, an appetite-suppressing hormone, at night, enabling her to sleep for longer periods without feeding, as long as she receives sufficient food during the day.

> A newborn baby can become so physically exhausted from lack of sleep during the day that she sleeps through the night without feeding at an earlier age. However, if she misses out on night-time feeds due to exhaustion this could negatively impact on her growth.

Three to six months

By three to four months of age, a baby's nervous, endocrine and digestive systems have matured sufficiently to stabilise her circadian rhythms in a 24-hour pattern, enabling her to wake each morning, nap during the day, and be ready for bed at night at similar times each day.

The average sleep for a baby of this age is around 15 hours in any 24- hour period. The largest portion of a baby's sleep should happen during the night. Most babies will sleep between 10 to 12 hours at night. A well-nourished baby at this stage may be down to one feed per night, but more than that is fine. By now, she may have one long stretch, between six and nine hours, of uninterrupted sleep during the night, and nap on average three times during the day, from 30 minutes to two and a half hours.

Over six months

By six months of age, a healthy, thriving baby averages a total of 14.2 hours sleep, and her circadian rhythms have developed to where she can sleep for 10–12 hours during the night without feeding. She will have two or three day-time naps ranging from 40 minutes to two hours each.

Table 14.1:   Examples of children's sleeping patterns

Age	Day-time sleep 7 am–7 pm	Night-time sleep 7 pm–7 am
Birth–2 weeks		
2–6 weeks		
6–12 weeks		
3–6 months		
6–9 months		
9 to 12–18 months		
12–18 to 3.5–5 years		
3.5–5 years and up		

Between six and nine months, most babies will drop to two naps per day. Between 12 and 18 months, most toddlers only need one nap. The pattern of one nap per day continues until three to five years, when the child no longer requires a regular day-time nap.

This graph is provided solely to demonstrate how children's sleep patterns change as they mature. If your baby's feeding and sleeping patterns don't bother her or you, then whether her pattern is typical is irrelevant. However, if you or your baby is unhappy and her sleeping pattern is quite different to that described or shown, there may be steps you can take to improve the situation, starting with assessing her sleep associations. Her associations will have a profound effect on her sleeping patterns, which in turn influence her feeding patterns and circadian rhythm development.

What can begin as one sleep problem owing to negative sleep associations can progress into a circadian rhythm sleep problem and/or an infant feeding problem. Once a circadian rhythm sleep problem has developed, sleep training to change your baby's sleep associations may not be enough to resolve all your baby's sleep issues. It depends on the type of circadian rhythm sleep problem.

Sleep problems and circadian rhythms

There are five types of circadian rhythm sleep problems that commonly affect babies:

- **Day-night sleep dysrhythmia:** baby is awake for hours in the middle of the night.
- **Erratic sleep-wake patterns:** baby's sleeping pattern is markedly different every day.
- **Late-sleep phase sleeping pattern:** baby refuses to fall asleep until very late at night and sleeps until late in the morning.
- **Early-sleep phase sleeping pattern:** baby is down for the night by mid-afternoon, waking ready to start her day in the wee hours of the morning.
- **Seasonal sleep problems:** baby wakes too early or settles too late during the summer months.

Day-night sleep dysrhythmia

A newborn baby's inner body clock is not in sync with a 24-hour cycle, and won't be for weeks, because her endocrine system is not yet mature. Also, because she's not long out of the womb, she may not yet have had sufficient exposure to the external sensory cues that support her to stabilise her circadian rhythms into a day-night pattern. Thus, it's typical for newborn babies to have wakeful periods during the night for the first few weeks. Parents are often told there's little or nothing they can do but wait until their newborn outgrows the problem. But what is often overlooked is the impact that external cues have on the development of a baby's circadian rhythms. There are often things a parent can do to help their newborn begin to establish a day-night sleeping pattern.

Teaching baby the difference between day and night

You play a key role in how your baby learns to differentiate between night and day. By using some of the suggestions below, you may see a difference in as little as few days.

During the day

- Keep the room bright, with shades or curtains open to encourage more awake time during the day, but reduce lighting at times you want baby to sleep.
- Don't limit normal household noises, ie, vacuum, dishwasher or telephone, except when encouraging her to sleep.
- Wake her if she is still asleep at feeding time.
- Stimulate her by talking to her and using direct eye contact.
- When she's awake and alert, play with her, watching closely for and stopping when behavioural cues indicate she's getting tired. Too much sensory stimulation can distress newborns.

During the night

- Dim the lights.

- Don't chat to her too much, and use a quiet, soothing voice when you do.
- Turn off the TV when feeding at night.
- Move slowly.
- Avoid too much eye contact.
- Resist playing with her when she wakes for a feed.
- Be as boring as possible.

Although at six weeks of age, a normal healthy baby's endocrine system has often matured sufficiently to promote longer sleep periods during the night, this does not mean she's going to sleep through the night at this stage. Most babies require night-time feeds during the first six months of life. But it does mean that she's likely to want to return to sleep as soon as she's finished feeding.

If, after six weeks, your baby starts or continues to be wakeful for long periods during the night beyond feeding, this could be because she has not received the external cues she needs to enable her internal clock to track a normal day-night pattern.

Baby Samuel

By the age of four months, Samuel suffered from sleep deprivation owing to having learned to rely on his mother, Gabrielle, to cuddle him to sleep. Gabrielle resolved this problem by encouraging Samuel to settle to sleep independently. Catching up on much-needed sleep, Samuel was much happier. He would only whine when he became tired, and, once placed into his cot, would fall asleep without a fuss. He napped three times during the day. By 6 pm he was tired and slept, waking at 11 pm when Gabrielle would breastfeed him, then return him to his cot where he would almost immediately fall asleep again. Gabrielle was delighted. However, when Samuel reached five months, he started to protest profusely when returned to his cot after his 11 pm breastfeed. Over several weeks, he remained awake longer and longer during the night, eventually staying awake from 11 pm until 2 or 3 am. Gabrielle tried many things to get him to go back to sleep sooner. She tried rocking Samuel's cot, patting him, singing to him, and offering infant formula and solids, which Samuel refused. One night she took Samuel for a drive. He enjoyed the ride but did not fall asleep. She tried taking Samuel into bed with her, which Samuel thought was fun but he stayed awake, wanting to play. In desperation, one night she left Samuel in his cot to cry it out. He cried for over two hours but did not fall asleep any sooner than the previous night. Nothing she tried worked. Eventually Gabrielle and her husband began taking turns getting up and allowing Samuel to play until he got tired, between 2 and 3 am. Then, when placed into his cot, he immediately settled down, fell asleep unaided, and slept soundly until 8 or 9 am, when he was ready to start the day.

Upon reflection, Gabrielle connected the extended night-time wakefulness with Samuel sleeping later in the mornings and longer day-time naps. She had encouraged this as a way to catch up on the sleep he had lost the previous night. However, by allowing him to sleep longer during the day, she inadvertently reinforced his atypical sleep pattern and encouraged him to remain awake for a good part of the night. Samuel was simply not tired between 11 pm and 3 am. The solution was to reduce his day-time sleep to encourage him to sleep through the night.

If your baby demonstrates a similar pattern, reducing the amount of sleep she gets during the day should help. It may be necessary to wake her in the mornings and/or shorten her day-time naps or aim for a later bedtime or a combination of all three. An age-appropriate routine may help you decide where to make changes. These are described in Chapter 17.

Attempting sudden huge, sweeping changes in sleep schedules will only upset your baby. Try making minor alterations, of 15 to 30 minutes each day, as they're usually more effective. It may take days, even a week or more, of consecutively shortening your baby's day-time sleep before her night-time sleeping pattern changes.

Erratic sleep-wake pattern

An erratic sleep-wake pattern means a baby's sleeping pattern differs, with the number, duration and timing of day-time naps from day to day. One night, baby might fall asleep early, the next night late. She wakes at random times during the night and at different times in the morning. Her feeding patterns may also be affected, with her appetite and milk/food intake differing considerably each day.

This is another circadian rhythm problem that is often dismissed as normal behaviour. Although it is common for newborn babies to feed and sleep at unpredictable times, you can still improve the situation.

While biological reasons can cause unpredictable sleeping patterns in newborn babies that must be accepted, there can often be behavioural reasons that, when addressed, improve the situation. Behavioural reasons that cause erratic sleeping patterns occur when:

- infant behavioural cues are misinterpreted, as they easily can be, thus, the care we provide is not consistent with baby's needs
- many parents unknowingly teach their baby to rely upon them to fall asleep, unaware that this means they become responsible for regulating their baby's sleeping patterns. If they misinterpret baby's 'tired signs' or fail to recognise when baby wakes too soon, owing to missing sleep associations, this means her sleeping patterns may not align with her circadian rhythms. Because sleeping patterns influence feeding patterns, these and her ability to self-regulate her dietary intake can also be affected. (See Chapter 15 for more information on how feeding is affected by sleep.)
- babies don't receive the external cues they need from parents to stabilise their circadian rhythms.

Newborns have the most to gain from being supported to self-regulate their feeding and sleeping patterns. This is because newborn babies are especially vulnerable to the Big Os: overtiredness, overstimulation, oversupply syndrome and overfeeding. These problems indicate that the baby requires more support from parents or caregivers to self-regulate her sleeping pattern and dietary intake. These problems can be readily resolved when parents make the appropriate adjustments to their infant feeding and settling practices.

A hectic and unpredictable family life is another reason a baby might develop an irregular sleeping or feeding pattern, denying her the chance to sleep when or as long as she needs. Sometimes this is beyond a parent's ability to control; sometimes it's not. Either way, it can destabilise baby's circadian rhythms.

Tanya, a mother of two girls, often needed to wake her baby in order to drop off and pick up her older child from school, whereas Amelia stated she simply got bored being home and would spend most days out and about with her baby, expecting her baby to sleep wherever she happened to be at the time.

To successfully resolve a circadian rhythm sleep problem, your baby must first be able to self-regulate her sleeping patterns, and settle to sleep by herself. If she can't do this yet, consider starting with sleep training. This must be done *before* changing the timing of your baby's sleeps. You may even find that this single strategy resolves all your baby's sleeping issues.

Step 1: Follow the Golden Rules of infant settling, removing any barriers that may prevent baby from self-regulating her sleep.

Step 2: If under four months old, use a cyclical pattern to harmonise her feeding and sleeping patterns with her circadian rhythms. If over four months old, follow an age-appropriate daily routine to support her to stabilise her circadian rhythms in a 24-hour pattern. See Chapters 16 and 17 for more about cyclical patterns and daily routines.

Late-sleep phase sleeping pattern

Is your baby alert and energetic during the evening hours, where she doesn't settle to sleep until late into the night? Does she also sleep late in the mornings? Is it difficult, if not impossible, to get her to stay awake in the mornings if you wake her? If the answers to these questions is 'yes', your baby may have what's called a late-sleep phase sleeping pattern. A baby's or toddler's sleeping patterns can easily drift towards this type of sleeping pattern unless you establish a regular bedtime in the evenings and wake-up time in the mornings. Elly and Madison both developed a late-sleep phase sleeping pattern, a problem for one family, but not for the other.

Baby Elly

At 10 months of age, Elly was considered a night owl, remaining awake in the evenings until after midnight, and sleeping until 10.30 or later each morning, followed by two naps each day. A well-meaning family member told her mother, Karen, 'It's bad for babies to be up this late.' In fact, this situation suited her family's lifestyle because her husband, Matthew, was a shift worker who enjoyed spending time with their only child after work. Elly was a happy, healthy, thriving baby. Despite her unusual sleeping pattern, she was by no means sleep-deprived. Because Matthew did not start work until noon and Karen did not have an outside job, the whole family would sleep until mid-morning. Elly's sleeping pattern was not causing her harm and she and her parents were happy with this arrangement, so there was no need to change.

Baby Madison

Madison, aged 11 months, had developed a similar sleeping pattern to Elly's, however, Madison's sleeping pattern was causing considerable distress for her entire family. Both parents were chronically sleep-deprived because of Madison's late nights. Madison's father, Ryan, rose at 5 am for work and her mother, Janene, was up at 6 am to care for Madison's three-year-old sister, Taleah, who had cystic fibrosis. Janene allowed Madison to sleep until late in the mornings as this allowed her to provide treatment for Taleah, but Madison's nocturnal wakefulness meant both Janene and Ryan were physically exhausted. They argued often. Janene felt guilty that she had no energy to play with her children and was often impatient with them, and Ryan in particular. Ryan felt his tiredness was impacting his work and feared he would lose his job. Janene was recently diagnosed with postnatal depression.

Although Madison's sleeping pattern did not cause her any direct harm, she was affected by the strain it placed on her family. Thus, changing her sleeping pattern for the sake of the entire family was vital.

If your baby's late-phase sleeping pattern is troubling you, then you must start bringing her evening bedtime forward. The best way to achieve this is to wake her earlier in the mornings and tweak the timing of her daytime naps.

- Wake your baby 15–30 minutes earlier than normal for a few days.
- Expose her to sun or other bright light in the morning, to increase her alertness.
- Schedule nap times and bedtime earlier in the day. If possible, avoid late afternoon naps. If she must have a late afternoon nap, wake her after 30 minutes.
- Avoid boisterous playful activity from the mid-afternoon onwards. Encourage only subdued play activities for an hour or more before bedtime.
- Dim the lights an hour prior to bedtime to induce melatonin production.
- Continue inching her bedtime, nap times and wake-up times earlier until she's going to bed and rising at the desired time.

Early-sleep phase sleeping pattern

Does your baby wake before the sparrows and think it's time to get up and start her day? Has she run out of steam by mid-afternoon and want to crash, even though it's not yet night? If she has this type of sleeping pattern, she'll probably be very sleepy by the afternoon and you might find it impossible to keep her awake, and equally impossible to get her to go back to sleep after she's woken in the early hours of the morning.

Baby Laura

Starting at three months, Laura's evening bedtime had progressively shifted earlier. By five months, Laura was so tired by 3 pm that she would fall sleep while breastfeeding and sleep solidly until 7 pm, at which time Desiree would attempt to breastfeed her again. Laura was not interested, returning to sleep instead. She then slept soundly until 3 am, rising bright and cheery to remain awake until 6 am, at which time Laura's sister, a toddler, would awaken while Laura wanted a nap. She would nap again at 11 am for 30 minutes. After weeks of this, Desiree was physically exhausted. Her children's nap times did not coincide, so she had no chance of resting, and her chronic sleep deprivation was severely impacting her relationship with her husband, her patience to care for her children and her physical health.

Desiree tried many things: preventing Laura from falling asleep at 3 pm – impossible – and waking her at 5 pm to keep her up, also unsuccessful. She tried keeping Laura awake when feeding her at 7 pm but that also didn't work. Laura would simply fall back to sleep. She tried feeding her at 3 am and leaving her to cry, and offering her more solids during the day. Nothing worked.

Laura was a healthy, thriving baby. She just wasn't getting enough sleep during the day so, by 3 pm, she was physically exhausted. The reason was because breastfeeding had become a sleep association for Laura. As Desiree had a toddler to care for, she wasn't able to sit or lie with Laura for long enough to ensure she got the sleep she needed. To successfully adjust the timing of Laura's sleep Desiree needed to prevent Laura from falling asleep while breastfeeding and encourage her to settle to sleep independently in her cot. After learning to settle by herself, Laura was then able to move from one sleep cycle to the next independently. This enabled her to self-regulate her sleeping patterns and get the amount of sleep she needed during the day. Once Laura got enough sleep during the day, Desiree could

> gradually move her naps and bedtime back to a later time in the day. After two weeks, Laura was finally going to bed at 7 pm and sleeping solidly during the night, getting up at 6.30 am. She now had three naps with a combined day-time sleep of around three hours, and Desiree regained her sleep.

The early-sleep phase sleeping pattern typically develops and continues when a baby doesn't get enough sleep during the day. Correcting problems causing day-time overtiredness must come before changing the timing of baby's night-time sleeping pattern. Supporting your baby to self-regulate her sleeping patterns, by achieving the Golden Rules when she settles to sleep, may help her to achieve better sleep quality and adjust her sleep-wake cycles into a typical day-night sleeping pattern without further guidance from you. If not, she's going to require your help to get her body clock back on track. To encourage a shift so that she has the longest sleep beginning in the evening instead of mid-afternoon, move all of her naps and bedtime later by 15-minute increments each day until you achieve the desired time. As with late-sleep phase problem, making too abrupt a change by attempting to keep your baby awake for many hours is likely to worsen the situation if she becomes overtired. Exposing her to daylight and providing stimulating play-time activities in the middle of the afternoon can also help to move her bedtime back to a reasonable hour.

Seasonal sleep problems

Babies can experience seasonal sleep problems owing to climate or other environmental changes. These often present as bedtime battles, early morning awakenings and day-time and/or night-time sleep disturbances. Seasonal sleep problems typically happen during the summer months due to:

- **Reduced hours of darkness:** can diminish production of melatonin, a sleep-inducing hormone (see box on page 239).
- **Increased daylight hours:** sunlight plays a significant role in regulating our circadian rhythms. Extended daylight hours can delay bedtime for many babies.

- **Change of routine:** longer daylight hours can mean a change in baby's routine, with family activities extending later into the afternoon or evening. This change in routine can re-program baby's circadian rhythms.
- **Noise:** can trigger early morning awakenings. In the summer months, birds are more active and often noisy during early morning, as are people, compared to other seasons.
- **Hot weather:** summer is also a time for hot weather, which can disturb sleep. The ideal sleeping temperature is between 18 and 22 degrees Celsius (65–70 degrees Fahrenheit); temperatures above 28 degrees Celsius (82 degrees Fahrenheit) can make sleeping difficult.

Seasonal sleep problems often resolve spontaneously as nights become longer and temperatures drop. To minimise the impact of climate or environmental factors causing sleep disturbance, try these suggestions:

- Use a fan or air-conditioner. If you don't have air conditioning, dress your baby appropriately, eg, in only a nappy in warm climates or light-weight muslin wraps if baby is swaddled for sleep.
- Maintain a regular daily routine suitable for baby's stage of development, which includes regular bedtime (see Chapters 16 and 17).
- Avoid boisterous activities before bedtime.
- Reduce lighting at least an hour before bedtime, perhaps moving baby indoors and drawing curtains or dimming lights.
- Use block-out blinds or curtains in baby's bedroom to reduce evening and early morning light.
- If noise is troublesome, try using a constant white noise throughout the night, such as a fan, to block out morning sounds.

Melatonin

Melatonin is a sleep-regulating hormone secreted at night by the pineal gland in your brain to help time and maintain our sleep. As light dims and night falls, melatonin is released. Come morning, as light increases, your brain produces less melatonin. Reducing the amount of light in a baby's room means her body will continue melatonin production uninterrupted, making her less likely to wake early. Babies begin producing melatonin from about six to nine weeks.

What to expect

While encouraging your baby to adjust her internal body clock, she may become a little out of sorts. It takes time to reset her body clock. It could take days to adjust to small changes or up to a week or more if big changes are required.

Key points

- Babies and young children are more susceptible to circadian rhythm sleep problems because they depend on others to provide the external cues they need to maintain their body rhythms in a normal day-night pattern.

- A baby requires guidance and support from parents and caregivers to correct a circadian rhythm sleep problem.

- Body clock problems tend to develop gradually; they also take time to resolve. Gradual changes over a period of a few days to two weeks are often more effective and less distressing than making sudden, large changes.

- To resolve a circadian rhythm sleep problem, you might need to first resolve any sleep-association problem.

15

Feeding and circadian rhythms

Topics

The link between feeding and sleeping.
When to feed your baby.
Feeding problems and circadian rhythms.

As a lactation consultant it frustrates me when I hear health professionals advising parents to feed their babies at set times. It doesn't take a rocket scientist to work out that babies need to be fed when they're hungry... – Sharon

Sharon makes a valid point, but it's not always easy for a parent, or health professional, to tell when a baby is hungry. While feeding a baby at set times can potentially cause baby-care problems, so too can demand feeding, especially when infant behavioural cues are misinterpreted as hunger.

Feeding is only one component, albeit an important one, in caring for a baby. However, a baby's contentment and ability to sleep soundly is not solely dependent on having his nutritional needs met. You need to provide for all his needs, starting with nutrition, sleep and sensory stimulation, at times that harmonise with his natural biological rhythms. When I advise parents on how to promote their baby's contentment, feeding and how it affects their baby's sleep is a topic I always cover.

Feeding and sleeping relationship

Infant sleep and feeding are intimately related. Sleeping patterns influence feeding patterns, and feeding patterns influence sleeping patterns. If a baby is prevented from self-regulating his sleeping patterns (owing to learned dependence on negative sleep associations) this can make it more difficult for him to self-regulate his dietary intake in a way that harmonises with his circadian rhythms. If baby is grazing or feeding erratically, this can disrupt his sleeping patterns.

Diagram 15.1:   Feeding and sleeping are related

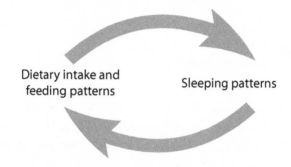

Dietary intake and feeding patterns

Sleeping patterns

The relationship between feeding and sleeping is so closely linked that it's important to consider the other when resolving either an infant sleeping or feeding problem.

- An overfed baby may become sleepless or wakeful owing to abdominal discomfort. Overfed babies can give the appearance of hunger because they often want to suck to soothe their aching bellies.
- *Sleep deprivation* can lead to overeating, as it increases the release of a hormone called ghrelin which stimulates hunger. Alternatively, a sleep-deprived baby can become too distressed or too exhausted to feed effectively, leading to underfeeding.
- A grazing pattern, where a baby takes small but frequent feeds, can affect sleeping patterns. Some babies, after feeding too much

during the night because of a feeding-sleep association, eat less during the day, reversing the natural circadian rhythm pattern.

Just as a baby needs support to self-regulate his sleeping patterns, we must also support him to self-regulate his dietary intake.

When to feed baby

Health care providers, lactation consultants and baby-care book authors advise parents to use one the following feeding regimes, varying only based upon the advisor's personal or professional preference:

- demand feeding
- semi-demand feeding
- scheduled feeding.

Demand feeding relies on interpretation of infant behavioural cues, scheduled feeding is governed by the clock, and semi-demand feeding uses both.

In general, lactation consultants and breastfeeding counsellors recommend demand feeding, while most health professionals seem to recommend semi-demand feeding. Meanwhile, many baby book authors promote either demand feeding or scheduled feeding.

The purpose of each is the same, to provide for a baby's nutritional needs, but babies have different needs, therefore no single feeding regime will match the needs of every baby. An ideal feeding regime for your friend's baby could prove to be problematic for your baby and vice versa. Also, some parents are more experienced and therefore more confident in interpreting their baby's behavioural cues than others.

Demand feeding

Demand feeding, also called cue feeding, means baby is offered a feed whenever he displays 'hunger cues'. In *The Womanly Art of Breastfeeding* by La Leche League International, hunger cues are described as, 'eyes moving beneath eyelids, eyelids fluttering before they even open, hands coming toward face, mouth movement'.[103] Subsequent cues are described as, 'tension in body and mouth, fast breathing and crying'. Other descriptions of hunger cues include licking or sucking of lips, tongue, fingers or fists, turning the head and opening the mouth wide when stroked or touched around the mouth, fussing or crying.

Demand feeding undoubtedly works well for many babies and their parents. Many babies who are fed 'on demand' naturally fall into a semi-predictable feeding pattern, making it easier for parents to accurately identify when their baby is hungry. However, these so-called hunger cues can also be attributed to reasons other than hunger. For example, when a baby is in a REM sleep stage, his eyes will move beneath his eyelids, which will flutter as he's beginning to wake. This doesn't mean he's hungry. A baby can have tension in his mouth, breathe fast and cry for all sorts of reasons, most of which have nothing to do with hunger. A newborn baby will turn his head when the side of his mouth is stroked because this triggers his rooting reflex. He will do this whether he's hungry or not. Young babies in particular have a strong urge to suck whenever they're tired, uncomfortable, bored, as a way to soothe and simply because babies are in an oral stage of development and love to suck. It doesn't mean a baby is hungry every time he wants to suck. Babies who develop a feeding-sleep association will appear hungry whenever they're tired and ready to sleep. The point is, while a baby will display these behavioural cues when he's hungry, they are not exclusive to hunger.

A demand feeding regime is likely to provide for a baby's nutritional needs, and beyond. Demand feeding can be likened to tuna fishing with a drag net. You're going to catch more than just tuna in the net. Offering your baby a feed every time he wants to suck, fusses or cries means sometimes he'll be offered feeds for the wrong reasons.

Parents are often reassured by such claims as, 'You can't overfeed a baby', or 'Your baby will stop when he's had enough', but this is not true in every case. Offering your baby a feed based on behavioural cues without understanding how sleep associations and infant reflexes may affect a baby's behaviour increases the risk of feeding and sleeping problems. It also increases parental distress owing to confusion about the reasons for baby's behaviour.

Without understanding the effects of sleep associations and the role parents and caregivers play in developing them, many parents inadvertently teach their babies to associate feeding with sleeping. When a baby becomes sleepless or wakeful because his sleep associations have altered, hunger is typically the first thing blamed, and a feed offered for the wrong reasons.

Newborns are especially vulnerable to overfeeding. We are all born with certain infantile reflexes, actions beyond our voluntary control, that fade within the first few months of life. Many infantile reflexes relate to feeding. These enable a baby to feed effectively without having to first learn how.

Infantile reflexes

- **Rooting reflex:** turning of the head and opening the mouth, seeking something to suck on; triggered by stroking a baby's cheek near his mouth.

- **Hand-to-mouth:** flexing the arm towards the mouth; triggered by either stroking the cheek or palm.

- **Suck reflex:** making sucking motions; triggered by pressure on the lips, tongue or roof of mouth.

- **Swallowing reflex:** an accumulation of milk in baby's mouth stimulates sensory receptors situated in his hard palate and the back of his mouth, these trigger his swallowing reflex.

These automatic movements are often misinterpreted by parents and others as a sign that the baby is hungry. Once a newborn baby's suck reflex is trigged, he can appear to be hungrily guzzling his feed, more so if his mother has a forceful milk ejection reflex, called 'let-down', or if the flow of milk from a bottle is too fast. Because a baby has no voluntary control over his suck reflex, he will continue to suck and swallow whether he wants to or not. So if a newborn baby is offered a feed every time he cries, wakes too soon, or starts to suck, he's likely to overfeed. A newborn has an immature digestive system unable to digest this excess nutrition. Symptoms associated with overfeeding include frequent milk regurgitation, other symptoms associated with overnutrition, which occurs when a baby overfeeds, include watery or sloppy bowel motions, which may at times be green in colour, excessive, often foul-smelling flatulence, intestinal cramps and infant distress and sleep disturbance owing to abdominal discomfort pain.

Breast-fed babies are less likely to overfeed compared to bottle-fed babies but they can still overfeed, despite claims to the contrary.[104] The newborn period is often a time when many breastfeeding mothers have an overly abundant supply of breast milk and a forceful let-down. (See pages 11–14 for more on oversupply syndrome and overfeeding.)

The problems associated with misinterpreting a baby's behavioural cues as hunger are not confined to newborn babies. Feeding a baby too soon or for the wrong reasons can also be problematic for babies fully capable of self-regulating their dietary intake. These potential problems are just a few examples:

- **Grazing:** small frequent feeds. When the suck reflex fades, a baby can control his milk intake. The more often he is fed, the less he needs to take. Grazing, while not a health risk, can affect a baby's sleeping patterns, preventing him from having long naps or sleeping for long periods during the night.

- **Fussy feeding behaviour:** a baby whose suck reflex has faded might refuse to feed if he's not hungry. Or he might take a little (graze) and then fuss during the feed if parents try to persist in getting him to take more than he wants. Because it was believed that he was hungry, then this normal infant behaviour which indicates he is not is often misinterpreted as baby experiencing problems or pain while feeding. Many healthy, thriving babies get diagnosed with medical conditions like acid reflux, to explain their fussy feeding behaviour, when in most cases the actual reason for the baby's behaviour is that parents are misinterpreting their baby's hunger and feeding cues.

- **Excessive or continued night-time feeding:** baby feeds more often during the night or continues to demand night-time feeds well beyond the average age. Although not usually problematic for the baby, it can be an issue for parents (see pages 252–254).

- **Dysrhythmic day-night feeding pattern:** a baby over three months consumes very little milk or solids during the day and feeds more often than expected during the night. As long as his nutritional needs are met during the 24 hours, this is not problematic unless parents try to coerce or pressure him to feed more during the day. (See pages 255–259.)

These problems are by no means exclusive to a demand feeding regime, but the risk of these problems occurring is greater if a baby's behavioural cues are misinterpreted. Denyse's story below illustrates how misinterpreting a baby's behavioural cues could lead to premature cessation of breastfeeding.

Denyse's story

Denyse was concerned she had low milk supply and was considering giving up on breastfeeding her baby, Cooper, aged eight weeks. Cooper, was thriving, active and alert and had numerous wet nappies and bowel motions every day, all signs of a well-nourished baby. Denyse, however, stated that Cooper never appeared to be satisfied, demanding breastfeeds 12–20 times in a 24-hour period. When asked how Cooper fell asleep, Denyse stated it was while breastfeeding. Denyse's milk supply was fine; she had simply misinterpreted Cooper's frequent desire to suck as unsatisfied hunger.

I explained the effects that infantile reflexes and sleep associations are likely to have on Cooper's behaviour. Denyse then decided to discourage his feeding-sleep association by no longer breastfeeding him to sleep. I suggested she follow the cyclical feeding pattern described in Chapter 16 to build her confidence in recognising Cooper's behavioural cues. Denyse continued to successfully breastfeed Cooper until he was 15 months.

The most common reason breastfeeding mothers give for stopping breastfeeding is that they believe they are not producing enough milk to satisfy their baby. In most instances, their baby's discontentment likely had nothing to do with hunger, and everything to do with misreading their baby's behavioural cues.

Demand feeding can also increase the risk of underfeeding for some babies. Consider the small percentage of babies too weak or unable to demand feeds, for example, premature, malnourished babies or babies with neurological problems. Some healthy babies with placid, undemanding temperaments display behavioural cues that are easily overlooked. These babies sleep well and appear to be so content that parents are often unaware that anything is wrong. It is poor growth rather than poor sleep that will usually ring alarm bells in the case of undemanding babies.

When faced with the dilemma of infant irritability, erratic feeding and sleeping patterns, grazing, excessive or continued night-time feeds, or concern that a baby is overfeeding, many parents are enticed by the promises that strict feeding and sleeping schedules will turn their screaming, uncomfortable little bundles into contented babies.

Scheduled feeding

Scheduled feeding involves offering baby feeds at pre-set times. Baby is offered a feed at three, three and half or four hourly intervals depending on age. The clock rather than the baby's hunger determines when a feed will be offered. Following this type of feeding pattern means your baby is offered a feed at specified times of the day irrespective of his behavioural cues.

Biologically, newborn babies in general don't cope well with a structured 24-hour routine or schedule.[105] A newborn baby's endocrine system, which produces hormones that regulate sleep and appetite, is still maturing. Babies of the same age will vary in growth rates, energy/caloric requirements and the volume of milk their stomachs can hold. So they can't be treated the same, which is what a pre-set schedule does.

Of course there are always exceptions: some newborn babies can be content and thrive on a set feeding schedule, if the timing of feeds happens to match the baby's biological needs. But if it doesn't, or if he does not take enough to sustain him until the next feed, problems can arise, including underfeeding and poor growth. These are less likely to occur when a baby is bottle-fed. A newborn bottle-fed baby can be easily enticed into taking more milk than he needs, or that his stomach can comfortably hold, while his suck reflex is present.

A scheduled feeding regime can cause a baby distress if:

- his behavioural cues are ignored
- he's kept waiting for a feed when hungry
- his parents try to control how much he eats.

Rigid feeding regimes can be especially problematic for breast-fed babies because the amount of milk a breast-fed baby takes varies from feed to feed, as does the nutritional composition of each feed. Breastfeeding mothers differ in their storage capacity (the amount of milk their breasts can hold) and how quickly they produce milk. Milk removal is the primary control mechanism for milk production and supply. A mother's breasts will decrease production if they're not drained often enough to maintain supply. Your baby may appear to cope at the time if he has an easy temperament, but the consequences of an inappropriate feeding regime, such as poor growth and insufficient milk supply, are seldom immediately apparent, especially if the baby has a generous layer of body fat at the time, or the mother initially has an oversupply of milk. It may only become apparent as your baby's body fat reserves deplete.

Semi-demand feeding

A semi-demand feeding regime sits between demand feeding and scheduled feeding. It is similar to demand feeding in that the goal is to feed your baby when he's hungry, however, parents also use the clock to assess baby's behavioural cues. A semi-demand feeding regime encourages parents to consider reasons beyond hunger for a baby's behaviour, and, if appropriate, to soothe their baby using other means rather than automatically feeding him every time he fusses, cries or wants to suck. Many parents, including experienced breastfeeding mothers, use a semi-demand feeding regime to help them decide when to offer their baby a feed.

A semi-demand feeding regime reduces the risk of overfeeding and grazing versus demand feeding. It also minimises the chances of underfeeding versus scheduled feeding. But no feeding regime can completely eliminate the potential for problems.

A semi-demand feeding regime is both predictable and flexible. The predictability of this feeding regime supports those babies inclined to feed erratically to stabilise their internal body clocks, and help parents anticipate when their baby is likely to become hungry, gaining greater accuracy when interpreting their baby's behavioural cues. Its flexibility accommodates day-to-day variations in a baby's appetite, and those in feeding patterns that occur due to increased maturity. A semi-demand feeding regime is flexible enough to provide for a baby's nutritional needs when he's hungry, instead of waiting until the clock says it's time.

The semi-demand feeding regime works by setting a minimum and maximum timeframe, encouraging feeding at the following intervals:

- **Breast-fed babies:** For babies under three months, any time from two to three and a half hours, timed from the beginning of one feed to the beginning of the next. For babies aged three to nine months, cycles can vary between two and a half to four hours.
- **Bottle-fed babies:** From birth until around nine months, cycles range from every three to four hours. By nine months, intervals increase to five or six hours, in addition to three meals and one or two snacks per day, plus water or other fluids.

If your baby displays a desire to suck or cries before the minimum time for feeds has lapsed, before assuming the reason is hunger, you will assess other reasons for his behaviour. It could be he's unsettled because he's tired, uncomfortable, overstimulated, bored, wants to suck or have a cuddle. Try other strategies like settling him to sleep, giving him quiet time if he's overstimulated or attention if he's bored, or let him suck on your little finger. If these methods fail to soothe him, by all means feed him.

If baby has not demanded a feed by the maximum timeframe, you would offer him one. You may need to wake him up (day-time only). If you can't wake him, you can let him go a little longer.

The suggested timeframes are just that – suggestions – and are intended for babies who are healthy and thriving. They're given as a guide to encourage you to consider possibilities other than hunger and soothing methods other than feeding.

These timeframes might not be appropriate for preterm babies, babies struggling to gain sufficient weight, special needs babies or those experiencing feeding problems which may prevent them from self-regulating their dietary intake. If you have any concerns about your baby's health, growth or your milk supply, consult your healthcare provider for feeding advice.

You may find these timeframes impossible to achieve on a consistent basis if your baby relies on feeding as a way to fall asleep, as he may refuse to fall asleep and become distressed due to overtiredness if he's not fed to sleep. If you plan to stop his feeding-sleep association, this can be done while following a semi-demand feeding regime.

True or false?

Breast milk is digested in around 90 minutes, therefore a breast-fed baby needs to be fed more frequently than a bottle-fed baby.

TRUE and FALSE: Yes, breast milk is digested much faster than infant formula, however, it's the dropping of a baby's blood sugar levels that triggers hunger. This will vary depending on the volume and composition (in particular the fat content) of the milk consumed. A low blood sugar level triggers the release of the hormone ghrelin, which causes the gnawing sensation of hunger, prompting a baby to fuss or cry when wanting another feed. If breast-fed babies needed feeding every 90 minutes, then every breast-fed baby would demand to feed this often, day and night.

If the feeding regime you're currently using is working for your baby, ie, he's happy, healthy and thriving, then there's no need to change. If your baby is not happy or thriving, or if you're confused by his behavioural cues, switch to a cyclical pattern, which includes the semi-demand feeding regime, if he's less than four months old, or a flexible daily routine if he's more than four months old. Chapters 16 and 17 discuss cyclical patterns and flexible daily routines in detail.

Before switching, let's discuss circadian rhythm feeding problems first.

Feeding problems and circadian rhythms

Two common circadian rhythm feeding problems can increase parental stress and indirectly affect a baby's contentment:

- excessive night-time feeding
- dysrhythmic day-night feeding pattern.

Excessive night-time feeding

What is excessive when it comes to night-time feeds? The number of feeds required by babies at night varies based on their stage of development. As a baby's body clock matures and stabilises, night-time feed frequency decreases. When a healthy, thriving baby demands more feeds at night than average, whether it is excessive depends on the individual baby's growth pattern.

> Issac will be 8 months old next week, and he still doesn't sleep through the night. He gets up three times a night for a breastfeed, more than when he was a newborn. He's around 9 kilos [19 lbs 13 oz] now so it's not like he's not getting enough. My husband thinks I should switch him to formula and leave him to cry himself back to sleep. I don't want to do either. There has to be some way to get him to go longer between breastfeeds at night. – Cate

Issac is feeding more than expected for a thriving, eight-month-old, indicating there may be reasons besides hunger for him to want to feed this often. Parents often ask how many times their baby should feed at night. The following table depicts the average number of night-time feeds for healthy, thriving, full-term babies according to age.

Table 15.1: Average night-time feeds

Age	Average overnight feeds	Average hours between overnight feeds
Birth–3 months	2–3	3–5*
3–6 months	1–2	5–8*
6–9 months	0–1	8–12
9+ months	0	10–12

*This is during one time period only, and not between all night-time feeds.

Babies born preterm, those who aren't gaining sufficient weight, sick, disabled or have growth-affecting medical conditions may need to feed more often than average during the night. Babies who struggle to gain sufficient weight may benefit from continued feeds overnight. In Issac's case, as with most healthy babies, additional night feedings will do little to increase his daily intake. He will likely graze at night or feed well at night but then take less during the day, as can occur with dysrhythmic day-night feeding patterns.

Reasons

As their circadian rhythms develop, babies can go for longer periods of time without feeding at night, and eventually go through the night without feeding. But despite being developmentally and physically mature enough to achieve this, not all babies do. If a healthy, thriving baby feeds more often than average during the night, check for these underlying reasons:

- Baby's normal awakenings between sleep cycles at night are mistaken for hunger. A baby under three months may accept a feed whenever it is offered, regardless of hunger, due to his suck reflex.
- Feeding has become your baby's sleep association. He'll want to feed to go back to sleep.

- Baby has developed a dysrhythmic day-night feeding pattern, so he's hungrier and eats more than he needs to at night and less than he could during the day.

These problems are not mutually exclusive. A baby might feed for more than one of these reasons.

How to discourage excessive night-time feeds

- If your baby repeatedly falls asleep while feeding, this must change before you can successfully resolve the problem of excessive night-time feeds. This means no longer feeding baby to sleep during the day as well as during the night. Doing so intermittently may confuse, frustrate, anger or distress him at the times you don't. Once he no longer associates feeding with sleeping – a process that usually takes three to five days or more of consistently no longer being fed to sleep, day or night – he may stop demanding extra feeds during the night and no further action is necessary.
- If there's no feeding-sleep association, then the reason could be a body clock/circadian rhythm issue. If your baby's internal body clock has now become programmed to trigger increased hunger at night, gradually cut back on the volume you offer during those feeds considered as excessive. If you breastfeed, start by offering only one breast rather than both during the feeds you plan to discourage, or restrict the time you allow baby to feed and remove him from your breast after a certain number of minutes. Gradually reduce the minutes over time. If you bottle-feed, gradually cut back the volume of milk offered during those feeds you plan to discourage by 20 or 30 millilitres/half to one full ounce every night or every other night. These strategies will slowly readjust his internal body clock and restore a normal hormonal balance so that he's not woken by gnawing hunger pangs. You could also go cold turkey by abruptly omitting the feeds you wish to discontinue. This would readjust baby's body clock more quickly, but may be a little traumatic for both of you. Offering water instead of a feed seldom works, but it won't hurt to try.

Caution – Don't cut back night-time feeds to below the average for your baby's age.

Dysrhythmic day-night feeding pattern

Dysrhythmic day-night feeding pattern is what I call an infant feeding pattern that is out of sync with a normal 24-hour day/night cycle. A dysrhythmic feeding pattern involves:

- A well-nourished baby more than three months old.
- Disinterest in some day-time feedings. Breastfeeds are brief; bottle-feeds are less than expected. Alternatively, baby might refuse to feed for unusually long periods during the day.
- Demands for night-time feeds exceeds what is expected. (See Table 1.1 for average feeds.) He appears to be ravenous when he wakes at night and feeds well.

This phenomenon, where baby appears to get his day and night turned around in regards to his feeding, can be very confusing for parents and health professionals alike. Although common, it is often overlooked and hence poorly managed.

> I am fully breastfeeding my 5-month-old son, Bennett. The past week he's refusing to eat practically anything during the day. He only nibbles for one to three minutes at a time until around 7 pm when he manages a decent feed. He feeds two or three times during the night; these are usually good long feeds. Today he's probably eaten for a total of 10 minutes and it's been about 10 hours since he had a proper feed. He doesn't seem to be sick. I'm at my wits' end. What can I do to make him eat? – Marjorie

Bennett is a healthy, thriving baby. He has six or more wet nappies in a 24-hour period, indicating he's well-hydrated despite his brief feeds during the day. It is likely that his decreased appetite during the day is caused by his feeding more often than he needs to during the night. Marjorie must first reduce the amount she feeds him at night in order to get him eat more during the day.

> I am desperate. I think my 4-month-old, Ashton, is on a hunger strike. It's been getting progressively worse over the last few weeks. He used to drink 150 ml [5 oz] every four hours. Now he only drinks

60 to 90 ml [2–3.5 oz] at a time during the day. Once he has had that he stops, pushes the teat out. I sit him up and burp him. As soon as I lay him back down to finish his bottle he cries and carries on. If I stop and sit him he's happy again. I am so confused. He just doesn't seem to be hungry but he should be. 60 to 90 ml is not enough. Even if we leave him for five hours between feeds it makes little difference. He will scoff a 200 ml [6.7 oz] bottle of formula in about 10 minutes twice during the night. Could it be reflux? How can I get him to drink more during the day? – Robyn

If it was painful for Ashton to feed he would not feed contentedly through the night. He is receiving a reasonable amount of milk over a 24-hour period for a four-month-old; it's just that he drinks more at night. Ashton was not getting enough sleep during the day and I suspect this is why his feeding pattern initially got turned about. Robyn needed to fix his sleep problem before she could resolve his feeding issues.

What is typical?

Newborn babies normally feed and sleep at regular intervals throughout the day and night. Starting at six to 10 weeks, most healthy, thriving babies begin to demonstrate a difference between their day and night feeding patterns. At this stage, their circadian rhythms, which influence appetite, have matured to a level where there will be one period in a 24-hour cycle when they feel less hungry. This period will initially run about four or five hours with occasional fluctuations. By three months of age, many now extend this single period to six to nine hours between feeds, and, between the ages of six and nine months, most healthy babies will have one period of 10 to 12 hours of decreased appetite. Ideally, this time of decreased appetite will occur during the night, but not always.

Reasons for a dysrhythmic feeding pattern

Learned dependence on feeding as a means to fall asleep is the number one reason for this reversed pattern. If your baby uses feeding to sleep, when he wakes during the night, he will want to feed in order to go back to sleep. If, when doing so, he consumes a significant proportion of his daily kilojoule/calorie intake, the period of decreased appetite will shift to the day-time. If you were to rise in the middle of the night to eat your dinner and then go back to bed, you likely would eat less during the day.

It is also common, particularly around the ages of four, seven and nine months, to confuse waking with hunger. Babies at these ages are more likely to wake frequently during the night due to developmental reasons, but are instead offered additional feeds. As a result of taking these additional feeds baby needs to consume less the next day. Because baby feeds less during the day, the next night he wakes one or more times to and demands a feed. It becomes a perpetuating cycle.

This atypical feeding pattern could also occur when a baby is not getting enough sleep during the day, and becomes too tired to feed effectively. Once his feeding pattern is reversed he then needs to eat less during the day because he's eating more during the night.

Baby Max

Max was a healthy, thriving seven-month-old baby who slept nightly with his mother, Kellie, and would wake every one to two hours demanding breastfeeds, during which he would fall back asleep. From morning until mid-afternoon, he did not seem interested in feeding, only accepting a breastfeed at naptime, at which time Kellie would lie down on the bed and feed him until he was asleep. Max was at an age where he could reasonably go for much longer periods during the night without feeding.

To encourage this, Kellie tried to coax Max to feed more often during the day, even offering him infant formula and solid foods in the hope that he might go for longer periods between breastfeeds during the night. Max was not interested.

Although Max had established a typical day-night sleeping pattern, in which the bulk of his sleep occurred during the night, and have two or three naps during the day, his feeding pattern was reversed. His dependence on feeding to fall asleep had disrupted the natural progression of his feeding patterns.

He would consume a significant proportion of his daily intake during the night and wasn't particularly hungry during the day as a result.

As long as Max relied on breastfeeding to fall asleep, there was little Kellie could do to change this situation. Once she taught him to fall asleep without her breast as a prop, she could then gently persuade him to go for longer periods during the night without feeding.

Thus, Max became hungrier during the day. After two weeks, Max was only waking once during the night for a breastfeed. Kellie and Max happily continued to bed-share at night.

If your baby is not feeding or eating enough during the day, it's tempting to think he needs feeding during the night, which will reinforce this inverted feeding pattern. This does not apply to newborns, however, as they require regular feeding during the night. Most babies require one or two feeds nightly until six months of age.

Effects

A dysrhythmic feeding pattern causes no physical harm to a baby provided he continues to gain sufficient weight. However, not recognising what's happening, you might be tempted to employ some not-so-helpful strategies to fix the situation, and inadvertently create new problems. For example, you might mistakenly attribute your breast-fed baby's reversed feeding pattern to low milk supply and take steps to increase it. When this fails to resolve the problem, which it will, you might mistakenly believe that your baby would feed and sleep better if he was bottle-fed, which is unlikely.

If you try to pressure your baby to feed when he's no longer hungry, he'll get increasingly upset, possibly screaming and arching his back. Pressuring a baby to feed is a common cause of fussy feeding behaviour. If it gets extreme baby may even develop a behavioural feeding aversion.

More than 90 per cent of the babies I see with a dysrhythmic day-night feeding pattern are mistakenly diagnosed as suffering from reflux to explain their fussy feeding behaviour during the day. But they don't have reflux, they're simply not hungry. The medication to treat reflux will alter the natural balance in baby's digestive tract. This will not improve baby's behaviour and can potentially create additional problems for him.

With this reversed feeding pattern, you might be tempted to start your baby on solid foods too soon, either by spoon or by adding cereal to his bottles. Don't. If he's healthy and thriving, it means he's already getting enough to eat. He's just consuming it at night instead of during the day. If you give him solids too soon, you might disrupt the nutritional balance of his diet; and jeopardise your milk supply if breastfeeding.

The solution lies in getting the diagnosis right. Once you identify a dysrhythmic feeding pattern, it's simply a matter of switching the bulk of your baby's feeding back to day-time.

How to resolve a dysrhythmic day-night feeding pattern

If your baby's growth and number of wet nappies demonstrates that his nutritional needs are being met, you will not entice him to take more food during the day until you begin to give him less during the night. Before trying to alter his feeding pattern, you need to first work out why this feeding pattern has developed. If he wants to feed solely to go back to sleep, then you need to begin by settling him without the help of your breast or bottle. Next, you need to reduce the excessive night-time feeds (those not required for your baby's stage of development – see Table 15.1 page 253). Once you do, he will become hungrier during the day. It may take a number of days or weeks for his circadian rhythms to realign into a normal day-night feeding pattern, depending on how significant the changes are and how quickly you make them. Once this is achieved you may find that following a flexible daily routine helps him to maintain his feeding in normal day-night feeding pattern.

Key points

- Any feeding pattern that meets the nutritional needs of your baby is one that works; no single feeding regime will suit every baby.

- Most babies under the age of five months have a strong desire to suck.

- All newborns have reflexes that can be triggered at times unrelated to hunger.

- The most common reason for atypical feeding patterns is because baby is feeding for the wrong reasons.

- An atypical feeding pattern does not cause a baby any harm, but it can cause unnecessary confusion and frustration for parents, who may take steps that create problems for baby.

- The single most common reason for atypical feeding patterns is associating falling asleep with feeding, something that must be addressed first if you want to adjust baby's feeding pattern.

Cyclical patterns

Annalise is six weeks old and I still don't know what I'm doing. Every time she cries I immediately feel tense. I don't trust myself to tell if she's hungry, tired or if she has got a pain. I must be the worst mother in the world. It's no wonder she's so unhappy when her own mother doesn't know what she wants. Am I the only mother who cannot tell what her baby's cries mean? – Carolyn

Many new parents find it difficult to recognise what their baby wants or needs by their cries. Becoming a mother doesn't mean you'll instinctively know why your baby is upset. Parenting is something you learn as you go, 'on the job' as they say. With Annalise being a newborn it's especially challenging because, during the newborn period, body movements are controlled mostly by reflex actions. Carolyn can gain increased accuracy in recognising her baby's various wants and needs through trial and error. Alternatively, she can fast-track the learning process and minimise the risk of error by following a cyclical pattern to help decide what Annalise might need at any point in time.

Babies who have the most to gain when their parents follow a cyclical pattern include:

- newborn babies, especially those who feed and sleep erratically
- healthy, thriving babies who experience gastrointestinal symptoms due to overfeeding
- babies who graze, taking small frequent feeds
- babies troubled by broken sleep.

A cyclical pattern can support your baby to stabilise her feeding and sleeping patterns in a way that matches her biological needs. It could also help you to anticipate her needs and gain greater accuracy and confidence in recognising the reason for her cries and other behavioural cues.

What is a cyclical pattern?

A cyclical pattern involves providing care in the same or similar order in recurring cycles over the course of the day. There are many variations, but all fit into two groups:

- **Basic cycles:** parents are simply advised to provide baby's cares in a set order, eg, feed–play–sleep.
- **Full-care cycle:** includes timeframes for feeding, sleeping and awake time.

As a parenting educator, I favour the full-care cycle. I believe this offers a balanced approach to providing baby care. It helps parents to gain greater accuracy in interpreting their baby's behavioural cues. They can avoid the 'feed baby every time she fusses, cries or wants to suck' scenario, which has to potential to cause a newborn distress due to overfeeding. It also minimises the risk of infant distress which can occur when parents try to adhere to strict feeding and sleeping schedules that do not match baby's biological needs. Baby gains contentment because she's supported to stabilise her feeding and sleeping patterns in harmony with her needs. When baby is content, the parent gains increased confidence and enjoyment in their parenting role. So it's a win-win situation, in most cases. But it won't suit every baby or parent.

How effective is a cyclical pattern?

A cyclical pattern works well for most healthy, thriving babies. It will be more effective if your baby is supported to self-regulate her sleeping patterns by independently falling asleep in her bed, without unreliable props or aids.

If you prefer to actively assist your baby to fall asleep, or to provide her with sleep aids like a pacifier, then utilising a cyclical pattern will be more challenging, because she may wake prematurely. (See page 72 for the effects of negative sleep associations.) However, following a cyclical pattern may help to identify those times when she wakes too soon and requires your assistance or her sleep aid to return to sleep.

I don't recommend using a cyclical pattern if your baby has developed a feeding-sleep association. In this situation, it won't work. Baby will want to feed to sleep. Delaying feeds at times of tiredness will increase the risk of overtiredness. If you prefer to settle your baby to sleep by feeding her, a demand feeding pattern is better suited. If you plan to discourage your baby's feeding-sleep association, then achieve this first.

A cyclical pattern may no longer be useful when a baby has dropped to two naps per day, generally around the age of seven to nine months, because feeds now exceed the number of naps she requires each day.

How full-care cycles work

A full-care cycle involves following baby's behavioural cues, but using timeframes as a guide to help you interpret her cues. Timeframes are flexible to avoid upsetting baby. They provide a guide only and are not meant to be adhered to rigidly. The advantage of timeframes is that you can anticipate your baby's needs and prepare in advance. Timeframes also help you to assess your baby's behaviour within the context of the situation. For example, when she fusses or wants to suck, a timeframe can help you to decide if she's likely to be hungry versus other reasons for her behaviour, like tiredness, boredom, discomfort or overstimulation.

The three key elements of a full-care cycle are:

- feeding
- awake time
- sleeping.

Feeding

With full-care cycles, feeding is the pivotal point around which all other baby cares are coordinated. Baby is supported to self-regulate her dietary intake by means of a semi-demand feeding pattern:

- **Breast-fed babies:** Less than three months, cycles range from two to three and a half hours; ages three to nine months, cycles range between two and a half to four hours.
- **Bottle-fed babies:** From birth until around nine months, cycles range from three to four hours.

The aim is to feed baby when she's hungry. Timeframes help to minimise the risk of overfeeding, which can occur when a newborn baby's behavioural cues are mistaken as hunger, and avoid underfeeding, which can occur when a hungry baby is kept waiting until 'it's time' for a feed. (See page 249 for more on how to use a semi-demand feeding pattern.)

Once you have some guidelines on when to expect that baby is likely to be hungry, the next step is to anticipate when she's likely to need to sleep.

Awake time

Knowing the average awake time for a baby based on her age may help you:

- interpret baby's behavioural cues
- anticipate baby's sleep needs and organise her care
- coordinate the care of other children
- plan outings or appointments.

The length of awake time can vary. In general, babies tend to have shorter awake periods in the mornings versus afternoons and evenings. You must be alert for signs of tiredness, using the timeframes as guides only.

If your baby is not getting sufficient sleep, she may exhibit signs of tiredness much sooner than average. Some babies have such placid temperaments that they don't give clear signals of tiredness until they become overtired. A baby could become so excited by boisterous play-time activities or lots of activity that she might not display early signs of tiredness.

Table 16.1:   Average awake time

Age	Average awake time including feeds
2–6 weeks	1–1¼ hours
6 weeks–3 months	1–2 hours
3–6 months	1½–2½ hours
6–9 months	2–3 hours
9–12 months	3–3½ hours

Once overtired, baby may then find it harder to get to sleep, so you may want to provide an opportunity to sleep even without clear signals of tiredness if nearing the end of the estimated timeframe. This way she has a little quiet time to unwind before going off to sleep.

Don't automatically assume fussiness during awake time indicates hunger or tiredness. She could be uncomfortable, bored or overstimulated. Ask yourself:

- When did she last feed and how well?
- When did she last sleep and for how long? How much sleep has she had so far?
- Should I change her nappy? Could she be feeling cold or hot?
- Has she been on her own for a while? Could she be bored?
- Have I been playing with her? Could she be overstimulated and need some quiet time?

Awake time activities
Awake time activities can be similar or different for each cycle, and include feeding time as well as various play-time activities, bath-time, walks in the pram, shopping, etc.

Sleeping
A cyclical pattern encourages your baby to nap at some point between every feed, minimising the risk of her becoming overtired. But you will

need to provide her with a low stimulus sleep environment; along with her familiar, consistent sleep associations so she will stay asleep. See Table 4.1 on page 54 for a reminder of what baby needs to sleep well.

The average number of day-time naps gradually decreases from four to five when first born to two per day when she reaches six to nine months. By the time your baby has dropped to two naps a day, a cyclical pattern is no longer feasible as she will not be napping between every feed.

Settling baby to sleep

The quickest way to settle a baby is to follow the same settling practices each time, whether for day-time naps, evening bedtime and after interim night-time awakenings.

How long will baby sleep?

The length of each nap can vary, but most babies require at least one or more lengthier naps during the day. Being guided by a semi-demand feeding pattern and the average awake time may help you to decide if your baby has woken too soon or if she's sleeping too long.

Just because your baby has woken doesn't necessarily mean she's had sufficient sleep. A baby can wake prematurely if she's hungry, uncomfortable, because her sleeping environment is too stimulating or has changed somehow, or if her sleep associations are missing. If she has only had a brief nap, ask yourself whether she still looks tired or has had less sleep than normal. As a guide, if your baby has slept less than an hour, give her a chance to return to sleep, after checking her comfort needs and ensuring her sleep associations are present, but only if she's not due for a feed. If, after five or 10 minutes, she doesn't look like she's going to go back to sleep, get her up.

Knowing how long babies can comfortably tolerate being awake can help you decide whether she needs more sleep or not. If getting her up means the average awake time will lapse before she's next due for a feed, you have three choices:

- encourage her to return to sleep
- get her up but provide an opportunity for her to go back down for another nap at some point before her next feed or
- bring her feed forward.

It might be necessary to wake a sleeping baby at times in order to maintain her circadian rhythms in a day-night pattern. Newborn babies are particularly vulnerable to getting their day and night switched around, and babies experiencing certain types of circadian rhythm sleep problems might sleep too long during the day. During 7 am to 7 pm, if she has not woken, wake your baby and offer her a feed after four hours from when she began her previous feed. After her feed, try to encourage some awake time. During the night, leave her to go as long as she wants between feeds, unless she weighs less than three kilograms/six and a half pounds, or if you have been advised by your health care provider to wake her at set times for night-time feeds.

True or false?

You should never wake a sleeping baby.

FALSE: A baby's circadian rhythms can get out of sync with normal day-night patterns if she does not receive external cues to distinguish between day and night. A baby will not sleep well during the night if she has slept too long during the day. You can reduce the amount of sleep she has during the day by waking her. Once her body clock adjusts to the normal day-night sleeping pattern appropriate for her stage of development, she will start waking naturally on her own.

How to gently wake baby
Remove her blankets and open the curtains or turn on the lights, and allow noise to enter her room. If this doesn't wake her within five minutes, then pick her up and hold her in an upright position and talk to her in animated tones.

The cyclical pattern described uses the order of feeding, awake time, and sleeping to help parents avoid having their baby fall asleep while feeding. However, you can provide your basic baby-care tasks in any order you feel appropriate. It is okay to feed your baby directly before sleep time provided you ensure she does not fall asleep while feeding. Use feed times as a marker to indicate when the next cycle begins.

What to do at night

$$\text{Sleep} \rightarrow \text{feed} \rightarrow \text{sleep}$$

Don't encourage awake time during the night beyond what's necessary for feeding; avoid too much sensory stimulation. Just quietly feed your baby and then pop her back to bed to encourage her to go back to sleep.

It can take a newborn baby a number of weeks to synchronise her circadian rhythms into a day-night pattern and quickly return to sleep once night-time feeds have been completed. You can help your newborn baby to learn to recognise the difference between day and night by following the tips on pages 229–230.

If you have an older baby who experiences long periods of sleeplessness during the night, and you suspect a circadian rhythm sleep problem, see Chapter 14 for more information.

Key points

- A cyclical pattern is a guide to help you more accurately interpret your baby's behavioural cues.

- A cyclical pattern should not be rigid if it upsets your baby.

- Maintaining negative sleep associations means your baby may wake more frequently and require more support from you to regulate her sleeping patterns in harmony with her biological needs.

- A cyclical pattern is generally unworkable when a baby has a feeding-sleep association.

Daily routines

Topics

Benefits of a routine.
Sample daily routines for babies at different stages of development.
How to modify a routine to suit your baby.
How to establish a routine.
How to maintain a routine.
How to tell when baby is ready for a new routine.

[At five months] Harrison's feeding and sleeping patterns are all over the place. I can't plan anything because every day is different. I feel like I am housebound because he won't sleep while we are out and I never know when he's going to want to nap. I asked my health nurse about a routine for him. She said I should follow his lead. I told her that's what I have been doing but it's not working. She said I can't expect Harrison to fit my lifestyle. I am not. I just want to know what to expect. Is it unreasonable to expect him to have a routine by now? – Eileen

It's not unreasonable to expect some degree of predictability in a five-month-old baby's day. The fact that Harrison's feeding and sleeping patterns differ every day to the point where Eileen feels she cannot leave the house may indicate that he requires more guidance from her. A routine would probably be helpful.

The topic of routines is another hotly debated parenting issue. Based on my professional experience, I support routines for babies over four months of age. I find that following an age-appropriate daily routine is the most helpful thing parents can do to promote their baby's contentment, after encouraging independent settling.

Babies' needs have not changed, but today's society and family life have changed significantly, moving at a faster pace, very different to past generations. Most babies are taken on frequent outings with parents each week, and it can be unsettling for a baby if the care he receives is not consistent with his biological needs or if it does not maintain his circadian rhythms. Most parents I meet don't expect their baby to fit into their lifestyle; they simply want guidance on how to adjust their lifestyles to promote their baby's contentment.

Daily routines

A daily routine means feeding, sleeping, awake time, play time, bathing, outings, etc, occur at similar times each day. This provides the external sensory cues that help a baby to stabilise his circadian rhythms into a 24-hour pattern. An age appropriate daily routine is one that matches the baby's biological needs at his current stage of development.

Benefits of a routine

- **Physical:** The more stable your baby's internal body clock is, the better he eats, sleeps and feels, and the fewer digestive problems he experiences.
- **Developmental:** The predictability helps baby learn what to expect, aiding memory development. As his ability to remember increases, he will begin to recognise when his needs are about to be met, reducing the need to cry.
- **Emotional:** Assist you to anticipate baby's needs and more accurately interpret his behavioural cues, minimising crying time. All babies are comforted when care is consistent and predictable. The structure and predictability makes a baby feel safe and secure. Consistency among caregivers may reduce stress when separated from his mother.
- **Relationships:** Baby's siblings benefit when a baby has a routine. The appearance of a new brother or sister can be very unsettling, and adjusting can be even harder when life is unpredictable and the new baby is taking up all of Mum's time. Siblings benefit when

you're able to coordinate their care with the care of the baby, as they may wait more patiently, knowing their own needs will soon be met.

- **Parental:** You benefit by being able to prioritise your baby's needs and plan your day, enhancing your ability to coordinate the care of family members and/or synchronise the care of multiple birth babies.

True or false?

1. Routines will reduce breast milk supply.

FALSE: Successful breastfeeding can be maintained while following a daily routine, however, reduced supply can occur when breastfeeding mothers follow too a strict feeding schedule. Page 283 explain how to adapt a routine to suit a breast-fed baby.

2. Routines are restrictive.

FALSE: Caring for a distressed, chronically overtired baby is restrictive. A daily routine usually provides greater contentment for babies, which means more freedom for parents. A routine enables parents to identify suitable times for outings, appointments, time for extended family member visits, and time for themselves.

3. Babies are not ready for a routine before six months of age.

FALSE: A routine is flexible; it is not the same as a strict schedule. Babies of all ages, even newborns, benefit from the familiarity, support and predictability that routines provide. However, any routine needs to be appropriate for a baby's stage of development. A cyclical pattern is better suited to babies under the age of four months.

Keys to a great routine

A routine or schedule might fail for numerous reasons. Here are some hints to help plan a successful routine.

1. Before you start

If your baby currently depends on negative sleep associations, this may prevent him from self-regulating his sleeping patterns and his sleeping patterns may remain erratic. You may find that despite your best efforts it's impossible for him to follow any sort of routine. Any negative sleep association problem your baby might be experiencing must be resolved before you attempt a daily routine. A cyclical pattern can be used during the learning phase of sleep training, after which you can switch to a daily routine. If you prefer to continue to help your baby fall asleep, using a cyclical pattern may be more practical in this situation.

If your baby is troubled by poor growth, check with your health care provider before attempting to follow a routine.

2. Record baby's feeding and sleeping patterns

Once you feel confident your baby can self-regulate his sleeping patterns, record both his feeding and sleeping patterns over three days in the sleep diary provided in the Appendix. This should help you plan adjustments that might prove beneficial. After comparing the three-day pattern with the routine appropriate for your baby's stage of development, you may discover a routine has already been established and it's simply a matter of supporting baby to maintain this pattern.

3. Choose a suitable routine

> I have three children. Two are at school. I often need to wake my baby to take him with me to drop off or pick up my other children. Needless to say he's not happy about this. I have tried to get him to nap earlier; it's not working. What can I do to change the timing of his naps to match the times I need to drop off and pick up my children from school? – Janelle

A routine is geared to harmonise with a baby's circadian rhythms, not convenience the family. If what you want to achieve doesn't match your baby's circadian rhythms, then it's probably not going to work. However, while a routine needs to match your baby's biological needs, there may be ways to coordinate your baby's cares with family life. See page 282 for more on how to vary a routine.

As your baby grows and matures, his circadian rhythms will change. This means the routine must also change, possibly three or more times during his first 18 months. Trying to stick to a routine that he has outgrown will upset your baby. It's best to watch for signs that indicate when it's time to switch to a new routine, rather than sticking to a routine that's no longer working.

4. Make gradual changes

Even when a routine is suitable at baby's current stage of development, it may take time for his circadian rhythms to stabilise. If you attempt to enforce rapid or dramatic changes – such as trying to make him sleep when he's not tired, or feed when he's not hungry – this can frustrate or distress him. You don't want to make a hungry or tired baby wait for too long either. Making multiple, small changes over a period of days or weeks is usually best.

Allow at least a week for your baby to adjust to a routine, longer if he's troubled by a circadian rhythm feeding or sleep problem. If his present feeding or sleeping pattern indicates a circadian rhythm sleep or feeding problem this could take up to two weeks to resolve, depending on how far you want his pattern to shift and how quickly he adjusts to the changes. Don't try to push things too fast.

5. Balance consistency with flexibility

Do you go to bed at exactly the same time each night and get up at the same time each morning? Do you eat at the same time every day? Do you consume the same amount of kilojoules/calories at each meal? Probably not. Babies experience the same variations in appetite and energy levels from one day to the next. Daily routines are designed to guide rather than control what baby does. Unlike schedules, you're encouraged to respond to your baby's behavioural cues and if necessary deviate from the routine.

An effective daily routine requires a balance between flexibility with consistency. While flexibility when following a routine is encouraged, there comes a point where too much flexibility means there's no consistency and therefore no routine. You need to gauge the right balance between consistency and flexibility to suit both your baby and your family. The proposed timeframes supplied in the sample routines below are a good starting point, but you must judge how flexible or structured you need to be to promote your baby's contentment.

Sample routines

Four basic daily routines will cater to a healthy, thriving bottle-fed baby's changing needs at various stages of development. (Recommendations for adapting these routines to breastfeeding appear on page 283.)

- 4–7 months   3 nap/5–6 feed routine
- 5–8 months   3 nap/4 feed routine
- 7–10 months   2 nap/4 feed routine
- 8 to 12–18 months   2 nap/3 meals plus snacks routine

The age recommendations overlap because babies develop at different rates. If your baby was born preterm, choose a routine to match his 'corrected age', the age he would have been had he been born at term.

How can you tell which routine will best suit your baby? The following sample routine descriptions contain tell-tale behaviours that your baby will display when ready to progress to the next routine.

Babies aged four to seven months

Table 17.1: Four to seven months: 3 nap/5–6 feed routine

Suggested start time	Activity	How to encourage adjustment
7 am	Wake-up time Milk feed	If baby wakes earlier than 6 am, encourage returning to sleep; if he sleeps past 7.30 am, wake him, to regulate his sleeping pattern for the rest of the day. Offer another feed soon after your baby wakes, regardless of what time his last feed was. This sets his feeding pattern for the rest of the day. Don't expect a full feed if not long since prior feed.

Suggested start time	Activity	How to encourage adjustment
8.30 am	Nap 1	Keep it brief, between 30 and 60 minutes. Wake after one hour if necessary.
10.30 am	Milk feed	
11.30 am	Nap 2	Most important nap of the day; ideally 1.5–2.5 hours. If your baby wakes before 1.5 hours, encourage returning to sleep. When possible, be at home for this nap to ensure sufficient length.
2 pm	Milk feed	
4 pm	Nap 3	Adjust to earlier if previous nap was short. This brief nap is ideally about 30–60 minutes. Wake after 60 minutes, if necessary. If starting this nap late, wake by 5 pm, to encourage settling to sleep at 7 pm bedtime.
5.30 pm	Milk feed	
6 pm	Bath/ Bedtime routine	
7 pm	Bedtime	
Overnight	Demand feed overnight	Allow to sleep as long as he wants between overnight feeds. Resettle if he wakes less than 3 hours from the start of the prior feed. Some parents prefer to wake their baby to offer a late evening feed before retiring.

Late evening feeds

As your baby's endocrine system matures his body will release leptin (the hormone which suppresses appetite) for increasingly longer periods during the night. By four months of age, most healthy, thriving babies can go for one period of five to nine hours without feeding, ideally at some point during the night. This could be the early or latter part of the night.

Parents are often advised to wake their baby and offer a late evening feed, generally sometime between 10 pm and midnight or a feed while he is still asleep, in the hope that he might then sleep through the remainder of the night without requiring another feed. It may be possible to encourage a baby to shift his sleeping pattern to take the longer sleep in the later part of the night instead of the early part of the night. It can take a number of weeks of offering a late evening feed to achieve this, and there are no guarantees that it will.

A half-asleep breast-fed baby may not take the breast into his mouth sufficiently to feed or might comfort suck rather than feed. This will make no difference in his night-time feeding pattern.

Waking a baby for a late evening feed or offering a feed while he is sleeping is not something I generally recommend because it has the potential to interfere with the natural progression of baby's circadian rhythms. If a healthy, thriving baby is not waking to demand a feed in the late evening of his own accord, then he probably does not need one. He might take the feed even if he doesn't need it if his suck reflex is still present or if he has a feeding-sleep association. Whether he be a breast-fed or bottle-fed baby if he feeds more often at night than he would otherwise, he may eat less the next day and eventually end up with a dysrhythmic feeding pattern, wanting to eat mostly at night.

Signs that baby is ready to cease night-time feeds

Most but not all healthy, thriving babies will cease night-time feeds on their own when they're developmentally ready, exceptions being when a baby has a feeding-sleep association or has developed a dysrhythmic feeding pattern. One or more of the following patterns often indicates that a healthy, thriving baby is ready to reduce or cease night-time feeds:

- uninterested in late evening feed when woken
- starts taking less during late evening feed
- takes less milk or goes for more than four hours between day-time bottle-feeds

- starts to be less interested in breastfeeds during the day, but continues to feed regularly and contentedly during the night. (Healthy growth and six or more wet nappies a day indicates his fussiness is not a supply problem.)

If your healthy, thriving baby has not ceased night-time feeds by seven months of age, then you can encourage him to do so, if you wish. See page 254 for strategies.

Babies aged five to eight months

With this routine, night-time feedings, including late evening feed, stop; subtle changes are made to nap times and inclusion of solid foods at around six months of age.

Table 17.2: Five to eight months: 3 nap/4 feed routine

Suggested start time	Activity	How to encourage adjustment
7 am	Wake time Milk feed Solids	If baby wakes before 6 am, encourage returning to sleep; otherwise, try to wait until 7 am to feed, to encourage longer sleeps in mornings in the future. Wake by 7.30 am, if necessary. Offer solids around 15–20 minutes after completing milk feed.
9 am	Nap 1	A 30–40 minute nap. Wake after 45 minutes, if necessary.
11 am	Milk feed Solids	Offer solids either now, 15–20 minutes after finishing milk feed, or the next feed.
12 midday	Nap 2	Most important nap of the day. When possible, be at home for this nap to ensure sufficient length, ideally 1.5–2 hours. Encourage returning to sleep if less than 1 hour.
3 pm	Milk feed Solids	Offer solids 15–20 minutes following milk feed, only if you did not offer after the 11 am feed.

Suggested start time	Activity	How to encourage adjustment
4 pm	Nap 3	Adjust to earlier if previous nap was short. This brief nap should be about 30–40 minutes. Wake after 45 minutes, if necessary. If starting this nap late, wake by 5 pm, to encourage settling to sleep at 7:30 pm bedtime.
6 pm	Solids	
6.30 pm	Bath/ Bedtime routine	
7 pm	Milk feed	
7.30 pm	Bedtime	
Overnight		If baby wakes, encourage returning to sleep without feeding. Check comfort needs and offer water if necessary. If baby is under 7 months and still wakes for night-time feeds he might not be ready for this routine. Return to routine for 4–7 months.

Signs that baby is ready to switch to a 2 nap routine

Somewhere between the ages of seven to 10 months, watch for behaviour patterns which may indicate your baby is ready to switch to a 2 nap per day routine:

- he takes longer to fall asleep at nap times and/or in the evenings
- he refuses to settle to sleep for one of his naps
- he protests more than usual when he goes down for his sleeps
- he starts to wake earlier in the mornings or wakes early from his second nap.

Some babies will demonstrate readiness to move to the 2 nap routine below and change feeding patterns at the same time. If this is the case for you, you can skip the routine in Table 17.3 and move directly to the daily routine shown in Table 17.4.

Babies aged seven to 10 months

Table 17.3:   Seven to 10 months: 2 nap/4 feed routine

Suggested start time	Activity	How to encourage adjustment
7 am	Wake time Milk feed Solids	If baby wakes before 6 am, encourage returning to sleep; otherwise, try to wait until 7 am to feed, to encourage longer sleeps in mornings in the future. Wake by 7.30 am, if necessary. Offer solids around 15–20 minutes after completing milk feed.
9.30 am	Nap 1	40 minutes–2 hours.
11 am	Milk feed Solids	Offer solids 15–20 minutes after this feed or the next.
1 pm	Nap 2	40 minutes–2 hours. If baby had a longer earlier sleep, delay this nap's start time until 2 or 2.30 pm. If earlier nap was short, encourage a longer nap now. If starting this nap late, wake by 5 pm, to encourage settling to sleep at 7:30 pm bedtime.
3 pm	Milk feed	
6.30 pm	Solids	
6.30 pm	Bath Bedtime routine	
7 pm	Milk feed	
7.30 pm	Bedtime	
Overnight		If baby wakes, encourage returning to sleep without feeding. Check comfort needs and offer water if necessary.

Please note: Once your baby starts to eat solid foods he may benefit from being offered a little water between feeds. Allow him to take as much or as little as he wants.

Signs that baby is ready for a change in feeding pattern

Behavioural signs that indicate a healthy, thriving baby is ready for a new routine include:

- drinking less milk during bottle feeds
- progressively extending time between milk feeds to five or six hours
- refusing or shows little interest in some breastfeeds.

Babies and toddlers aged eight to 12–18 months

By this age, solid foods play a significant role; the number of milk feeds has reduced and morning and afternoon snacks are introduced.

Table 17.4:   Eight to 12–18 months: 2 nap/3 meal + 2 snack routine

Suggested start time	Activity	How to encourage adjustment
7 am	Wake-up Offer solids before or after milk feed	If baby wakes before 6 am, encourage returning to sleep; otherwise, try to wait until 7 am to feed, to encourage longer sleeps in mornings in the future. Wake by 7.30 am, if necessary.
9.30	Morning snack Water or diluted juice	Snacks are optional. Your baby might not always want a snack.
10 am	Nap 1	Wake him after 90 minutes.
12.00	Lunch Milk feed	Offer solids before milk feed.
2 pm	Afternoon snack Water or diluted juice	If too tired for a snack, offer it after 2.30 pm nap.
2.30 pm	Nap 2	Move forward if baby had only a brief nap earlier. Combined sleep for both naps should total 2.5–3 hours. If starting this nap late, wake by 5 pm, to encourage settling to sleep at 7:30 pm bedtime.
5 pm	Dinner	
6/6.30 pm	Bath Bedtime routine	
7 pm	Milk feed	
7.30 pm	Bedtime	If baby wakes, encourage returning to sleep without feeding. Check comfort needs and offer water if necessary.

Signs your child is ready to move to a one nap routine

Somewhere between 12 and 18 months of age, your child will begin displaying signs that he is ready to eliminate one of his day-time naps, by either taking a long time to fall asleep for his morning nap or refusing an afternoon nap.

By this age, children are very active and easily distracted. They often go through a long transitional phase as they move from two naps to one nap per day. Your child might want two naps one day and one nap the next and two the following day, with no predictable pattern for a few weeks, before finally settling into a one nap a day routine. Most children will then continue this way until between the ages of three and a half years to five years of age. When your child is ready to switch to one nap per day, move lunch time earlier, to 11 or 11.30 am, and offer a nap directly afterwards.

How to vary sample routines

These sample routines are designed to match a baby's natural biological rhythms at various stages of development. However, babies differ in their rate of development, so it's important not to be rigid. It is not essential that your baby follow a routine exactly. You also need to be guided by your baby's behavioural cues. Leeway of half to one hour on either side of the recommended times are generally okay. Beyond that range, the benefits may be lost.

By four months of age, a baby's suck reflex will have faded and he can now self-regulate milk intake to meet his nutritional needs, meaning you can be more flexible regarding feed times compared to sleep times. If necessary, give your baby a little something to tide him over until the next recommended feed time, but try to avoid a grazing feeding pattern as this may negatively impact on his sleep.

You can change the recommended wake-up times of a routine, provided all sleep and feeding times are changed accordingly. If the desired wake-up time is quite different to your baby's current wake-up time, you will need to take things slowly to allow his body clock to adjust. Remember the conditions need to be conducive to sleep. Use block out blinds if you want him to sleep beyond dawn.

The main purpose behind following a routine is to support your baby to stabilise his internal body clock to a 24-hour pattern by providing care, such as feeding and sleeping, at similar times each day. If you find these sample routines too restrictive, a cyclical pattern may suit better.

It's simply not possible to include every variation that can be made to a routine. Your challenge is to work out what works best for your baby and your family. Use the recommended times as a guide only.

Adapting routines to suit a breast-fed baby

The recommended feeding times provided in the sample routines above are for bottle-fed babies. Parents of breast-fed babies can still follow a daily routine, however, greater flexibility is required.

For babies over four months of age, infant sleeping patterns are the key to supporting a baby to stabilise circadian rhythms into a 24-hour pattern. The number of feeds or timing of baby's feeds is not as relevant as the timing and duration of baby's sleep. You can breastfeed on demand or follow a semi-demand feeding regime and still use a routine to support your baby's sleeping patterns.

Try to avoid allowing your baby to constantly graze as this may negatively impact his sleeping patterns, or letting him fall asleep while breastfeeding, as this will encourage a feeding-sleep association which may then prevent him from being able to follow a routine.

How to establish a routine

Compare your baby's sleeping pattern, which you recorded in the sleep diary, with the routine recommended for his age and decide if any adjustments are needed.

To encourage a change in a baby's feeding patterns might involve gradually extending the time between feeds, increasing the amount of milk offered in some day-time feeds, or reducing the amount or number of feeds offered overnight.

To adjust sleeping patterns may involve one or more of the following changes, depending on how you want to adjust them:

- Give him an opportunity to resettle back to sleep if he wakes too early in the morning or from a nap; or wake him in the morning or from a nap if he sleeps too long.

- Place him into bed a little earlier or later than normal.
- Keep him awake a little longer than normal before naps or bedtime.

When you first start to follow a routine, remember that a baby will not sleep if he's not tired and you should not attempt to make him to eat if he indicates he's not hungry.

It is unrealistic to expect your baby to instantly adapt to changes in his routine, especially if the changes are significant. Making adjustments gradually, in 15- or 30-minute increments daily over a three- to seven-day period will permit his body clock to adapt, and minimise any resulting crankiness.

What to expect as baby's body clock adjusts

Establishing a routine can require a number of days for your baby's circadian rhythms, which influence all of his physical functions, to adjust. Some people, when travelling to different time zones, feel a little out of sorts for a few days until circadian rhythms adjust. It's the same for babies, which is a good reason to take things slowly.

How to maintain a routine

Once your baby's circadian rhythms have adjusted, he may comfortably follow the routine with only minimal guidance from you. You may still need to provide the external cues he needs to maintain his circadian 24-hour pattern. While flexibility is encouraged, consistency is what's necessary.

Baby Harry

Harry, aged five months, had once been a crying, restless baby. However, once his mother, Julie-Anne, encouraged him to learn to self-settle, his naps lengthened and he was much happier. The only time he then fussed or cried was when he was hungry or tired. Julie-Anne took my suggestion to try a flexible daily routine suitable for Harry's developmental age to see if this would help to reduce his crying further, and found that Harry had no need to fuss to let her know he was hungry or tired. By way of the routine Julie-Anne was able to anticipate when Harry would become hungry or tired and offer food or a sleep, pre-empting his need to fuss or cry. He happily accepted the food and would often drop off to sleep without a whimper. Julie-Anne noticed that, if she deviated from the routine too much, Harry would start to fuss and cry again.

Harry's routine would need to change as he matured, I pointed out, and told her when to expect these changes, and what signs to watch for, like him taking longer to settle to sleep or going for longer periods between breastfeeds. When Julie-Anne would observe signs indicating Harry was getting ready to change to a new routine, it would typically take him a week or so to settle into it.

Key points

- A daily routine must match your baby's natural biological rhythms.

- A baby's routine will change many times in his first year of life.

- A routine means doing things at similar times each day. A routine should not be confused with a schedule, which dictates fixed times to provide baby care.

- Routines require flexibility, but too much flexibility erases the benefits and can be unsettling for your baby.

- Baby is best guided to self-regulate sleeping patterns and settle to sleep independently, without unreliable props or aids, before attempting to following a routine.

Conclusion

Congratulations.

By now, you will:

- have enhanced your ability to identify infant behavioural cues that indicate tiredness
- recognise how babies behave when they become overtired
- understand the impact of sleep associations on a baby's ability to sleep
- realise there's more than one way to change a baby's sleep associations and
- appreciate your role in supporting your baby to stabilise his circadian rhythms.

You now possess the tools to resolve any behavioural infant sleep problems your baby may be experiencing. If you have difficulty implementing the recommended strategies, there are places you can turn for one-on-one information, advice and support.

Where to find more help

If you need more help check out my Babycare Advice website: www.babycareadvice.com

There you will find qualified child health nurses, lactation consultants and other health professionals, hand picked by me because of their extensive experience and expertise in dealing with baby-care problems. These health professionals are available to provide individualised parenting advice and follow-up support through our consultation service.

You'll also find articles on other baby-care issues and an up-to-date list of organisations qualified to help you deal with various baby-care problems.

Also see my *Your Baby Series* website at www.yourbabyseries.com. There you will find my blog, parents' message board, extracts from existing and upcoming publications written by me on baby care topics such as breastfeeding, bottle-feeding, understanding your baby's needs and behavioural cues, and reasons and solutions to infant irritability.

Appendix

Sleep diary

Fill out this sleep diary for one week, labelling asleep, awake, feeding and crying times. This will give you a clearer picture of what's troubling your child. You can see if baby is sleeping disproportionate amounts of time during the day. Or you might find crying is more intense in the afternoons if baby has had inadequate naps for his age group during the day.

Once you have this clearer picture if you feel you need more help you can inform your health care provider, so together you can take appropriate action. Or you can try strategies from within the book.

Day	7am	8am	9am	10am	11am	12pm	1pm	2pm	3pm	4pm	5pm	6pm	7pm	8pm	9pm	10pm	11pm	12am	1am	2am	3am	4am	5am	6am

Asleep   **Awake**   **F Feeding**   **C Crying**   **Half Hour**

Day	7am	8am	9am	10am	11am	12pm	1pm	2pm	3pm	4pm	5pm	6pm	7pm	8pm	9pm	10pm	11pm	12am	1am	2am	3am	4am	5am	6am
Monday		F	F			F	C				F						F				F			F

References

1   OG Jenni, HZ Fuhrer, I Iglowstein, L Molinari and RG Largo, 'A longitudinal study of bed sharing and sleep problems among Swiss children in the first 10 years of life', *Pediatrics*, 2005, 115, pp 233–40; P Lam, H Hiscock and M Wake, 'Outcomes of infant sleep problems: A longitudinal study of sleep, behavior, and maternal well-being', *Journal of Pediatrics*, 2003, 111, pp 203–07.

2   KH Archbold, KJ Pituch, P Panahi and RD Chervin, 'Symptoms of sleep disturbances among children at two general pediatric clinics', *Journal of Pediatrics*, 2002, 140, pp 97–102; JA Owens, A Spirito, M McGuinn and C Nobile, 'Sleep habits and sleep disturbance in elementary school-aged children', *Journal of Developmental and Behavioral Pediatrics*, 2000, 21, pp 27–36.

3   SR Goldfeld, M Wright and F Oberklaid, 'Parents, infants and health care: Utilization of health services in the first 12 months of life', *Journal of Paediatrics and Child Health*, 2003, 39(4), pp 249–53.

4   A Host, 'Cow's milk allergy', *Journal of the Royal Society of Medicine*, 1997, 90(S30), pp 34–39.

5   M Wake, K Heskethand and J Lucas, 'Teething and tooth eruption in infants: A cohort study', *Pediatrics*, 2000, 106, pp 1374–79.

6   KL Armstrong, N Previtera and RN McCallum, 'Medicalizing normality? Management of irritability in babies', *Journal of Paediatrics and Child Health*, 2000, 36(4), pp 301–05.

7   WH Frey and M Langseth, *Crying: The mystery of tears*, Winston Press Inc, Minneapolis, 1985.

8   MV Woodridge and C Fisher, 'Colic "overfeeding", and symptoms of lactose malabsorption in the breast-fed baby: A positive artifact of feed management?', *Lancet*, 1988, pp 383–84.

9   *The Merck Manuals*, Online Medical Library, http://www.merck.com/mmpe/sec19/ch286/ch286b.html (cited 7/11/11); PH Casey, 'Management of children with failure to thrive in a rural ambulatory setting', *Clinical Pediatrics*, 1984, 23(6), pp 325–30; RH Sills, 'Failure to thrive: The role of clinical and laboratory evaluation', *American Journal of Diseases of Children*, 1978, 132(10), pp 967–69.

10 H van de Rijt-Plooij and F Plooij, *The Wonder Weeks*, Kiddy World Promotions, BV, The Netherlands, 2003.

11 W Damon and RM Lerner, *Handbook of Child Psychology: Social, emotional, and personality development*, John Wiley & Sons, Hoboken, New Jersey, 2006, p 28.

12   BJ Sadock and VA Sadock, *Kaplan & Sadock's Concise Textbook of Clinical Psychiatry*, Lippincott, Williams and Wilkins, Philadelphia, PA, 2008, p 662.

13   K Spiegel, R Leproult and E van Cauter, 'Impact of sleep debt on metabolic and endocrine function', *Lancet*, 1999, 354, pp 1435–39; R Leproult, G Copinschi, O Buxton and E van Cauter, 'Sleep loss results in an elevation of cortisol levels the next evening', *Sleep*, 1997, 20, pp 865–70.

14   JM Siegel, 'Functional implications of sleep development', *PLoS Biology*, 2005, 3(5), pp 756–58.

15   NL Rogers, MP Szuba, JP Staab, DL Evans and DF Dinges, 'Neuroimmunologic aspects of sleep and sleep loss', *Seminars in Clinical Neuropsychiatry*, 2001, October, 6(4), pp 295–307.

16   M Rutter (ed), *Developmental Psychiatry*, American Psychiatric Press, Washington DC, 1987, p 124.

17   TF Anders, 'Night-waking in infants during the first year of life', *Pediatrics*, 1979, 63, pp 860–64.

18   R Ferber and M Kryger, *Principles and Practice of Sleep Medicine in the Child*, Saunders, Philadelphia, 1995.

19   TF Anders, LF Halpern and J Hua, 'Sleeping through the night: A developmental perspective', *Pediatrics*, 1992, 90(4), pp 554–60; BL Goodlin-Jones, MM Burnham, EE Gaylor and TF Anders, 'Night-waking, sleep organization, and self-soothing in the first year of life', *Journal of Developmental & Behavioral Pediatrics*, 2001, 224(6), pp 226–33.

20   P Franco, N Seret, JN van Hees, S Scaillet, J Groswasser and A Kahn, 'Influence of swaddling on sleep and arousal characteristics of healthy infants', *Pediatrics*, 2005, 115(5), pp 1307–11, http://pediatrics.aappublications.org/cgi/content/abstract/115/5/1307 (cited 24/3/11).

21   CM Gerard, KA Harris and BT Thach, 'Spontaneous arousals in supine infants while swaddled and unswaddled during rapid eye movement and quiet sleep', *Pediatrics*, 2002, 110(6), p 70, http://pediatrics.aappublications.org/cgi/content/full/110/6/e70 (cited 24/3/11).

22   J Piaget and B Inhelder, *Memory and Intelligence*, Routledge and Kegan Paul Ltd, London, 1973.

23   MM Burnham, BL Goodlin-Jones, EE Gaylor and TF Anders, 'Use of sleep aids during the first year of life', *Pediatrics*, 2002, 109(4), pp 594–601, http://pediatrics.aappublications.org/cgi/content/full/109/4/594 (cited 24/3/11).

24   I Paret, 'Night waking and its relationship to mother-infant interaction in nine month old infants', in J Call, E Galenson, R Tyson (eds), *Frontiers of Infant Psychiatry*, Basic Books, New York, NY, 1983, pp 171–78.

25   RH Passman, 'Providing attachment objects to facilitate learning and reduce distress: The effects of mothers and security blankets', *Developmental Psychology*, 1977, 13, pp 25–28.

26   Anders, et al, 'Sleeping through the night…', pp 554–60.

27   American Academy of Pediatrics, 'Sleeping and eating issues; Practice guide', http://www.aap.org/sections/scan/practicingsafety/Modules/Sleeping Feeding/SleepingEatingIssues.pdf - 2010-03-12 (cited 17/10/11).

28   Archbold, et al, 'Symptoms of sleep disturbances ...', pp 97–102; Owens, et al, 'Sleep habits and sleep disturbance ...', pp 27–36.

29   P Franco, S Chabanski, S Scaillet, J Groswassera and A Kahnaet, 'Pacifier use modifies infant's cardiac autonomic controls during sleep', *Early Human Development*, 2004, 77(1–2), pp 99–108.

30   CR Howard, FM Howard, B Lanphear, S Eberly, EA deBlieck, D Oakes and RA Lawrence, 'Randomized clinical trial of pacifier use and bottle-feeding or cup-feeding and their effect on breastfeeding', *Pediatrics*, 2003, 111, pp 511–18.

31   CW Binns and JA Scott, 'Using pacifiers: What are breastfeeding mothers doing?', *Breastfeed Review*, 2002, 10, pp 21–25.

32   RO Mattos-Graner, AB de Moraes, RM Rontani and EG Birman, 'Relation of oral yeast infection in Brazilian infants and use of a pacifier', *ASDC Journal of Dentistry for Children*, 2001 January–February, 68(1), pp 33–36, 10; E Comina, K Marion, F Renaud, J Dore, E Bergeron and J Freney, 'Pacifiers: A microbial reservoir', *Nursing & Health Sciences*, 2006, 8(4), pp 216–23.

33   MM Roversa, ME Numansa, E Langenbacha, DE Grobbeea, TJM Verheija and AGM Schilderb, 'Is pacifier use a risk factor for acute otitis media? A dynamic cohort study', *Journal of Family Practice*, 2008, 25(4), pp 233–36; JJ Warren, SM Levy, HL Kirchner, AJ Nowak and GR Bergus, 'Pacifier use and the occurrence of otitis media in the first year of life', *Pediatric Dental Journal*, 2001, 23, pp 103–07.

34   LL Shotts, DM McDaniel and RA Neeley, 'The impact of prolonged pacifier use on speech articulation: A preliminary investigation', *Contemporary Issues in Communication Science and Disorders*, 2008, 35, pp 72–75.

35   JJ Warren and SE Bishara, 'Duration of nutritive and nonnutritive sucking behaviors and their effects on the dental arches in the primary dentition', *American Journal of Orthodontics and Dentofacial Orthopedics*, 2002, 121, pp 347–56; E Larsson, 'Sucking, chewing, and feeding habits and the development of crossbite: A longitudinal study of girls from birth to 3 years of age', *Angle Orthodontics*, 2001, 71, pp 116–19.

36   P Franco, S Scaillet, V Wemenbol, F Valente, J Groswasser and A Kahn, 'The influence of a pacifier on infants' arousals from sleep', *Journal of Pediatrics*, 200, 136, pp 775–79.

37   TB Brazelton and J Sparrow, *Touchpoints: Your child's emotional and behavioral development, Birth to 3 – The essential reference for the early years*, Perseus Books Group, New York, NY, 2009.

38   M Weissbluth, *Your Fussy Baby*, Ballantine Books, New York, NY, 2003, p 93.

39   KD Ramos and DM Youngclarke, 'Parenting advice books about child sleep; Co-sleeping and cry it out', *Sleep*, 2006, 29(12), pp 1610–23.

40   M Weissbluth, *Healthy Sleep Habits, Happy Child*, Ballantine Books, New York, NY, 2003, p 103.

41   R Ferber, *Solve Your Child's Sleep Problems*, Simon & Schuster Inc, New York, NY, 1985, p 62.

42 JA Mindell, *Sleeping Through the Night*, HarperCollins Books, New York, NY, 2005, pp 99–104.

43 H Hiscock, 'Randomised controlled trial of behavioural infant sleep intervention to improve infant sleep and maternal mood', *British Medical Journal*, 2002, 324, pp 1062–65.

44 BR Kuhn and AJ Elliott, 'Treatment efficacy of behavioral pediatric sleep medicine', *Journal of Psychosomatic Research*, 2003, 54, pp 587–97; PWL Ramchandani, V Webb and GA Stores, 'Systematic review of treatments for settling problems and night waking in young children', *British Medical Journal*, 200, 320, pp 209–13.

45 Ramos, et al, 'Parenting advice books ...', pp 1610–23.

46 M Sunderland, *The Science of Parenting*, Dorling Kindersley Ltd, London, 2006, p 79.

47 W Sears, *Nighttime Parenting*, Penguin Books, New York, NY, 1999, p 77.

48 W Sears and M Sears, *The Fussy Baby Book*, Little, Brown and Company, New York, NY, 1996, p 39. 49 R Grille, *Parenting for a Peaceful World*, Longueville Books, Sydney, 2005, p 311.

50 A Gethin and B Macgregor, *Helping Your Baby to Sleep*, Finch Publishing, Sydney, 2007, pp 57, 93.

51 P McKay, *100 Ways to Calm the Crying*, Thomas C Lothian Pty Ltd, Melbourne, 2002, pp 13–14.

52 K McGeown, 'Life in Ceausescu's institutions', *BBC News*, 12 July 2005, http://news.bbc.co.uk/2/hi/europe/4630855.stm (cited 25/3/11); K McGeown, 'What happened to Romania's orphans?', *BBC News*, 8 July 2005, http://news.bbc.co.uk/2/hi/europe/4629589.stm (cited 25/3/11); HT Chugani, ME Behen, O Muzik, C Juhász, F Nagy and DC Chugani, 'Local brain functional activity following early deprivation: A study of postinstitutionalized Romanian orphans', *Neuroimage*, 2001, 14(6), pp 1290–301.

53 KG France, 'Behavior characteristics and security in sleep-disturbed infants treated with extinction', *Journal of Pediatric Psychology*, 1992, 17(4), pp 467–75; B Eckerberg, 'Treatment of sleep problems in families with young children: Effects of treatment on family well-being', *Acta Paediatria*, 2004, 93(1), pp 126–34; VI Pickert and CM Johnson, 'Reducing nocturnal awakening and crying episodes in infants and young children; A comparison between scheduled awakenings and systematic ignoring', *Pediatrics*, 1998, 81, pp 203–12; JL Owens, KG France and L Wiggs, 'Behavioural and cognitive-behavioural interventions for sleep disorders in infants and children', *Sleep Medicine Reviews*, 1999, 3(4), pp 281–302.

54 Murdoch Institute, 'Research news: "Controlled crying" technique safe for babies', http://www.mcri.edu.au/pages/research/news/2010/3/controlled-crying-technique-safe-for-babies.asp (cited 24/3/11).

55 AN Schore, 'The experience-dependent maturation of regulatory system in the orbital prefrontal cortex and the origin of developmental psychopathology', *Development and Psychopathology*, 1996, 8, pp 59–87; AN Schore, 'The effects of early relational trauma on right brain development, affect

regulation, and infant mental health', *Infant Mental Health Journal*, 2001, 22, pp 201–69.

56 BD Perry, RA Pollard, TL Blakely and D Vigilante, 'Childhood trauma, The neurobiology of adaptation and "use-dependent" development of the brain: How "states" become "traits"', *Infant Mental Health Journal*, 1995, 16(4), pp 271–91.

57 SE Hyman, *The Science of Mental Health: Stress and the brain*, Routledge, London, Vol 9, 2001, p 3.

58 DA Lott, 'Brain development, attachment and impact on psychic vulnerability', *Psychiatric Times, Online*, 1998, 15(5).

59 I Bretherton, 'The origins of Attachment Theory: John Bowlby and Mary Ainsworth', *Developmental Psychology*, 1992, 28, pp 759–75, http://www. psychology.sunysb.edu/attachment/online/inge_origins.pdf (cited 24/3/11).

60 Eckerberg, 'Treatment of sleep problems ...', pp 126–34.

61 H Hiscock, JK Bayer, A Hampton, O Ukoumunne and M Wake, 'Long-term mother and child mental health effect of a population-based infant sleep intervention: Cluster-randomized, controlled trial', *Pediatrics*, 2008, 122, pp 621–27.

62 JJ McKenna, 'Babies need their mothers beside them', *Natural Child*, http:// www.naturalchild.org/james_mckenna/babies_need.html (cited 2/1/11).

63 UNICEF, 'Childhood under threat. The state of the world's children 2005', http://www.unicef.org/sowc05/english/index.html (cited 2/1/11).

64 Australian Breastfeeding Association, *Breastfeeding Naturally*, Australian Breastfeeding Association, Malvern, Vic, 2009, p 105; La Leche League International, *The Womanly Art of Breastfeeding*, 8th edition, La Leche League International, New York, NY, 2010, p 231.

65 JJ McKenna, SS Mosko and CA Richard, 'Bedsharing promotes breastfeeding', *Pediatrics*, 1997, 100(2), pp 214–19.

66 McKenna, et al, 'Bedsharing promotes breastfeeding', pp 214–19.

67 LH Amir and SM Donath, 'Socioeconomic status and rates of breastfeeding in Australia: Evidence from three recent national health surveys', *Medical Journal of Australia*, 2008, 189(5), pp 254–56.

68 R Li, SB Fein, J Chen and LM Grummer-Strawn, 'Why mothers stop breastfeeding: Mothers' self-reported reasons for stopping during the first year', 2008, http://pediatrics.aappublications.org/cgi/content/full/122/ Supplement_2/S69 (cited 25/11/11); K Schwartz, HJ D'Arcy, B Gillespie, J Bobo, M Longeway and B Foxman, 'Factors associated with weaning in the first 3 months postpartum', *Journal of Family Practice*, 2002, 51(5), pp 439–44.

69 Australian Breastfeeding Association, *Breastfeeding Naturally*, p 105; La Leche League International, *The Womanly Art of Breastfeeding*, p 231.

70 Sears, *Nighttime Parenting*, p 34; MJ Heinig, 'Bed sharing and infant mortality: Guilt by association?', *Journal of Human Lactation*, 2000, 16, pp 189–91.

71 G Puig and Y Sguassero, 'Early skin-to-skin contact for mothers and their healthy newborn infants: RHL commentary', revised 9/11/2007, *The WHO Reproductive Health Library*, Geneva, World Health Organization, http://apps.who.int/rhl/newborn/gpcom/en/index.html (cited 10/11/11).

72 A Maslow, 'Hierarchy of needs', in C Zastrow and KK Kirst-Ashman, *Understanding Human Behavior and the Social Environment*, 8th edition, Book/Cole, Cengage Learning, Belmont, CA, 2010, p 448.

73 T Lewis, F Amini and R Lannon, *A General Theory of Love*, Vantage Books, New York, NY, 2000, p 75.

74 ES Buchholz, *The Call of Solitude: Alonetime in a world of attachment*, Simon & Schuster, New York, NY, 1997.

75 DW Winnicott (1958) 'The capacity to be alone', in DW Winnicott, *The Maturational Processes and the Facilitating Environment*, International University Press, New York, NY, 1980, pp 29–36.

76 'Back to sleep public education campaign', *National Institute of Child Health and Human Development*, http://www.nichd.nih.gov/sids/ (cited 10/1/11).

77 JJ McKenna and T McDade, 'Why babies should never sleep alone: A review of the co-sleeping controversy in relation to SIDS, bedsharing and breast feeding', *Paediatric Respiratory Reviews*, 2005, 6, pp 134–52.

78 S Mosko, C Richard and JJ McKenna, 'Maternal sleep and arousals during bedsharing with infants', *Sleep*, 1997, 20(2), pp 142–50; JJ McKenna and SS Mosko, 'Sleep and arousal, synchrony and independence, among mothers and infants sleeping apart and together (same bed): An experiment in evolutionary medicine', *Acta Paediatrica Supplement*, 1994, 397, pp 94–102.

79 JJ McKenna, E Thoman, T Anders, A Sadeh, V Schechtman and S Glotzbach, 'Infant-parent co-sleeping in evolutionary perspective: Implications for understanding infant sleep development and the Sudden Infant Death Syndrome (SIDS)', *Sleep*, 1993, 16, pp 263–82.

80 JJ McKenna, 'Is sleeping with my baby safe? Can it reduce the risk of SIDS?', *The Natural Child Project*, http://www.naturalchild.org/james_mckenna/sleeping_safe.html (cited 12/1/11).

81 PS Blair, P Sidebotham, C Evason-Coombe, M Edmonds, EMA Heckstall-Smith and P Fleming, 'Hazardous cosleeping environments and risk factors amenable to change: Case-control study of SIDS in south west England', *British Medical Journal*, 2009, 339:b3466 http://*www.bmj.com/content/339/bmj.b3666.full.pdf+html (cited 5/2/11)*.

82 PS Blair, PJ Fleming, IJ Smith, M Ward Platt, J Young, P Nadin, PJ Berry and J Golding, 'Babies sleeping with parents: Case-control study of factors influencing the risk of the Sudden Infant Death Syndrome. CESDI SUDI Research Group', *British Medical Journal*, 1999, 319, pp 1457–61.

83 PS Blair, 'Sudden Infant Death Syndrome epidemiology and bed-sharing', *Paediatrics and Child Health*, 2006, 11, pp 29–31; C James, H Klenka and D Manning, 'Sudden Infant Death Syndrome: Bed-sharing with mothers who smoke', *Archives of Disease in Childhood*, 2003, 88(2), pp 112–13.

84   JS Kemp, B Unger, D Wilkins, RM Psara, TL Ledbetter, MA Graham, M Case and BT Thach, 'Unsafe sleep practices and an analysis of bed sharing among infants dying suddenly and unexpectedly: Results of a four-year, population-based, death scene investigation study of Sudden Infant Death Syndrome and related deaths', *Pediatrics*, 2000, 106(3), p 41, http://pediatrics. aappublications.org/cgi/content/full/106/3/e41 (cited 11/11/11).

85   FR Hauck, SM Herman, M Donovan, S Iyasu, C Merrick Moore, E Donoghue, RH Kirschner and M Willinger, 'Sleeping environment and the risk of Sudden Infant Death Syndrome in an urban population: The Chicago Infant Mortality Study', *Pediatrics*, 2003, 111, pp 1207–14.

86   PJ Fleming, PS Blair and J McKenna, 'New knowledge, new insights and new recommendations', *Archives of Disease in Childhood*, 2006, 91(10), pp 799–801.

87   Kemp, et al, 'Unsafe sleep practices ...', p 41.

88   PJ Fleming, PS Blair, C Bacon and PJ Berry (eds), *Sudden Unexpected Deaths in Infancy: The CESDI SUDI studies, 1993–1996*, The Stationary Office, London, 2000. 89   Hauck, et al, 'Sleeping environment and the risk ...', pp 1207–14.

90   RG Carpenter, LM Irgens, PS Blair, P Fleming, J Huber, G Jorch and P Schreuder, 'Sudden unexplained infant death in 20 regions in Europe: Case control study', *Lancet*, 2004, 363, pp 185–91; DM Rappin, R Ecob and H Brooke, 'Bedsharing, room sharing and sudden infant death syndrome in Scotland: A case controlled study', *Journal of Pediatrics*, 2005, 147, pp 32–37; JH Ruys, GA De Jonge, R Brand, AC Engelberts and BA Semmekrot, 'Bed-sharing in the first four months of life: A risk factor for sudden infant death', *Acta Paediatrica*, 2007, 96(10), pp 1399–403.

91   McKenna, 'Is sleeping with my baby safe?...'.

92   EA Mitchell, 'Sudden Infant Death Syndrome: Should bed-sharing be discouraged?', *Archive of Pediatric and Adolescent Medicine*, 2007, 161, pp 305–06; EA Mitchell, 'Risk factors for SIDS', *British Medical Journal*, 2009, http://www.bmj.com/content/339/bmj.b3466.full (cited 25/11/11); C McGarvery, K McDonnell and M O'Reagan, 'An 8-year study of risk factors for SIDS: Bedsharing versus non bed-sharing', *Archive of Disease in Childhood*, 2006, 91, pp 318–23.

93   EA Mitchell and JM Thompson, 'Cosleeping increases the risk of sudden infant death syndrome but sleeping in the parent's bedroom lowers it', in TO Rognum (ed), *Sudden Infant Death Syndrome: New trends in the nineties*, Scandinavian University Press, Oslo Norway, 1995.

94   SIDS and Kids National Scientific Advisory Group (NSAG), 'Information statement – Sleeping with a baby', SIDS and Kids http://www.sidsandkids. org/wp-content/uploads/Room_Sharing.pdf (cited 25/11/11).

95   Task Force on Sudden Infant Death Syndrome, 'The changing concept of Sudden Infant Death Syndrome: Diagnostic coding shifts, controversies

regarding the sleeping environment, and new variables to consider in reducing risk', *Pediatrics*, 2005, 116(5), pp 1245–55.

96 'CDC: Infant suffocation, strangulation deaths quadruple over 20 years', FOX News, 26 January 2009, http://www.foxnews.com/story/0,2933,483064,00. html#ixzz1Aa2hUKU4 (cited 25/11/11); CK Shapiro-Mendoza, M Kimball, KM Tomashek, RN Anderson and S Blanding, 'US infant mortality trends attributable to accidental suffocation and strangulation in bed from 1984 through 2004: Are rates increasing?', *Pediatrics*, 2009, 123(2), pp 533–39.

97 M Willinger, C Ko, HJ Hoffman, RC Kessler and MJ Corwin, 'Trends in infant bed sharing in the United States, 1993–2000', *Archives of Pediatric and Adolescent Medicine*, 2003, 157, pp 43–49.

98 G Lower, 'Co-sleeping puts babies' lives at risk, inquest told', *The Australian*, 22 October 2009, http://www.theaustralian.com.au/news/co-sleeping-puts-babies-lives-at-risk-inquest-told/story-e6frg6p6-1225789767962   (cited 25/11/11).

99 'Co-sleeping a risk for young babies', *Daily Telegraph*, 30 September 2010, http://www.dailytelegraph.com.au/news/breaking-news/co-sleeping-a-risk-for-young-babies/story-e6freuz0-1225932454850 (cited 25/11/11).

100 Armstrong, et al, 'Medicalizing normality? ...', pp 301–05.

101 T Lange, S Dimitrov and J Born, 'Effects of sleep and circadian rhythm on the human immune system', *Annals of the New York Academy of Sciences*, 2010, 1193, pp 48–59.

102 Canadian Centre for Occupational Health and Safety, 'Rotational shiftwork', http://www.ccohs.ca/oshanswers/ergonomics/shiftwrk. html#_1_4 (cited 16/07/2011); LC Antunes, R Levandovski, G Dantas, W Caumo and HP Hidalgo, 'Obesity and shift work: Chronobiological aspects', *Nutrition Research Reviews*, 2010, 23(1), pp 155–68.

103 La Leche League International, *The Womanly Art of Breastfeeding*, p 455.

104 M Woolridge, 'Colic, overfeeding, and symptoms of lactose malabsorption in the breast-fed baby: A possible artifact of feed management?', *The Lancet*, 1988, 332, pp 382–84.

105 OG Jenni and MA Carskadon, 'Normal human sleep at different ages: Infants to adolescents', in *SRS Basics of Sleep Guide*, Westchester, Illinois, Sleep Research Society, 2005, pp 11–19.

Index

CPSIA information can be obtained
at www.ICGtesting.com
Printed in the USA
BVHW08s0150160618
519073BV00002B/202/P